70-1187

PR
6023
A93
S7

Tedlock

D.H. Lawrence and
sons and lovers.

Date Due

		JUL	2000
		JUN	2004
		JUL	00
		JUL X X	2015
	WITHDRAWN		

D. H. *Lawrence and* Sons and Lovers

D. H. Lawrence and
Sons and Lovers:

SOURCES AND CRITICISM

Edited by E. W. Tedlock, Jr.

NEW YORK UNIVERSITY PRESS 1965

COPYRIGHT © 1965 BY NEW YORK UNIVERSITY PRESS
LIBRARY OF CONGRESS CARD CATALOG NO. 65–22471
MANUFACTURED IN THE UNITED STATES OF AMERICA

ACKNOWLEDGMENTS

In addition to the permissions and copyrights cited in the footnotes at the beginning of each article, the publishers are pleased to make the following acknowledgments:

All quotations from Lawrence's writings, including his letters, and from the letters of Frieda Lawrence, appear by permission of William Heinemann, Ltd. and Laurence Pollinger, Ltd.

D. H. Lawrence: A Personal Record by Jessie Chambers is published in the United States of America by Barnes & Noble, Inc., and an excerpt from it is reprinted with their permission.

The Revised Edition of *D. H. Lawrence: His Life and Works* by Harry T. Moore is copyrighted (© 1964 by Harry T. Moore).

The Mirror in the Roadway by Frank O'Connor is quoted by permission of A. D. Peters & Co.

Two excerpts from *The Love Ethic of D. H. Lawrence* by Mark Spilka appear by permission of Dennis Dobson.

Twelve Original Essays on Great English Novels, from which "The Unattainable Self" by Louis Fraiberg is reprinted, is copyrighted (© 1960 by Wayne State University).

Introduction   1

I.   Origins   7
    1. *From Lawrence's Letters*   12
    2. *From a Letter by Alice Dax ("Clara")
      to Frieda Lawrence*   33
    3. *From Letters by Frieda Lawrence*   36
    4. Jessie Chambers ("Miriam"): *From
      D. H. Lawrence: A Personal Record*   39
    5. Harry T. Moore: *The Genesis as Re-
      vealed in the Miriam Papers*   43
    6. Harry T. Moore: *A Postscript*   63
    7. E. W. Tedlock, Jr.: *A Report on the
      Final Manuscript*   66

II.   Freudian Connections and Approaches   73
    8. Alfred Booth Kuttner: *A Freudian
      Appreciation*   76
    9. Frederick J. Hoffman: *Lawrence's
      Quarrel with Freud*   101
    10. Daniel A. Weiss: *The Mother in the
      Mind*   112

II.   Freudian Connections and Approaches
      —Continued
      11. Frank O'Connor: *D. H. Lawrence,*
          Sons and Lovers   137

III. Technique and Values   147
      12. John Middleton Murry: *Son and Lover* 151
      13. Mark Schorer: *Technique as Discovery* 164
      14. Dorothy Van Ghent: *On* Sons and
          Lovers   170
      15. Mark Spilka: *How to Pick Flowers*   188
      16. Mark Spilka: *Counterfeit Loves*   200
      17. Louis Fraiberg: *The Unattainable Self* 217
      18. Alfred Kazin: *Sons, Lovers and*
          Mothers   238

To Agnes, Dennis, Susan, and David

Introduction

For some fifty years now, after its first impact and vogue, *Sons and Lovers* has held a place on the lists and shelves of modern classics. Like all books that apply unique insights to familiar human relationships, it has been both a revelation and a mystery. The criticism that has followed it has interpreted the former with considerable consistency and treated the latter as not requiring unlimited respect. The novel is successful, but the disturbed and disturbing young man is too much in it; it contains the residue of his own confusions and, it might be added, cruelty to what blocked him from his destiny, as he ultimately saw it. Past and future collide, and the provincial microcosm trembles.

All these years, the text of the novel has not fully represented Lawrence's final correction and revision. He left to his distinguished and personally sympathetic and befriending editor Edward Garnett the final and quite extensive cutting of a manuscript that was too long to seem profitable to the publisher. The cutting was wisely and skilfully done; but some day, perhaps, we can have in addition to the current text the fuller one that Lawrence laid down. (See "A Report on the Final Manuscript.")

This collection has been designed to give the reader of *Sons and Lovers* an opportunity to range through the problems of meaning and technique that have been connected with it, and the solutions that have been offered. To help him make a more informed judgment, he is also given certain materials having to do with the origins of the novel—its life connections —and its evolution through many drafts. The book is not on trial, though one wonders about the ultimate implications of certain challenges—those of Murry and Schorer, for example— of its artistic detachment and its values. At any rate, here are the considerations, the talk that has gone on. The selection from reviews, essays, and chapters in books has been made in the interests of both quality and coverage. The latter consideration ruled out some interesting but repetitive or discursive things. As for the divisions, the second, consisting of pieces that emphasize psychology (or, as some prefer, psychoanalysis), is not so exclusively separate from the last, on technique and values, as may at first appear; but the crossing of the line is usually tentative and brief.

I. Origins

Lawrence's letters have much to say about the personal problems in which the novel is rooted, and make important statements of intention, attitude, and later reaction. Even the reader who is convinced of the essential autonomy of such a novel's richly organized world may feel that the following passages furnish a helpful commentary. They not only reveal Lawrence's "real life" responses but in their "sense-making" constitute a subsidiary part of the process that created the novel.

The unpublished foreword expounds the novel's theme in parabolic language that assigns religious meaning to this nothing more than a fiction, turning Christian modes to vitalistic uses. It reveals a Lawrence who through a tremendous effort of consciousness, understanding, and activity has at least partially transcended the predicament of his fictional counterpart; its "artful" manner is one of the indications. Along with all more than perfunctory forewords, it belongs to the tradition of the right, as well as the need, of further exploration and clarification of the potentiality of the Jamesian *donné*. No doubt it also stems from the transaction going on between Lawrence and his editor, Edward Garnett, who pressed him hard for clarity and form, so that partly it may have been a way of teasing this powerful and helpful man to whom he was grateful, but from whom he was soon to break when the pressure threatened his sense of growth. At any rate, it helped put that stage of continuous imaginative realization that *Sons and Lovers* represents behind him, just as earlier letters helped him towards it.

In general, the statements in the letters become part of the transaction between book and reader at the stage, beyond the immediate impact, of the question of ultimate meaning. And the other material in this book makes evident that there is a great deal to think about as one considers the novel's strange and passionate presentation of sacrosanct and usually safely ordinary relationships. Even in an age familiar with depth psychology—the new predestinarianism, from which Lawrence fought clear—the book contains experiences that shake us. The latest man, full of the latest self-knowledge, is still susceptible to Paul Morel's predicament.

With the letters the reader can begin with something resembling the border of a jigsaw puzzle, the easier part. Lawrence leaves, or seems to leave, little doubt about his feelings—about what he wants from his girls, and what he finds them lacking in; about the nature of his attachment to his mother, and her exclusive possession of his soul; about his hard feelings towards his father; about his share of guilt and suffering in broken relations; about his astonishment at and liking for the miners; about his fight for success in his relationship with Frieda while he was revising the novel; about his pride in the book, and, in a sense, its message; about his rebellion against fixed notions of novelistic form; and about his not caring much, or so he said, what was cut as Garnett undertook a final polishing, so that the final supervision was another's and the question of the extent to which we have Lawrence's total creation can be raised, as it is in "A Report on the Final Manuscript." Noteworthy also is his fear that the novel has cost him a friend, presumably because that friend had attached to Lawrence personally, there and then, something of shame in the book; and his explanation that "one sheds one's sicknesses in books" makes literature very personal indeed, and as Freudianly therapeutic as Lawrence is likely to come. Finally, there is his beautiful reaction to a review by a professional psychologist (possibly the one by Alfred Booth Kuttner represented in this volume), in which he says that as art his book was "a fairly complete truth" out of which a half-lie has been carved.

The woman other than his mother who was most crucially involved in Lawrence's son-lover problem was Jessie Chambers. The extent to which Lawrence was able to do her justice in the role of Mirian—that is, to present accurately the degree of responsibility the mother and he must accept for her defeat —is the ultimate and concluding issue in her *D. H. Lawrence: A Personal Record*. It is also the issue in much of the criticism. The excerpts from Lawrence's letters show how profoundly shaken he was when her view was first made articulate, in fictional form, in 1913. The critical concern with this issue is usually, and properly, based on internal evidence—contradictory characterization and disorganization of themes—but it seems likely that the skill and power with which she presented her side of the story has to some extent stimulated, if not prompted, this critical approach. The novel even bears the marks of her collaboration in its early stages, before she was alienated by the treatment of Miriam, and the nature and extent of her role are discussed in Harry T. Moore's "The Genesis as Revealed in the Miriam Papers." It has not been possible to obtain permission to present here an adequate representation of her own book; but the passage obtained suggests the kind of help and confidence, in the root sense, she was able to give Lawrence, and at the same time her, to him, painful inaccessibility as mistress or wife because she stood for soul, the "Psyche" of the passage, and consequently appealed to that part of his nature that irrevocably belonged to his mother. The reader will recall passages in the novel that parallel this real-life conflict. For Jessie Chambers the part of the novel that develops the Paul Morel-Miriam relationship merely repeated Lawrence's inability to love fully—that is, spiritually as well as sexually. His tendency to make the sexual relationship supreme, or at least to argue so, came out of his inability to fully understand and transcend his commitment to his mother. The brief excerpt from his letter to Jessie Chambers, first published in her book, that speaks of the mutual death involved in their alienation, refers to the episode in the novel, presented also in her book, in which the adolescent boy, at the prompting of the mother, announces that henceforward on their walks and other meetings they must always have someone with them. This, to her, was as he said, the slaughter

of the foetus in the womb. Other passages in her book parallel
his novel: his, to her, obsession with analyzing their relationship;
his objection to her touching flowers and insistence on detachment; his recurrent reaction against her soulfulness and passional
inadequacy. She felt that all this was essentially untruthful; to
her not only Lawrence's creation, Paul Morel, but Lawrence
himself was victimized by the split between soul and passion
mentioned in the letter to Garnett on his intention, and blindly
and cruelly made her a scapegoat.

The final draft of the novel was written during the difficult
early months of his relationship with Frieda—a mixture of
passion, happiness, and profound disturbance over her separa-
tion from her children, and the question of her part in his
creative life. His mother and Jessie Chambers lay in his immediate past; she could not enter his kind of life-based fiction
until the next book. Asked how a woman might feel in certain
situations, she wrote out bits for him. When his work did not
go well, the cause might be her distraction and distance. The
excerpts from her letters reveal all this, and her essential
antagonism to the influence of both the mother and Jessie
Chambers. It does not seem likely that, particularly at this
advanced stage of the novel, her attitude could have caused
basic changes. Frieda's view of Jessie Chambers' part in the
novel is as critical argument completely *ad hominem,* but it
raises legitimate questions if the critic relies on Jessie Chambers'
account.[1]

The excerpt from the letter by Alice Dax on the occasion
of Frieda's *Not I But the Wind* is included because it indicates
poignantly the kind of severe limitation of the capacity for love
that Lawrence encountered during the period of his life covered
by the latter pages of the novel. It may contain a parallel to
the relation between Clara and Baxter Dawes. Alice Dax and
Louie Burrows and one other apparently formed the real-life

[1] The reader who wishes to learn more about the effect on Jessie
Chambers of the break with Lawrence should see the portrait of her by
Helen Corke in *D. H. Lawrence's Princess: A Memory of Jessie Chambers*
(Thames Ditton, Surrey: Merle Press, 1951; soon to be reissued by the
University of Texas Press).

bases of the character of Clara, a composite perhaps of Louie Burrows' warmth and spontaneity, as Lawrence describes her in the excerpt from his letter, and the complex nature of Alice Dax, aroused but troubled, intelligent, emancipated, in a sense the new woman of her day.

1 · From Lawrence's Letters

To Blanche Jennings, January 28, 1910

What do you want me to tell you about—my latest love? Well—she's off again—I don't like her. She's rather a striking girl with much auburn hair. At first, she seems a person of great capacity, being alert, prompt, smart with her tongue, and independent in her manner. She is very popular with men, and goes out a good bit. Now I'm tired of her. Why?—She's so utterly ignorant and old fashioned, really, though she has been to college and has taught in London some years. A man is—or was, a more or less interesting creature, with whom one could play about with smart and silly speech—no more—not an animal —*mon dieu*, no!—I have enlightened her, and now she has no courage. She still judges by mid-Victorian standards, and covers herself with a wooly fluff of romance that the years will wear sickly. She refuses to see that a man is a male, that kisses are the merest preludes and anticipations, that love is largely a physical sympathy that is soon satisfied and satiated. She believes men worship their mistresses; she is all sham and superficial in her outlook, and I can't change her. She's frightened. Now I'm sick of her. She pretends to be very fond of me; she isn't really: even if she were, what do I care!—but if she were, she wouldn't be the timid duffer she is, declaring things dreadful, painful, hateful; life not worth living, like a degradation etc etc; she would be more interested in life; she lapses into sickly sentimentality when it is a question of naked life.

I have been sick of her some little time. At Christmas an old fire burned up afresh, like an alcohol flame, faint and invisible, that sets fire to a tar barrel. It is the old girl, who has been attached to me so long. It is most rummy. She knows me through and through, and I know her—and—the devil of it is, she's a hundred and fifty miles away. We have fine, mad little scenes now and again, she and I—so strange, after ten years, and I had hardly kissed her all that time. She has black hair, and wonderful eyes, big and very dark, and very vulnerable; she lifts up her face to me and clings to me, and the time goes like a falling star, swallowed up immediately; it is wonderful, that time, long avenues of minutes—hours—should be swept up with one sweep of the hand, and the moment of parting has arrived when the first kiss seems hardly overkissed. She is coming to me for a weekend soon; we shall not stay here in Croydon, but in London. The world is for us, and we are for each other—even if only for one spring—so what does it matter! . . .

Why are you sad?—tell me. What is the matter, that you have so discordant a note?—Tell me. What do you want? But what we all want, madly, is human contact. That I find more and more—not ideas;—transference of feeling—human contact.

To Sydney S. Pawling, October 18, 1910

. . . I will give you—with no intermediary this time—my third novel, *Paul Morel* [the early title of *Sons and Lovers*], which is plotted out very interestingly (to me), and about one-eighth of which is written. *Paul Morel* will be a novel—not a florid prose poem,[1] or a decorated idyll runnning to seed in realism:[2] but a restrained, somewhat impersonal novel. It interests me very much. I wish I were not so agitated just now, and could do more.

When you say "the plates of *The White Peacock* were sent from New York"—do you mean the plates of the cover design,

[1] Apparently a reference to his second novel, *The Trespasser*.
[2] Apparently a reference to his first novel, *The White Peacock*.

or what? I am a trifle curious. I *do* want that book to make haste. Not that I care much myself. But I want my mother to see it while still she keeps the live consciousness. She is really horribly ill. . . .

To Rachel Annand Taylor, December 3, 1910

I have been at home now ten days. My mother is very near the end.[3] Today I have been to Leicester. I did not get home till half past nine. Then I ran upstairs. Oh she was very bad. The pains had been again.

"Oh my dear" I said, "is it the pains?"

"Not pain now—Oh the weariness" she moaned, so that I could hardly hear her. I wish she could die tonight.

My sister and I do all the nursing. My sister is only 22. I sit upstairs hours and hours till I wonder if ever it were true that I was at London. I seem to have died since, and that is an old life, dreamy.

I will tell you. My mother was a clever, ironical delicately moulded woman of good, old burgher descent. She married below her. My father was dark, ruddy, with a fine laugh. He is a coal miner. He was one of the sanguine temperament, warm and hearty, but unstable: he lacked principle, as my mother would have said. He deceived her and lied to her. She despised him— he drank.

Their marriage life has been one carnal, bloody fight. I was born hating my father: as early as ever I can remember, I shivered with horror when he touched me. He was very bad before I was born.

This has been a kind of bond between me and my mother. We have loved each other, almost with a husband and wife love, as well as filial and maternal. We know each other by instinct. She said to my aunt—about me:

"But it has been different with him. He has seemed to be part of me."—And that is the real case. We have been like one, so sensitive to each other that we never needed words. It has been rather terrible and has made me, in some respects, abnormal.

3 Her death came on December 9th.

I think this peculiar fusion of soul (don't think me high-falutin) never comes twice in a life-time—it doesn't seem natural. When it comes it seems to distribute one's conscious-ness far abroad from oneself, and one understands! I think no one has got "Understanding" except through love. Now my mother is nearly dead, and I don't quite know how I am.

I have been to Leicester today, I have met a girl [4] who has always been warm for me—like a sunny happy day—and I've gone and asked her to marry me: in the train, quite unpre-meditated, between Rothley and Quorn—she lives at Quorn. When I think of her I feel happy with a sort of warm radiation —she is big and dark and handsome. There were five other people in the carriage. Then when I think of my mother:—if you've ever put your hand round the bowl of a champagne glass and squeezed it and wondered now near it is to crushing-in and the wine all going through your fingers—that's how my heart feels—like the champagne glass. There is no hostility be-tween the warm happiness and the crush of misery: but one is concentrated in my chest, and one is diffuse—a suffusion, vague.

Muriel [5] is the girl I have broken with. She loves me to madness, and demands the soul of me. I have been cruel to her, and wronged her, but I did not know.

Nobody can have the soul of me. My mother has had it, and nobody can have it again. Nobody can come into my very self again, and breathe me like an atmosphere. Don't say I am hasty this time—I know. Louie—whom I wish I could marry the day after the funeral—she would never demand to drink me up and have me. She loves me—but it is a fine, warm, healthy, natural love—not like Jane Eyre, who is Muriel, but like—say Rhoda Fleming or a commoner Anna Karenina. She will never plunge her hands through my blood and feel for my soul, and make me set my teeth and shiver and fight away. Ugh— I have done well—and cruelly—tonight.

I look at my father—he is like a cinder. It is very terrible, mis-marriage.

4 Louie Burrows, said by Jessie Chambers to have contributed to the composite character Clara Dawes in the novel.
5 Jessie Chambers, the real-life counterpart of Miriam in the novel.

To Helen Corke [?1911]

. . . Really, I have got a bit indifferent. Life seemed so paltry, so short of generosity. It would give its half measures with much benignity—very Christian-like. Really, the one beautiful and generous adventure left seemed to be death.

And this is not because I am inactive altogether. My soul has strenuous work in intimacies to do. But then I scorn the intimacy, when it's formed; it is always a lot short. . . .

To Helen Corke [?1911]

. . . I have begun Paul Morel again—glory, you should see it! The British public will stone me if ever it catches sight. . . .

To Jessie Chambers, Spring 1911

. . . You say you died a death of me, but the death you died of me I must have died also, or you wouldn't have gone on caring about me. . . . They tore me from you, the love of my life. . . . It was the slaughter of the foetus in the womb. . . . I've got a grinning skull-and-crossbones headache. The amount of energy required to live is—how many volts a second?

To Ada Lawrence Clarke,[6] April 26, 1911

My dear—I don't know what to say to you. There is nothing to do with life but to let it run, and it's a very bitter thing, but it's also wonderful. You never know what'll happen next. Life is full of wonder and surprise, and mostly pain. But never mind, the tragic is the most holding, the most vital thing in life and as I say, the lesson is to learn to live alone. . . . I have sent Mrs. Hopkin some of McLeod's books which I want you particularly to read. They are tragedies, but all great works are. Tragedy is beautiful also. This is my creed. But sometimes also it leaves me full of misery. Never mind, my dear. I am very sorry father is proving such a nuisance to you. Never mind, he will be much humbler when he has not got his own house to be boss in. Let him eat a bit of the bread of humility. It is astonishing how hard and bitter I feel towards him.

6 His sister, with whom he maintained a close relationship to the end of his life.

I am tired of life being so ugly and cruel. How I long for it to turn pleasant. It makes my soul heave with distaste to see it so harsh and brutal. I'm glad you like Louie. When she is a bit older she'll be more understanding. Remember she's seen nothing whatever of the horror of life, and we've been bred up in its presence: with father. It makes a great difference. . . . It was Louie's birthday on Monday, and I didn't know. I've bought her rather a pretty brooch of paste brilliants. Don't be jealous of her. She hasn't any space in *your* part of me. You and I—there are some things which we shall share, we alone, all our lives . . . you are my own *real* relative in the world—only you. I am yours: is it not so?

To Edward Garnett, March 6, 1912
. . . By the way, would you care to see the MS. of the colliery novel, when it is finished, before it goes to Wm. H.? [7] I have done two thirds or more. . . . Here, in this ugly hell, the men are *most* happy. They sing, they drink, they rejoice in the land. There were more "drunks" run-in from the Crown and the Drum here last week-end, than ever since Shirebrook was Shirebrook. Yesterday I was in Worksop. It is simply snyed with pals. Every blessed place was full of men, in the larkiest of spirits. I went in the Golden Crown and a couple of other places. They were betting like steam on skittles—the "seconds" had capfuls of money. There is some life up here this week, I can tell you. Everywhere you go, crowds and crowds of men, not unhappy, as they usually are.

To Edward Garnett, April 3, 1912
I was round with a friend delivering relief tickets yesterday. It's not that the actual suffering is so great—though it's bad enough—but the men seem such big, helpless, hopeless children, and the women are impersonal—little atlases under a load that they know will crush them out at last, but it doesn't matter. They aren't conscious any more than their hearts are conscious of their endless business of beating. They have no conscious life, no windows. It makes me ill. . . . I shall finish my col-

7 The publisher William Heinemann.

liery novel this week—the first draft. It'll want a bit of revising.
It's by far the best thing I've done.

[*The manuscript was sent to the publisher William Heinemann
near the first of June, 1912. When he rejected it, Edward Garnett
intervened, and the book went to Duckworth. Lawrence's letters
indicate that Garnett's editorial supervision had considerable to
do with the final form. A part of this impression may be due to
hyperbolic expression of Lawrence's feeling of gratitude, and there
are signs of resistance to Garnett's insistence on form. Towards
the end of this "collaboration" Lawrence seems to have given
his editor* carte blanche *to make a final cutting. (See the introduction.) The letters speak of another potential influence on the
novel, Frieda Weekley, the woman with whom fulfillment
seemed at last possible, and who had some knowledge of
Freudian theory.* E.W.T.]

I got *Paul Morel* this morning, and the list of notes from
Duckworth. The latter are awfully nice and detailed. What
a Trojan of energy and conscientiousness you are! I'm going to
slave like a Turk at the novel—see if I won't do you credit.
I begin in earnest tomorrow—having spent the day in thought (?)
. . . Here, in this tiny savage little place, F. and I have got
awfully wild. I loathe the idea of England, and its enervation
and misty miserable modernness. I don't want to go back to
town and civilisation. I want to rough it and scramble through
free, free. I *don't* want to be tied down. And I can live on a
tiny bit. I shan't let F. leave me, if I can help it. I feel I've got
a mate and I'll fight tooth and claw to keep her. She says I'm
reverting, but I'm not—I'm only coming out wholesome and
myself. Say I'm right, and I ought to be always common. I *loathe
Paul Morel*. F. sends love.
[P. S.] I'll do you credit with that novel, if I can.

[*On August 4th Lawrence thought revision would take three
months. September 7th he wrote Garnett that he would "re-cast
the first part altogether." That same month he wrote to an old
friend A. W. McLeod: "Paul Morel* is better than The White
Peacock *or* The Trespasser. *I'm inwardly very proud of it, though*

I haven't yet licked it into form—am still at that labour of love. Heinemann refused it because he was cross with me for going to Duckworth—refused it on grounds of its indecency, if you please." Then on October 30th, as if theme and form had crystallized in a phrase, Lawrence wrote to Garnett: " . . . Will Sons and Lovers do for a title? I've made the book heaps better—a million times." This was followed by the letter containing the incisive statement of intention that critics have had to weigh against the complexities of the imaginative statement of the novel, and that, on the whole, they have found incomplete. E.W.T.]

To Edward Garnett, November 14, 1912

    I hasten to tell you I sent the MS. of the *Paul Morel* novel to Duckworth registered, yesterday. And I want to defend it, quick. I wrote it again, pruning it and shaping it and filling it in. I tell you it has got form—*form*: haven't I made it patiently, out of sweat as well as blood. It follows this idea: a woman of character and refinement goes into the lower class, and has no satisfaction in her own life. She has had a passion for her husband, so the children are born of passion, and have heaps of vitality. But as her sons grow up she selects them as lovers— first the eldest, then the second. These sons are *urged* into life by their reciprocal love of their mother—urged on and on. But when they come to manhood, they can't love, because their mother is the strongest power in their lives, and holds them. It's rather like Goethe and his mother and Frau von Stein and Christiana—[sic] As soon as the young men come into contact with women, there's a split. William gives his sex to a fribble, and his mother holds his soul. But the split kills him, because he doesn't know where he is. The next son gets a woman who fights for his soul—fights his mother. The son loves the mother—all the sons hate and are jealous of the father. The battle goes on between the mother and the girl, with the son as object. The mother gradually proves stronger, because of the tie of blood. The son decides to leave his soul in his mother's hands, and, like his elder brother go for passion. He gets passion. Then the split begins to tell again. But, almost unconsciously, the mother realises what is the matter, and begins to die. The son casts off his mistress, attends to his mother dying. He is left in the end naked of everything, with the drift towards death.

It is a great tragedy, and I tell you I have written a great book. It's the tragedy of thousands of young men in England—it may even be Bunny's [8] tragedy. I think it was Ruskin's, and men like him.—Now tell me if I haven't worked out my theme, like life, but always my theme. Read my novel. It's a great novel. If *you* can't see the development—which is slow, like growth—I can. . . .

I should like to dedicate the *Paul Morel* to you—may I? But not unless you think it's really a good work. "To Edward Garnett, in Gratitude." But you can put it better. . . .

Have I made those naked scenes . . . tame enough? You cut them if you like. Yet they are so clean—and I *have* patiently and laboriously constructed that novel.

To A. W. McLeod, December 2, 1912

. . . This is the interlude between novels. The *Paul Morel* book—to be called, I think, *Sons and Lovers,* is being got ready for the printer—I'm resting a bit after having delivered it. It's quite a great work. I only hope the English nation won't rend me for having given them anything so good. Not that the English nation is likely to concern itself with me—but "England, my England" is for me, I suppose, "Critic, my Critic." Duckworth's going to give me £100 on account. I feel quite like a thief.

To Edward Garnett, December 19, 1912

I'm glad you don't mind cutting the *Sons and Lovers.* By the way, is the title satisfactory?

To Ernest Collings, December 24, 1912

. . . January sees my poems published, February my novel *Sons and Lovers.* Of course I admire both works immensely. I am a great admirer of my own stuff while it's new, but after a while I'm not so gone on it—like the true maternal instinct, that kicks off an offspring as soon as it can go on its own legs.

---

8 Garnett's son, David.

It all sounds very egoistic, but you don't tell me enough about yourself. It's good of you to be only thirty. These damned old stagers want to train up a child in the way it should grow, whereas if it's destined to have a snub nose, it's sheer waste of time to harass the poor brat into Roman-nosedness. They want me to have form: that means, they want me to have *their* pernicious ossiferous skin-and-grief form, and I won't. Do tell as many people as you can that I'm a great writer and that my influence is pure and sweet—also that I'm being published just now. I'm so afraid I shall have to take to teaching again.

To Edward Garnett, December 29, 1912

I'm glad to hear you like the novel better. I don't much mind what you squash out. I hope to goodness it'll do my reputation and my pocket good, the book. I'm glad you'll let it be dedicated to you. I feel always so deep in your debt.

To Edward Garnett, January 12, 1913

. . . I am afraid of being a nuisance. Do you feel, with me, a bit like the old man of the seas? If I weren't so scared of having no money at all, I'd tell you to shovel all my stuff on to Pinker,[9] get rid of the bother of me, and leave me to transact with him. The thought of you pedgilling away at the novel frets me. Why can't I do those things?—I can't. I could do hack work, to a certain amount. But apply my creative self where it doesn't want to be applied, makes me feel I should burst or go cracked. I couldn't have done any more at that novel—at least for six months. I must go on producing, producing, and the stuff must come more and more to shape each year. But trim and garnish my stuff I cannot—it must go.

[Also in January 1913, Lawrence sent Garnett the following foreword, which was not used, and which he seems to disavow in a later letter. It is an early example of the Lawrencean vitalistic jeu d'esprit, *here reversing the gospel according to John by making the flesh anterior to the word, and extending the novel's realistic meaning to religious proportions. Criticism*

9 J. B. Pinker, literary agent.

of the novel has, on the whole, paid little attention to it; yet it bears at least on that intensity, that taking of life in a profoundly serious way, that constitutes an important part of Lawrence's difference from his contemporaries. E.W.T.]

Foreword to *Sons and Lovers*

To Edward Garnett

John, the beloved disciple, says, "The Word was made Flesh." But why should he turn things round? The women simply go on bearing talkative sons, as an answer. "The Flesh was made Word."

For what was Christ? He was Word, or He became Word. What remains of Him? No flesh remains on earth, from Christ; perhaps some carpentry He shaped with His hands retains somewhere His flesh-print; and then His word, like His carpentry just the object that His flesh produced, is the rest. He is Word. And the Father was Flesh. For even if it were by the Holy Ghost His spirit were begotten, yet flesh cometh only out of flesh. So the Holy Ghost must either have been, or have borne from the Father, at least one grain of flesh. The Father was Flesh— and the Son, who in Himself was finite and had form, become Word. For form is the uttered Word, and the Son is the Flesh as it utters the Word, but the unutterable Flesh is the Father.

And the Word is not spoken by the Father, who is Flesh, forever unquestioned and unanswerable, but by the Son. Adam was the first Christ: not the Word made Flesh, but the Flesh made Word. Out of the Flesh cometh the Word, and the Word is finite, as a piece of carpentry, and hath an end. But the Flesh is infinite and has no end. Out of the Flesh cometh the Word, which blossoms for a moment and is no more. Out of the Flesh hath come every Word, and in the Flesh lies every Word that will be uttered. The Father is the Flesh, the eternal and unquestionable, the law-giver but not the law; whereas the Son is the mouth. And each law is a fabric that must crumble away, and the Word is a graven image that is worn down, and forsaken, like the Sphinx in the desert.

From *The Letters of D. H. Lawrence,* edited by Aldous Huxley. Copyright 1932 by The Estate of D. H. Lawrence, 1960 by Angelo Ravagli and Montague C. Weekley. Reprinted by permission of The Viking Press, Inc.

We are the Word, we are not the Flesh. The Flesh is beyond us. And when we love our neighbour as ourself, we love that word, our neighbour, and not that flesh. For that Flesh is not our neighbour, it is the Father, which is in Heaven, and forever beyond our knowledge. We are the Word, we know the Word, and the Word alone is ours. When we say "I," we mean "The Word I am." This flesh I am is beyond me.

So that if we love our neighbour, we love that Word, our neighbour, and we hate that Lie, our neighbour, which is a deformity. With that Flesh, our neighbour, We, the Word-Utterer, have nothing to do. For the Son is not greater than the Father. And if we love and subserve that Flesh, our neighbour, which is the Father, it is only by denying and desecrating the Father in ourselves. For the Father is the Almighty. The Flesh will feel no pain that is not upon itself, and will know no hurt but its own destruction. But no man can destroy the Almighty, yet he can deny Him. And pain is a denial of the Father. If then we feel the pain and suffering of our neighbour's flesh, we are putting destruction upon our own flesh, which is to deny and make wrathful the Father. Which we have done. For in loving our neighbour, the Flesh, as ourself, we have said, "There is no Father, there is only the Word." For it is the Word hath charity, not the Flesh. And it is the Word that answereth the cry of the Word. But if the Word, hearing a cry, shall say, "My flesh is destroyed, the bone melteth away," that is to blaspheme the Father. For the Word is but fabric builded of the Flesh. And when the fabric is finished, then shall the Flesh enjoy it in its hour.

But we have said, "Within this fabric of the Word the Flesh is held." And so, the Son has usurped the Father. And so, the Father, which is the Flesh, withdraws from us, and the Word stands in ruins, as Nineveh and Egypt are dead words on the plains, whence the Flesh has withdrawn itself. For the lesser cannot contain the greater, nor the Son contain the Father, but he is of the Father.

And it is upon the head of that nation that shall deny the Father. For the Flesh will depart from that collective Word, the nation, and that great nation shall remain as a Word in ruin, its own monument.

For who shall say, "No child shall be born of me and my wife. I, the Word, have said it?" And who shall say—"That woman whom my flesh, in its unquestionable sincerity, cleaveth toward, shall not come unto my flesh. But my Word shall come unto her. I, the Word have said it?" That is to usurp the flesh of my neighbour, and hold governance over it by the word. And who shall say, "That woman shall be Flesh of my Flesh. I, the Word, have said it?" For either the woman is Flesh of my Flesh, or she is not, and the Word altereth nothing, but can only submit or deny.

And when we burned the heretic at the stake, then did we love that Word, our neighbour, and hate that lie, the heretic. But we did also deny the Father, and say, "There is only Word." And when we suffer in our flesh the pangs of those that hunger, then we do deny the Flesh, and say, it is not. For the Flesh suffereth not from the hunger of the neighbour, but only from its own hunger. But the Word loveth its neighbour, and shall answer to the cry of the Word, "It is just, what thou askest." For the Word hath neither passion nor pain, but lives and moves in equity. It has charity, which we call love. But only the Flesh has love, for that is the Father, and in love he begets us all, of love are we begotten. But it was spoken, "They shall be one Flesh." Thus did the Word usurp the Father, saying, "I unite you one flesh." Whereas the Word can but confirm. For the twain are one flesh, whether the Word speak or not. And if they be not one twain, then the Word can never make them so, for the Flesh is not contained in the Word, but the Word in the Flesh. But if a man shall say, "This woman is flesh of my flesh," let him see to it that he be not blaspheming the Father. For the woman is not flesh of his flesh, by the bidding of the Word; but it is of the Father. And if he take a woman, saying in the arrogance of the Word, "The flesh of that woman is goodly," then he has said, "The flesh of that woman is goodly as a servant unto the Word, which is me," and so hath blasphemed the Father, by which he has his being, and she hath her being. And the Flesh shall forsake these two, they shall be fabric of Word. And their race shall perish.

But if in my passion I slay my neighbour, it is no sin of

mine, but it is his sin, for he should not have permitted me. But if my Word shall decide and decree that my neighbour die, then that is sin, for the Word destroyeth the Flesh, the Son blasphemeth the Father. And yet, if a man hath denied his Flesh, saying, "I, the Word, have dominion over the flesh of my neighbour," then shall the Flesh, his neighbour, slay him in self-defence. For a man may hire my Word, which is the utterance of my flesh, which is my work. But my Flesh is the Father, which is before the Son.

And so it was written: "The Word was made Flesh," then, as corollary, "And of the Flesh was made Flesh-of-the-Flesh, woman." This is again backward, and because the Son, struggling to utter the Word, took for his God the accomplishment of his work, the Uttered Word. Out of his flesh the Word had to come, and the flesh was difficult and unfathomed, so it was called the servant. And the servant of the servant was woman. So the Son arranged it, because he took for his God his own work when it should be accomplished: as if a carpenter called the chair he struggled with but had not yet made, God. But the Chair is not a god, it is only a rigid image. So is the Word a rigid image, parallel of the chair. And so the end having been chosen for the beginning, the whole chronology is upside-down: the Word created Man, and Man lay down and gave birth to Woman. Whereas we know the Woman lay in travail, and gave birth to Man, who in his hour uttered his word.

It is as if a bit of apple-blossom stood for God in his Wonder, the apple was the Son, as being something more gross but still wonderful, while the pip that comes out of the apple, like Adam's rib, is the mere secondary produce, that is spat out, and which, if it falls to the ground, just happens to start the process of apple-tree going again. But the little pip that one spits out has in it all the blossom and apples, as well as all the tree, the leaves, the perfume, the drops of gum, and heaven knows what else that we never see, contained by miracle in its bit of white flesh: and the tree, the leaves, the flowers themselves, and the apple are only amplifications of this little seed, spent: which never has amplified itself enough, but can go on to other than just five-petalled flowers and little brown apples, if we did but know.

So we take the seed as the starting point in this cycle. The woman is the Flesh. She produces all the rest of the flesh, including the intermediary pieces called man—and these curious pieces called man are like stamens that can turn into exquisite-coloured petals. That is, they can beat out the stuff of their life thin, thin, thin, till it is a pink or a purple petal, or a thought, or a Word. And when it is so beaten out that it ceases to be begetting stuff, of the Father, but is spread much wider, expanded and showy: then we say, "This is the Utmost!"—as everybody will agree that a rose is only a rose because of the petals, and that the rose is the utmost of all that flow of life, called "Rose." But what is really "Rose" is only in that quivering, shimmering flesh of flesh which is the same, unchanged for ever, a constant stream, called if you like rodoplasm, the eternal, the unquestionable, the infinite of the Rose, the Flesh, the Father—which were more properly, the Mother.

So there is the Father—which should be called Mother—then the Son, who is the Utterer, and then the Word. And the Word is that of the Father which, through the Son, is tossed away. It is that part of the Flesh in the Son which is capable of spreading out thin and fine, losing its concentration and completeness, ceasing to be a begetter, and becoming only a vision, a flutter of petals, God rippling through the Son till he breaks in a laugh, called a blossom, that shines and is gone. The vision itself, the flutter of petals, the rose, the Father through the Son wasting himself in a moment of consciousness, consciousness of his own infinitude and gloriousness, a Rose, a Clapping of the Hands, a Spark of Joy thrown off from the Fire to die ruddy in mid-darkness, a Snip of Flame, the Holy Ghost, the Revelation. And so, the eternal Trinity.

And God the Father, the Inscrutable, the Unknowable, we know in the Flesh, in Woman. She is the door for our in-going and our out-coming. In her we go back to the Father: but like the witnesses of the Transfiguration, blind and unconscious.

Yea, like bees in and out of a hive, we come backwards and forwards to our woman. And the Flowers of the World are Words, are Utterance—"Uttering glad leaves," Whitman said. And we are bees that go between, from the flowers home to the hive and the Queen; for she lies at the centre of the hive, and stands in the way of bees for God the Father, the Almighty, the Unknowable, the Creator. In her all things are born, both words and bees. She is the quick of all the change, the labour, the production.

And the bee, who is a Son, comes home to his Queen as to the Father, in service and humility, for suggestion, and renewal, and identification which is the height of his glory, for begetting. And again the bee goes forth to attend the flowers, the Word in his pride and masterfulness of new strength and new wisdom. And as he comes and goes, so shall man for ever come and go; to his work, his Uttering, wherein he is masterful and proud; come home to his woman, through whom is God the Father, and who is herself, whether she will have it or not, God the Father, before whom the man in his hour is full of reverence, and in whom he is glorified and hath the root of his pride.

But not only does he come and go: it is demanded of him that he come and go. It is the systole and diastole of the Heart, that shall be. The bee comes home to the hive, and the hive expels him to attend the flowers. The hive draws home the bee, the bee leaps off the threshold of the hive, with strength, and is gone. He carries home to the hive his essence, of flowers, his joy in the Word he has uttered, he flies forth again from the hive, carrying to the flowers the strength and vigour of his scrambling body, which is God Almighty in him. So he fetches and carries, carries and fetches.

So the man comes home to woman and to God, so God the Father receives his Son again, a man of the undying flesh; and so the man goes forth from the house of his woman, so God expels him forth to waste himself in utterance, in work, which is only God the Father realizing himself in a moment of forgetfulness. Thus the eternal working. And it is joy enough to see it, without asking why. For it is as if the Father took delight in seeing himself for a moment unworking, for a moment wasting himself that he might know himself. For every petalled flower, which alone is a Flower, is a work of productiveness. It is a moment of joy, of saying, "I am I." And every table or chair a man makes is a self-same waste of his life, a fixing into stiffness and deadness of a moment of himself, for the sake of the glad cry: "This is I—I am I." And this glad cry, when we know, is the Holy Ghost, the Comforter.

So, God Eternal, the Father, continues, doing we know not what, not why: we only know He is. And again and again comes the exclamation of joy, or of pain which is joy—like Galileo and Shakespeare and Darwin—which announces "I am I."

And in the woman is the eternal continuance, and from the man, in the human race, comes the exclamation of joy and astonishment at new self-revelation, revelation of that which is Woman to a man.

Now every woman, according to her kind, demands that a man shall come home to her with joy and weariness of the work he has done during the day: that he shall then while he is with her, be re-born of her; that in the morning he shall go forth with his new strength.

But if the man does not come home to a woman, leaving her to take account of him, but is a stranger to her; if when he enters her house, he does not become simply her man of flesh, entered into her house as if it were her greater body, to be warmed, and restored, and nourished, from the store the day has given her, then she shall expel him from her house, as a drone. It is as inevitable as the working of the bees, as that a stick shall go down stream.

For in the flesh of the woman does God exact Himself. And out of the flesh of the woman does He demand: "Carry this of Me forth to utterance." And if the man deny, or be too weak, then shall the woman find another man, of greater strength. And if, because of the Word, which is the Law, she do not find another man, nor he another woman, then shall they both be destroyed. For he, to get that rest, and warmth, and nourishment which he should have had from her, his woman, must consume his own flesh, and so destroy himself: whether with wine, or other kindling. And she, either her surplus shall wear away her flesh, in sickness, or in lighting up and illuminating old dead Words, or she shall spend it in fighting with her man to make him take her, or she shall turn to her son, and say, "Be you my Go-between."

But the man who is the go-between from Woman to Production is the lover of that woman. And if that Woman be his mother, then is he her lover in part only; he carries for her, but is never received into her for his confirmation and renewal, and so wastes himself away in the flesh. The old son-lover was Oedipus. The name of the new one is legion. And if a son-lover take a wife, then is she not his wife, she is only his bed. And his life will be torn in twain, and his wife in her despair shall hope for sons, that she may have her lover in her hour.

D. H. LAWRENCE

GARGNANO.
JAN., 1913

To Edward Garnett February 1, 1913
. . . Your sympathies are with your own generation, not with mine. I think it is inevitable. You are about the only man who is willing to let a new generation come in. It will seem a bit rough to me, when I am 45, and must see myself and my tradition supplanted. I shall bear it very badly. Damn my impudence, but don't dislike me. . . . We have to hate our immediate predecessors, to get free from their authority.

But Lord, I can't be sententious and keep my dignity.

I don't want *neither* a foreword nor a descriptive notice *publishing* to Sons and Lovers. I wanted to *write* a Foreword, not to have one printed. You can easily understand. I am fearfully satisfied with myself as it is, and I should die of shame if that Foreword were printed.

To Edward Garnett February 18, 1913
I corrected and returned the first batch of *Sons and Lovers.* It goes well, in print, don't you think? Don't you think I get people into my grip? You did the pruning jolly well, and I am grateful. I hope you'll live a long long time, to barber up my novels for me before they're published. I wish I weren't so profuse—or prolix, or whatever it is. But I shall get better.

To Edward Garnett March 3, 1913

. . . I finished and returned all the proofs of *Sons and Lovers*. I suppose they came all right. It is rather a good novel— but if anything a bit difficult to grip as a whole, at first. Yet it *is* a unified whole, and I hate the dodge of putting a thick black line round the figures to throw out the composition. Which shows I'm a bit uneasy about it.

To Edward Garnett March 11, 1913

We are most interested to hear of Miss Chambers' MS.,[10] and Frieda is more anxious to see it than I am. I think I will ask Jessie to send it along. I heard from her the other day in answer to the book of poems—a damned affected letter. But there, it isn't so easy to write naturally to a quondam lover.

I am anxious down to my vitals about the poems. I thought my friends in the field—de la Mare and so on—would review them decently for me. God help us, I've got the pip horribly at present. I don't mind if Duckworth crosses out a hundred shady pages in *Sons and Lovers*. It's got to sell, I've got to live.

To A. W. McLeod [postmark April 26, 1913]

Pray to your gods for me that *Sons and Lovers* shall succeed. People should begin to take me seriously now. And I do so break my heart over England when I read *The New Machiavelli*. And I am so sure that only through a readjustment between men and women, and a making free and healthy of this sex, will she get out of her present atrophy. Oh, Lord, and if I don't "subdue my art to a metaphysic," as somebody very beautifully said of Hardy, I do write because I want folk—English folk—to alter, and have more sense.

To Edward Garnett May 19, 1913

The copy of *Sons and Lovers* has just come—I am fearfully proud of it. I reckon it is quite a great book. I shall not write

---

10 The manuscript of her novel, *Eunice Temple*, covering the same ground as *Sons and Lovers*, was later destroyed. Her view of her relations with Lawrence, and her objections to his account in the novel, are given in her *D. H. Lawrence: A Personal Record*.

quite in that style any more. It's the end of my youthful period. Thanks a hundred times.

We got Miss Chambers' novel. I should scarcely recognise her—she never used to *say* anything. But it isn't bad, and it made me so miserable I had hardly the energy to walk out of the house for two days.

To Edward Garnett [?July 16, 1913]

Fussy old woman in the *Nation*! But I *did* touch her up, at any rate. Do *you* think the second half of *Sons and Lovers* such a lapse from the first, or is it moralistic blarney? Frieda agrees with them that Miriam and Clara and Paul's love affairs weren't worth writing about.

To A. D. McLeod October 27, 1913

. . . I am sure every man feels first, that he is a servant— be it martyr or what—of society. And if he feels that he has trespassed against society, and it is adverse to him, he suffers. Then the individual self comes up and says, "You fool."

Now again, only the sea—it is rather dark today, with heavy waves—and the olives matter to me. London is all smoke a long way off. But yesterday I was awfully grateful to you for your sane and decent letter. You must continue to believe in me— I don't mean in my talent only—because I depend on you a bit. One doesn't know, till one is a bit at odds with the world, how much one's friends who believe in one rather generously, mean to one. I felt you had gone off from me a bit, because of *Sons and Lovers*. But one sheds one's sicknesses in books—repeats and presents again one's emotions, to be master of them.

To Edward Garnett December 30, 1913

I shan't write in the same manner as *Sons and Lovers* again, I think—in that hard, violent style full of sensation and presentation.

To Edward Garnett January 29, 1914

Then about the artistic side being in the background. It is that which troubles me most. I have no longer the joy in creating vivid scenes, that I had in *Sons and Lovers*. I don't care much more about accumulating objects in the powerful light of emotion, and making a scene of them.

To Barbara Low September 11, 1916
    I hated the *Psychoanalysis Review* of *Sons and Lovers*.[11] You know I think "complexes" are vicious half-statements of the Freudians: sort of can't see wood for trees. When you've said *Mutter*-complex, you've said nothing—no more than if you called hysteria a nervous disease. Hysteria isn't nerves, a complex is not simply a sex relation: far from it.—My poor book: it was, as art, a fairly complete truth: so they carve a half lie out of it, and say "*Voilà*." Swine! . . .

    11 Lawrence may have been referring to the critical review by Alfred Booth Kuttner in the July, 1916, number of *The Psychoanalytic Review*. Kuttner's review may be found in this anthology in the section titled "Psychological Connections and Approaches." It was included to illustrate the nature and possibilities of an extensive professional application of Freudian theory to the novel. Lawrence's objection in the name of the more complete truth of art raises a question that perhaps none of the later, literary critics deal with completely.

2 · From a Letter by Alice Dax ("Clara")
to Frieda Lawrence

. . . The "Wind" nearly broke my heart with sadness and gladness and other conflicting emotions. And I was grateful to you—really grateful.

I had always been glad that he met you, even from the day after the event, when he told me about you, and I knew that he would leave me. I was never *meet* for him and what he liked was not the me I *was*, but the me I might-have-been— the potential me which would never have struggled to life but for his help and influence. I thank him always for my life though I know it cost him pains and disappointments. I fear that he never even enjoyed morphia with me—always it carried an irritant—we were never, except for one short memorable hour, whole: it was from that one hour that I began to see the light of life.

Unlike you, I could never quarrel with D. H., the probable truth being that I felt unsure of him and feared to lose him, whilst he in turn, I suppose equally unsure of me, rarely quarreled with me, but when he became extremely angry would turn and walk out. It was not honest—I know it, and I know too how much sooner I should have achieved myself had I given vent to the feelings I had, *when* I had them. And then I expected of him an honesty which I myself did not render, which was impertinence, so that always between us there were undercurrents which we could not cross. He needed *you*. I remember so well his words:—"You would like Frieda—she is direct and free, but I don't know how you would get on together" and his voice tailed off into "I wonder," whilst his mind compared us and his eyes left me in no doubt. You had, without doubt, all the things that he needed, and his sensitive soul knew it without an inventory.

My own childhood had been much nearer to D. H.'s than to yours, but even in his poverty he was richer than I, for the poverty of my life was shut in behind clean faces and gloved hands; a father's silk hat and frock coat, and a table which carried fair linen and crocheted doyleys even though every cake on it had to be halved or quartered to make them go round—a damnable crippling poverty, base and dishonest, which had no room for thought or books or recreation, but which demanded that every moment must be devoted to mending and making and scraping to keep up an appearance.

I happened to be the most unlucky bird of the brood—damned from before my birth and doubly damned after it. I was conceived during a long period of unemployment, and the sordid story of those pregnant months, as well as those which followed, I heard time after time after time repeated by my mother throughtout my childhood with tears of thankfulness to the good God who had always provided her with *bread*—she seemed to have had little else beside! When at last *knowledge* came to me, I loathed and detested my father (I had never been very fond of him); I swore vengeance on his sex when I should myself be married, and since *everyone* said that no man would ever marry me, I took the first who offered lest I should be cheated. Luckily for him I had developed a rather strong sense of justice before the marriage day so that he didn't suffer so much as he might have done. But this! All this! *Was* it the vessel from which D. H. might drink to his joy and well-being? I ask you! And I do believe that my revenge, unconsciously and unintentionally, hurt *him* far more than it has ever hurt my husband. Alas! I loved him. But now I think you will understand why I was so glad that you loved him too—you who could give him so much, but my cup was bitter when he wrote from Garda in the richness of fulfilment.

How bitterly I envied you that day! How I resented his snob-
bery and his happiness whilst I was suffering in body and sick
in soul, carrying an unwanted child which would never have
been conceived but for an unendurable passion which only *he*
had roused and my husband had slaked. So—life! . . .

3 · From Letters by Frieda Lawrence

To Edward Garnett [?*September 1912*]

. . . I think L. quite missed the point in "Paul Morel." He really loved his mother more than anybody, even with his other women, real love, sort of Oedipus; his mother must have been adorable. He is writing P. M. again, reads bits to me and we fight like blazes over it, he is so often beside the point. . . .

To Edward Garnett [?*September 1912*]

. . . I also feel as if I ought to say something about L.'s formlessness. I don't think he has no form. I used to. But now I think anybody must see in "Paul Morel" the hang of it. The mother is really the thread, the domineering note. I think the honesty, the vividness of a book suffers if you subject it to form. I have heard so much about "form" with Ernest; why are you English so keen on it? Their own form wants smashing in almost any direction, but they can't come out of their snail house. I know it is so much safer. That's what I love Lawrence for, that he is so plucky and honest in his work. . . . any new thing must find a new shape, then afterwards one can call it "art." I hate art, it seems like grammar, wants to make a language all grammar. . . . I quite firmly believe that L. is quite great in spite of his "gaps." Look at

Reprinted from Frieda Lawrence: The Memoirs and Correspondence, edited by E. W. Tedlock, Jr., by permission of Alfred A. Knopf, Inc. Copyright © 1961, 1964 by The Frieda Lawrence Estate.

the vividness of his stuff, it knock you down, I think. It is perhaps too "intimate," comes too close, but I believe that is youth. . . . Don't think I am impudent to say all this, but I feel quite responsible for "Paul." I wrote little female bits and lived it over in my own heart. . . .

To Edward Garnett [*May* 1913?]

. . . Miriam's novel is very lovable, I think, and one does feel so sorry for her, but it's a faded photograph of *Sons and Lovers*; she has never understood anything out of herself, no inner activity, but she does make one ache! I only just realized the amazing brutality of *Sons and Lovers*. How that brutality remains in spite of Christianity, of the two thousand years; it's better like that, than in the civilized forms it takes! It's only a top plaster, and I'm sure brutality ought to develop into something finer, out of *itself*, not be suppressed, denied! Paul says to his mother, when she is dying, "If I'd got to die, I would be quick about it, I would *will* to die." Doesn't it seem awful! Yet, one *does* feel like that, but not only that after all! . . .

To Harry T. Moore, January 30, 1951

. . . I was trying hard to remember about "Miriam." . . . L. felt unhappy about hurting her feelings. She *was* deeply hurt. She was the "sacred love," you know the old split of sacred and profane. She tries to defend her position by insisting on the "purity," which gives the show away. Humanly as a whole she wasn't the person his mother was, so the best horse won. She bored me in the end. There was some correspondence between L. and her about the book, but when she had read it, she never wrote again. In writing about her, he had to find out impersonally what was wrong in their relationship, when so much had been good. But what was insufficient in her, how could she admit or even see it. . . .

To Edward Gilbert, October 13, 1951

. . . You say Miriam was spiritual. She was intellectual. Her passion was the written word. She never realized L.'s potentiality. But he owed her much as a writer. For me the man came first. . . .

To Harry T. Moore, July 21, 1953

. . . I read Miriam's D. H. L. again, it is very good and charming, very well written. . . . That she could not face the incompleteness of her own nature, that one cannot expect. . . .

To Harry T. Moore, January 14, 1955

. . . I never told you about my friend, a young Austrian doctor who had worked with Freud and who revolutionised my life with Freud. Through him and then through me Lawrence knew about Freud. . . .

4·*From* D. H. Lawrence:
A Personal Record

by Jessie Chambers ("Miriam")

. . . Lawrence continued to bring, and when he left home to send his writings to me: poems frequently, and always the novel which ultimately became *The White Peacock*. It was at Christmas of this year on his first holiday from Croydon that he showed us the *English Review* for December, 1908. We were delighted with the journal. The very look of it, with its fine blue cover and handsome black type, was satisfying. Father thoroughly appreciated it, and we decided to subscribe to it amongst us. The coming of the *English Review* into our lives was an event, one of the few really first-rate things that happen now and again in a lifetime. I remember what a joy it was to get the solid, handsome journal from our local newsagent, and feel it was a link with the world of literature. I soon noticed that the Editor was prepared to welcome new talent. I drew Lawrence's attention to this and begged him to submit some of his work, but he refused absolutely. I asked what was to become of his writing if he made no attempt to place any of it.

"I don't care what becomes of it," he said stubbornly. "I'm not anxious to get into print. I shan't send anything. Besides they'd never take it."

"How do you know unless you try?" I persisted, and he suddenly said:

"*You* send something. Send some of the poems, if you like."

Reprinted by permission of Jonathan Cape, Ltd., and J. R. Wood.

"Very well, which shall I send?"

"Send whatever you like. Do what you like with them," he answered. Then, seeing I was in earnest, he added: "Give me a *nom de plume*, though; I don't want folk in Croydon to know I write poetry." And he would say nothing more.

I looked through the poems Lawrence had sent in letters to me since he left home, picked out what I thought were the best, and copied them out one beautiful June morning. I was careful to put the poem called "Discipline" first, not because I thought it was the best, but hoping that the unusual title might attract the Editor's attention. In "Dreams Old and Nascent" I knew he was trying to explain himself to me; and "Baby Movements" I sent because I loved it. It was about the baby in the family with whom he lived in Croydon. He was very fond of her and often spoke about her in letters. I enclosed also several other poems whose titles I don't remember. I wrote a letter to the Editor of the *English Review* saying that the author of the poems was a young man who had been writing for a number of years, and who would be very grateful for any recognition. I gave his name, of course, but said that if any of the poems were printed they should appear under the *nom de plume* of Richard Greasley (Richards was an unacknowledged name of Lawrence's and Greasley was his home parish). The next time I saw Lawrence he said:

"Did you send those poems to the *English*?" adding immediately, "They'll never print them."

The reply came in August when the Lawrences were on holiday at Shanklin in the Isle of Wight. It said, as nearly as I can remember, that the poems were very interesting and that the author had undoubted talent, but that nowadays luck played such a large part in a literary career, and continued, "If you would get him to come and see me some time when he is in London perhaps something might be done." The letter was signed Ford Madox Hueffer, a name that I knew only in connection with the first instalment of the serial story, A *Call*, in the current number of the *English Review*. I replied that Mr. Lawrence was away at the moment, but when school re-opened I was sure he would be glad to call on Mr. Hueffer.

Lawrence wrote to me from Shanklin, a long descriptive

letter about the island and the fun they all had bathing, but I
kept my news until he returned. When we were alone together
I said:

"Oh, I've got a letter for you."

He looked at me quickly, then his eyes narrowed:

"From the *English*? About the poems? Show it me."

I gave him the letter, and his face became tense.

"*You* are my luck," he murmured. Then he said with suppressed excitement, "Let me take it to show mother." And I
never saw it again.

In our talks that holiday Lawrence told me that his mother
and sister were not pleased with him. He was changing, they said,
and breaking away from the old things, and they hated him to
be different from what he used to be. He felt it was hard and
narrow on their part. He had to change, and leave the old things,
but he thought they might go on liking him just the same.

As I had not been away for a holiday I reminded Lawrence
of the project for making up a party and visiting the historic
remains of Nottingham. He looked worried for a moment, but
said he would like it, adding, "The others probably won't want
to, so if we go *à deux*, we go *à deux*." It was arranged that the
party (if there was one) should meet at his home. When I
called Lawrence was not ready, and his sister was nowhere to be
seen. I asked Mrs. Lawrence if A. was to accompany us, and she
replied shortly that she was not. I thought Mrs. Lawrence might
make some reference to Hueffer's letter, but she said nothing.
I seemed to be in disgrace. At the time I could not understand
why, and I can only surmise that Lawrence in self-defence told
his mother I had sent the poems without his knowledge, so that
in her eyes I was guilty of unwarrantable interference in his
affairs. Whatever the reason, the atmosphere suggested an im-
minent thunderstorm. I tried to take no notice and went on
talking, only to feel the air grow more oppressive. We set off
finally with the distinct sense of a rod in pickle, for either or
both of us.

As was usual when the home atmosphere was disturbed in
this way, Lawrence took refuge in an arrogance which I felt to be
a mask for his own wretchedness. I tried not to be affected by it,

but after a time my spirit flagged and I became a mere bundle of misery. It was the same at the café where we had tea. Lawrence's precise and distant manner withered my attempts at conversation. Afterwards he strode along to one of the picturesque old shops near the Castle, where he bought some photographs of Greek statuary. One was "Amor et Psyche," which he said ominously was for me. The remainder of the evening is a blank in my memory, but we must have been to a theatre, because it was late when we went home. I was to stay with my sister (who was now married) and on the walk from the station Lawrence poured out his accumulated spleen. It was the old story. There could never, *never* be anything between us but an association of the mind and the spirit. I was Psyche, I was the soul, and I had no other significance for him . . . But it was uttered with the dehumanized vehemence that was so devastating. At the gate he held out the picture of "Amor et Psyche."

"Take it," he said, "it is you. You are Psyche, you are the soul, and I leave you, as I *must*." He gazed at me for a moment with a face set in agony, then turned on his heel and began to stamp his way homeward. I felt terror-stricken, for both of us, but more for him. I ran for some steps after him and called, but his heel rang on the pavement so that it was impossible for him to hear me. I went back to the cottage.

In the morning I felt too ill to go home. My sister mercifully asked no questions, and later in the day we returned together. I learned afterwards that Lawrence arrived at the cottage soon after we had gone, and badly wanted to start in pursuit of us. He was assured that he could not overtake us, and remained hanging about, moody and silent. . . .

bers, and then used some of her sentences, but he greatly expanded the material—and illuminated it. Her effort is a commonplace account of an incident, the kind of writing almost any literate person could provide. Lawrence in adapting it does not produce a "great" passage, but he transmutes the material creatively and makes the episode one of the many living bits that contribute to the total effectiveness of *Sons and Lovers*.

In Jessie Chambers' version of this "Saturday Afternoon" fragment, Miriam and Agatha are dressing when they hear the "characteristic, click of the chain" as Paul flings open the gate and pushes his bicycle into the yard. Lawrence in *Sons and Lovers* sets the scene more fully; he does not merely have the girls "upstairs dressing," but describes the bedroom, which is above the stable: the Veronese reproduction on the wall, and the view from the windows. Lawrence "characterizes" the girls somewhat, contrasting not only their appearances but their ideas of values. In both Jessie's version and Lawrence's, the dialogue is identical when the girls briefly discuss the arrival of Paul, and in both accounts "Agatha was dressed first, and ran downstairs," but Lawrence's adaptation differs in many details. It is interesting to note that the comma before "and" in the sentence just quoted, technically incorrect in modern English, was omitted in Jessie's manuscript; a comma with the double predicate was habitual with Lawrence, probably because of his familiarity with the King James Bible, in which the use of commas in this construction is common. Jessie Chambers in her "Saturday Afternoon" fragment has Paul make no further appearance until Miriam descends and sees him in the parlor, where he is talking to Agatha. But in *Sons and Lovers* Lawrence, while keeping the focus on Miriam in this sequence, also keeps Paul within range: Miriam hears him talking in Midlands dialect to the "seedy" old horse in the yard below. Miriam also—in Lawrence's version—hears her sister gaily greeting Paul downstairs. In both versions, Miriam prays at this point, asking the Lord to keep her from loving Paul if it is not right for her to love him; Lawrence throughout the prayer sequence writes more skillfully than the girl who was here providing a part of her own autobiography, though now and then he takes over phrases and even whole sentences from her manuscript. He omits, however, Jessie's extravagant comparison between Miriam's plight and Gethesemane; at the end of the prayer he describes her as she kneels by the bed, "her black hair against the red squares of the patchwork-quilt." After she finishes her prayer, she gets up and goes to meet Paul:

> When she went downstairs Paul was lying back in an arm-chair, holding forth with much vehemence to Agatha, who was scorning a little painting he had brought to show her. Miriam glanced at the two, and avoided their levity. She went into the parlour to be alone.
>
> It was teatime before she was able to speak to Paul, and then her manner was so distant he thought he had offended her.

These two paragraphs are taken over almost verbatim from Jessie's narrative. The only difference in the first sentence, besides Lawrence's omission of the comma Jessie put after the opening adverbial clause and his altering of "the arm-chair" to "an arm-chair," is in Lawrence's slight improvement of the expression "talking in an animated way to Agatha." In the second sentence Miriam, in Jessie's version, "glanced at them, half afraid of their levity, and went into the parlour." Lawrence makes a separate paragraph of the next sentence, which is precisely as Jessie wrote it, with the very minor exception of Lawrence's making "teatime" one word instead of using Jessie's hyphenation.

. . . Jessie Chambers—in her *D. H. Lawrence: A Personal Record* (1935), for whose ascription of authorship she used the pseudonymous initials E. T.—said that when she gave Lawrence her reactions to the first draft of *Sons and Lovers*, he "asked me to write what I could remember of our early days, because, as he truthfully said, my recollection of those days was so much clearer than his." She suggested that his request was made in the autumn of 1911; she was wrong, however, in stating that Lawrence began the novel in that year, for in a letter to Sydney Pawling of Heinemann's on October 18, 1910, Lawrence speaks of the book—then entitled *Paul Morel*—as being one-eighth completed.

. . . The Miriam Papers apparently are concerned with improving the first version of the novel, the version which was begun in 1910 but not shown to Jessie Chambers until the autumn of the following year. This version will be referred to hereinafter as *Paul Morel* A.

Lawrence was violently ill by the end of that autumn of 1911, and was convalescent through most of the ensuing winter. At this time he was working on *The Trespasser*, which he completed in early February, for publication in May. In a letter to Edward Garnett on February 24, 1912, Lawrence spoke of his "third novel," which was obviously *Paul Morel*. He expected to complete it by May: he had not expected to meet Frieda.

Jessie Chambers said that Lawrence wrote *Sons and Lovers* in a frenzy, in about six weeks. This was probably the second draft, and it was doubtless this version of the manuscript he wrote of as practically completed, in May 1912, when he was alone in the Rhineland after he and Frieda had gone to the Continent and had temporarily separated. This version of the book that was to be *Sons and Lovers* will subsequently be referred to as *Paul Morel* B. Early in June Lawrence mailed the finished product to England; late in July he had received it back and by the middle of November had finished it in Italy— the *Sons and Lovers* that was published the following May.

It is necessary to point out once again that Jessie Chambers' contribution of various episodes to the novel was doubtless an attempt to improve the *first draft*, or *Paul Morel* A. Two more of these contributions remain to be discussed: they might be called "Easter Monday" and "Flower Sequence."

. . . "Easter Monday," which carries that title at the beginning, is a complete unit on four pages. Lawrence does not use this sequence in the "Lad-And-Girl Love" chapter, but in the second chapter afterward, "Defeat of Miriam."

Once again Lawrence takes a narrative outline from Jessie, using the same incidents and occasionally the same language, but once again the result is vastly different: her prose is lead, his quicksilver.

In "Easter Monday," Paul walks through the fields with Miriam, her mother, and two of the smaller children. At tea, Paul complains about a sermon he had heard on Good Friday. Later, he and Miriam sit under a haystack, and he reads from *Jane Eyre*. Then he and the girl discuss their status. When they go back indoors, Miriam's mother says that Paul is pale and that she is sure he has caught cold. He leaves, and two days later he sends Miriam a copy of *The Mill on the Floss.*

All this is familiar to readers of *Sons and Lovers,* where Lawrence scrambled the material somewhat, however; the mockery of the sermon Paul had heard in the Primitive Methodist Chapel comes early in the chapter, during Paul's visit to the farm on Easter Sunday. Jessie's "Easter Monday" sequence he gives to the following *Sunday.*

Once again, where Jessie Chambers provided the barest outline, Lawrence filled it in with living details. In her first "Easter Monday" paragraph, for instance, Paul finds a thrush's nest, and after carefully breaking away the thorns he holds the "eggs reverently in the hollowed palm of his hand." Then Jessie's narrative abruptly switches to Paul's later discussion of the sermon, at tea. But in *Sons and Lovers* Lawrence brings the whole scene alive, using it to develop story and character. The mother thrush has been frightened away by the approach of the human beings, and the eggs are still warm; Miriam's mother speaks sympathetically of the bird, and Miriam is compelled to touch the eggs, as well as Paul's hand, which "cradled them so well." She says it is a strange warmth, and he tells her it is blood heat. She watches him as he reaches through the thorns of the hedge, putting the eggs back, his hands carefully folded over them. "He was concentrated on the act. Seeing him so, she loved him; he seemed so simple and sufficient to himself. And she could not get to him."

Later, when Paul and Miriam have been reading by the haystack, he asks "Do you think—if I didn't come up so much—you might get to like somebody else—another man?" This is almost exactly as Jessie wrote it, and for two pages Lawrence closely follows her version of the conversation, occasionally changing a word or a phrase, adding "he blurted," or noting that "Miriam wanted to cry. And she was angry, too," and making similar additions.

When Paul and Miriam go back indoors, Miriam's mother exclaims, as previously mentioned, that Paul looks pale; in Lawrence's version, instead of merely stating that Paul has probably caught cold, she keeps the balance between all the characters by asking whether he does not feel that he has caught cold; Paul, kept in focus, laughs and says "Oh no!" Lawrence adds that Paul did, however, feel "done up," worn out by "the conflict in himself."

In Jessie Chambers' account, "While it was quite early and not yet dark, Paul rose to go. The family exclaimed at his going so soon. Miriam, sitting in the rocking-chair, near the wall of the stairs, was silent." In *Sons and Lovers* Lawrence breaks this paragraph up, intensifies the situation. Paul starts to leave while it is "quite early," and Miriam's mother "anxiously" asks "You're not going home, are you?" He replies that he had promised to be home early; he is "very awkward." Miriam's father steps into the little contest: "But this *is* early." Miriam sits in her chair; Paul hesitates beside it, expecting her as usual to walk out to the barn with him when he goes after his bicycle. When she does not join him, he is "at a loss," and he departs. In Jessie's story, as he passes the window he looks "at her with so much reproach that she" goes to the doorway to wave farewell to him. Lawrence is not content to have Paul merely look at Miriam with "much reproach": in *Sons and Lovers*, Miriam sees Paul "pale, his brows knit slightly in a way that had become constant with him, his eyes dark with pain."

The third section of the first part of the Miriam Papers is less interesting than the other two; it is a two-page fragment out of context, called "Flower Sequence" here.

Lawrence took over virtually all the material in this fragment, spreading it over three pages of *Sons and Lovers* in the "Lad-And-Girl Love" chapter. This "Flower Sequence" describes an episode in the Morels' garden, where Paul picks some sweet peas and pins them on Miriam's dress, saying "Don't let mother know." Miriam tells Paul that she will no longer call for him at his house on the Thursday evenings when she comes into town to the library; if Paul wants to be with her at the library he can meet her at some place in town; because he will not do this, the Thursday evenings at the library are "dropped." Paul's attitude in regard to "the glances and remarks of acquaintances is that such manifestations are unimportant: 'Let them talk.' "

Lawrence in *Sons and Lovers* again makes the situation more effective by dramatizing the material Jessie has provided, by adding opposing statements, and by swinging his camera around to catch peripheral but significant details. Instead of statements about Paul and Miriam arriving at decisions, Lawrence shows them in discussion, using tense, brief sentences. And where Jessie merely says that "the Thursday evenings at the library were dropped," Lawrence intensifies the situation by addition, deepening it particularly by introducing Paul's mother at the end of the paragraph: "So the Thursday evenings, which had been so precious to her, and to him, were dropped. He worked instead. Mrs. Morel sniffed with satisfaction at this arrangement."

Lawrence, however, took over a good deal of Jessie's text in this sequence. He even assimilates some of the descriptions and color: Jessie's sentence, "The sky behind the church was orange-red with sunset: the garden was flooded with a strange warm light that lifted every leaf into significance," goes into *Sons and Lovers* almost exactly as she wrote it.

The foregoing discussion of the first part of the Miriam Papers proves the truth of Jessie Chambers' assertion that she wrote what she modestly called "notes" to help Lawrence with the composition of *Sons and Lovers*. The comparison of her text with that of the published novel indicates that Lawrence advantageously used the material, greatly improving it in the process. It might be pointed out that Jessie Chambers was not trying to write a novel, that she was merely providing "notes," but actually she did use the narrative form, and there can be little doubt that her effort represents the best that she could do at the time: her *Personal Record*, written years later in direct autobiographical form, is superior in composition to her *Paul Morel* "notes." (She wrote an autobiographical novel, *Eunice Temple*, which she destroyed; the name character furnished the initials, E. T., which she used to signify the authorship of her later *Personal Record* of Lawrence.)

The questions remain, how much credit should she be given for collaboration on *Sons and Lovers*, and how far did her collaboration actually extend?

So far as credit for collaboration is concerned, Jessie Chambers in her essential modesty never put in a claim for any: her principal contention in regard to *Sons and Lovers* was that the book "betrayed" the beauty of her early relationship with Lawrence; she continually makes it clear that she cannot distinguish between biographical fact and the necessary fiction required for the novel-form. So far as the queston of combined authorship is concerned, the situation is certainly different from that of Lawrence's collaboration with M. L. Skinner, whose entire novel *The House of Ellis* was rewritten by Lawrence as *The Boy in the Bush*. It is doubtful that Jessie Chambers' contributions were much more extensive than the sections already surveyed. That Lawrence was an extremely resourceful, richly inventive writer cannot be gainsaid: occasionally he drew upon the recollections or reactions of others in order that parts of his writing not dealing with himself, or not dealing exclusively with himself, might have some of the immediacy of his purely objective passages. It has been mentioned in the body of the present book that Lawrence's wife says that he kept asking her, when he was writing about his mother in *Sons and Lovers*, what a woman would feel at certain times, in certain situations—and Frieda says that she wrote several passages of *Sons and Lovers*. Lawrence's reworking of Miss Skinner's book did not represent his only attempt at large-scale collaboration with women in the writing of novels: he wanted Mabel Luhan to work with him on a story about her life, and Catherine Carswell includes in *The Savage Pilgrimage* a vivid synopsis Lawrence prepared of a Scottish novel for which Mrs. Carswell was to supply the Caledonian background and the character of the heroine. In *Sons and Lovers*, however, Lawrence went far beyond the range of what Jessie Chambers could have supplied, or what Frieda might have provided as a description of the mother's feelings; indeed, Jessie was irritated because he went too far beyond her own ideas of reality and propriety in introducing Clara Dawes into the story and in giving the mother "the laurels of victory" in the conflict with Miriam.

Lawrence's originality can be defended easily: the re-creation of his own family background, for example, reveals a gift of selection by artistic principle, of inventiveness in which imagination dominates fact, and of sustained narrative intensity, all present in a high degree. Throughout the novel, the descriptions of the life of the coal miners, of the workers in an artificial-limb factory, of young people from Midlands farms and towns, all presented in a rich fullness, are testimony to Lawrence's surpassing ability to transmute fact into what might be called the imaginative reality of first-rate fiction. If Jessie Chambers provided him with some details about life at Haggs Farm, and even with some memories of the time she and Lawrence were living through their unhappy relationship, these raw materials were used by him in the same way as his own observations and remembered experiences.

It may be said, then, that while Jessie Chambers supplied a number of reminiscental passages which Lawrence assimilated into *Sons and Lovers,* she was in no true sense a collaborator. Her innate modesty did not merely prevent her from making such a claim: there is no hint in her book on Lawrence that she even remotely considered doing so. She was, indeed, as previously pointed out, hostile to *Sons and Lovers.* But in discussing the book, she mentions merely that she provided some notes and suggestions. That is what she did, and no more. Her material had an ancillary value; Lawrence's gift was the primary one, and he used the material creatively.

So far, Jessie Chambers' positive contributions have been considered; her appearances in the second part of the Miriam Papers are chiefly negative.

As previously pointed out, this second portion of the Miriam Papers comprises twenty-three pages of Lawrence's manuscript with comments by Jessie Chambers, plus her four-page critique of that section of the manuscript. It is quite possible, as will be shown later, that this part of Lawrence's manuscript was based on papers of Jessie's that are now missing.

Lawrence's twenty-three holograph sheets are numbered pp. 204–226. The first page begins with two words (". . . knock it.") ending a paragraph; p. 226, which apparently concludes a section, contains only five lines of writing. . . .

The material covered in this segment of manuscript corresponds for the most part to incidents in the "Lad-And-Girl Love" chapter (Chapter VII) of the final version; judging from Miriam's notations, this was Chapter IX in the earlier version, and entitled "Young Love." This manuscript evidently represents a fragment of the second stage of composition of *Sons and*

Lovers; as previously noted, the entire second *Paul Morel* manuscript will be designated hereafter as *Paul Morel B.* The manuscript described by Dr. Powell in *The Manuscripts of D. H.
Lawrence*—the crude early *Paul Morel* in which the father is
jailed for accidentally killing one of his sons—would then properly become *Paul Morel A,* as also previously noted. This *Paul
Morel A* was the product of 1910–1911. *Paul Morel B* was evidently written in the spring of 1912, completed in Germany
about the beginning of June. Between July and November, in
Germany, Austria, and Italy, Lawrence wrote what might be
designated as *Paul Morel C,* the actual manuscript of *Sons and
Lovers* as published. The segment of manuscript discussed here
as comprising the first section of the second part of the Miriam
Papers is apparently a section of *Paul Morel B;* it is probably
a variant, for Lawrence doubtless rewrote this chapter and

Sequence	Ms. pages
1. Paul, Miriam, and the swing	204
2. Paul discusses art	204–207
3. Paul teaches algebra	207–208
4. Paul and his mother	208–209
5. Paul walks with Miriam	211–214
6. Paul talks with his mother	214–216
7. The Good Friday hike	216–221
8. The broken umbrella	218–219
9. Easter Monday excursion	221–226
10. The blowing skirt	223

placed the revised version in the complete manuscript of *Paul
Morel B,* retaining the part under discussion and putting it away
with the other Miriam Papers, among which they were found
after his death. On the strength of this speculation, this holograph text of twenty-three pages will, in further references to it
here, be called *Paul Morel B*[1].

The table indicates the disposition of the principal sequences—episodes and narrative statements—of this part of *Paul
Morel;* that is, of *Paul Morel B*[1]. The pages on which the material appears in the manuscript are indicated in the column.
The table is of course a simplification, but it must serve until
such time as the material concerned is published in full. The
table cannot indicate transitions between sequences, which are

often made by means of minor narrative statements. In the ensuing discussion, these sequences will be referred to by the numbers in the left-hand column of the table which designate their order of appearance. One fact for the reader to keep continually in mind throughout this part of the Miriam Papers is that Jessie Chambers was completely unable to see Paul and Miriam as fictional characters. Everything must be according to fact. And twenty years later she still regarded *Sons and Lovers* in the same way: it was "bad" when it introduced imaginative elements.

Discussion of Sequences

1. Since this manuscript fragment begins with the tail end of a sentence, the swinging episode, of which that sentence is a part, cannot be fully compared with the later version in the published *Sons and Lovers*. The existing evidence, however, indicates that the earlier version is less intense: in *Sons and Lovers*, Miriam's ecstatic fear of the swinging seems rather sexual—the dread and excitation of sex felt by a Victorian girl inclined to virginity. In the *Paul Morel* manuscript of the second compositional stage, she is merely nervous. She notices that Paul enjoys swinging, and therefore she lets him have longer turns; this helps establish a sense of harmony between them. Jessie Chambers struck a line through the last thought and substituted a statement to the effect that the swinging incident showed her how deeply Paul could become absorbed in acivities that interested him, an idea Lawrence took over in *Sons and Lovers* and intensified: Paul becomes himself "swinging stuff," and "every particle of him" is involved.

2. In this B^1 version of *Paul Morel*, Paul tries to explain his painting to Miriam's brother Edgar, who mocks at him. In *Sons and Lovers* Edgar's comments are omitted; Paul makes a revised version of some of his explanations, to Miriam; she accepts them without mockery.

3. The algebra lessons are presented in somewhat more detail in *Paul Morel B*[1] than in *Sons and Lovers*. In the published novel, the account of the lessons is more general: Paul is described as storming at Miriam and becoming furious and abusive. In the earlier version, the sequence is presented chiefly in

dialogue: Paul shouts at her such names as duffer, fathead, and donkey. In the *Paul Morel B*[1] manuscript, Paul's "wrath, overcharged, would burst like a bubble. Then he would be very gentle, and she would want to cry. Once, in a real passion, he threw the soft covered algebra book full in her face." If this passage is compared with its improved version in *Sons and Lovers*, the superiority of the later text becomes evident at once. In *Sons and Lovers* Paul's anger still bursts like a bubble, and he throws a pencil rather than a book in Miriam's face; but the whole incident is made more vivid by the addition of details—significant, not irrelevant—and by intensification of emotion and concentration of focus. In the later version, for example, there is more concrete motive for one of Paul's spurts of anger than the mere statement that he was "in a real passion"; part of a single sentence will show how the material has been vivified: "When he saw her eager, silent, as it were, blind face, he wanted to throw the pencil in it; and still, when he saw her hand trembling and her mouth parted with suffering, his heart was scalded with pain for her." (In another passage he does, as previously mentioned, throw the pencil in her face.) Jessie Chambers wrote a suggestion on the manuscript of the original to the effect that the algebra sequence should be modified or left out; she had no personal objections to it, but she thought that readers might find it unintelligible or dull. And in a later paragraph she objected to Lawrence's saying that Paul and Miriam, at seventeen and sixteen, read Schopenhauer and Spencer and Nietzsche, "authors who," Lawrence wrote, "hurt her inexpressibly, and delighted him"; Lawrence subsequently omitted the reference to those authors.

4. A discussion between Paul and his mother about his frequent visits to Willey Farm stands out prominently in the *Paul Morel B*[1] manuscript. There are some general statements about Paul's attitude to his mother, including one that strikingly suggests the "blood-knowledge" doctrines Lawrence was to develop later: "Their connection was subconscious, physical, of the blood." (After Lawrence read Freud he stopped using the term *subconscious* and instead used Freud's term *unconscious*.) This particular mother-son sequence is not found in *Sons and Lovers*,

though various thoughts and phrases from it are applied or suggested throughout the book.

5. Paul's walk with Miriam on a summer evening is one of the romantic high points of *Sons and Lovers*. Like the other material taken over from *Paul Morel B*[1], it is greatly improved in the rewriting. The incidents are similar in both versions, but the treatment of the second is, once again, more vivid, intense, and living. For example, the sentence, "It was early June, and the red of sunset was being spun down behind the Derbyshire hills, as Paul and Miriam went between the young wheat on the high lands," becomes: "There was a yellow glow over the mowing-grass, and the sorrel-heads burned crimson. Gradually, as they walked along the high land, the gold in the west sank down to red, the red to crimson, and then the chill blue crept up against the glow." The landscapes throughout this sequence are touched up in this way, though occasionally a bit of the earlier picture is taken over without change, such as "the high road to Alfreton, which ran white between the darkening fields," the second "the" being the only addition to the later version. This version is not only enriched in the matter of landscape descriptions, but also in regard to the relationship of Miriam and Paul, which is considerably more intensified in *Sons and Lovers*. This sequence is particularly remarkable because it is one of the first successful large-scale attempts by Lawrence to fuse character and landscape. In the earlier version, Lawrence had included an erotic passage; in it, Miriam is so excited by "her" flowering rose-tree that she wants Paul to kiss her, "almost for the first time." But Paul feels that passion is sealed in him, his mood is "abstract, purely religious." Touching Miriam's lips would cause him great agony of spirit; he cannot give her "cool kisses." But Miriam, who "had made it impossible for him to kiss her," now wants his mouth. She wants him "to clasp her body," but it is her tragedy that she has "purified his love too much"; it is painful for him even to touch her. Jessie Chambers drew pencil marks across this passage and noted at the end that Lawrence in writing it had been guilty of an amazing misconception, for Miriam at sixteen was "as pure and fierce in virginity as Paul." Lawrence omitted the passage from *Sons and Lovers*.

6. Paul's talk with his mother after he gets back home on that summer evening is, like most of the other assimilated passages, expanded in *Sons and Lovers*. The dialogue at the beginning of the scene is almost the same in both texts—the mother sarcastically remarks that Miriam must be "wonderfully fascinating," she speaks against "boy-and-girl courtship," she insists she has nothing against Miriam, she angers Paul by referring persistently to courtship—but in *Sons and Lovers* Lawrence gives the episode more breadth by introducing references to Paul's sister Annie's "keeping company" with a young man. In the manuscript, Paul ends the scene by flinging his boots down, kissing his mother hastily "on the brow," and leaving; in the published novel, Paul exhibits more sympathy for his mother, who looks weary; she has not been strong since the death of Paul's older brother, "and her eyes hurt her." Paul stays with her for a while, trying to make peace, and as he kisses her forehead he notices the wrinkles on it, the greying hair, and "the proud setting of the temples." His hand lingers on her shoulder—he has forgotten Miriam. This ends the sequence in the book, where the transition passage to the Good Friday hike is different from the one in the manuscript. In the latter, Miriam is irritated because Paul is "at the beck and call of everybody." Jessie Chambers questioned this passage in a note at the bottom of the page, in which she protested that "Miriam revered Paul's love for his mother." She added that both Paul and Miriam were at this time "unconscious," not desiring "even love." Lawrence's statement that Paul was at this time a child, "just an unmanageable, tiresome child," was crossed out by Jessie Chambers, who noted: "Not until twenty-one."

7. Lawrence in *Sons and Lovers* makes Paul older in the Good-Friday-hike sequence than in *Paul Morel B* [1]; in the latter, the hike takes place when Paul is eighteen, but in *Sons and Lovers* he is a year older—perhaps Lawrence was weary of Jessie's marginal notes to the effect that Paul and Miriam were too young to have certain feelings. In the transition passage preceding the hike episode, Lawrence in *Sons and Lovers* has a long paragraph about Miriam's hypersensitiveness to the physical facts of life: grossness of any kind upsets her, and the men around the farm must be careful what they say in her presence;

they cannot even mention that the mare is in foal. The Good Friday hike itself is essentially the same in both manuscript and book; the latter is, as usual, more detailed and vivid. The sequence ends, in both accounts, with a discussion between Paul and Miriam; this is the "love begets love" dialogue that takes up about half a page in *Sons and Lovers*. This was a longer scene in *Paul Morel B*[1], but Jessie Chambers scratched out a good deal of it and pencilled in extensive comments. Lawrence did not use anything she had objected to here. He had originally cast the scene into "another day" (from the day of the hike), but Jessie wrote in "the same" above "another"—Lawrence put "another evening" into *Sons and Lovers*. In both cases, Paul and Miriam are walking under the trees at Nether Green; in *Sons and Lovers*, before he speaks about love's being necessarily reciprocal, he has been "talking to her fretfully," as if "struggling to convince himself." In the earlier text, Miriam has wanted Paul to acknowledge his love; she was sure of his love but desired to have him acknowledge it. Jessie Chambers drew pencil marks through this passage and wrote above it: "Oh dear no: the conversation was Paul's." Later she noted that Paul's remarks in this scene were self-justification; he was coming under the spell of "the second self that watches things." She wrote further that Miriam was at this time the stronger of the two because her love for Paul had not yet grown beyond control; the denial of it became terrible later, when "it became invested with holiness like religion and had behind it the whole force of the will to live."

8. The broken-umbrella sequence stands out importantly in *Sons and Lovers* and in Jessie Chambers' comments upon it. The scene is presented so vividly from Miriam's point of view in *Paul Morel B* [1] that it suggests that this manuscript was in part based on passages originally prepared by Jessie Chambers, as in the first part of the Miriam Papers—or that Jessie had perhaps mentioned emphatically to Lawrence how deeply she had been impressed by the incident when it actually occurred. She wrote of it in her *D. H. Lawrence: A Personal Record*, more than twenty years after the publication of *Sons and Lovers* and more than thirty years after the probable date of the incident itself. In her memoir she gives it the position of climax at the end

of her first chapter: a party of young people had been walking, and she had strayed away from the others. Suddenly she
saw Lawrence, a figure apart from the rest, bending over an
umbrella. "His stooping figure had a look of intensity, almost
of anguish," and he became to her "a symbolic figure"; she
dates their "awareness of sympathy for one another from that
moment." The situation in the previously mentioned passage in
Paul Morel B [1] is the same; in both accounts, the young man
explains that he is concerned because the umbrella belonged
to the older brother who had died, and the mother will be
grieved if it is broken. In *Sons and Lovers* the episode is, like
all the others assimilated into that work, greatly improved.
Again, the correct details are added to provide the most effective background and to sharpen the action in the foreground.
The positions of the figures concerned are made clearer—there
is no vague or merely half-defined wandering, but a distinct
geographic placing of the characters involved. And Lawrence
in his final version of the incident lifts it into poetry: Miriam
sees Paul "in dark relief" against "one rift of rich gold in that
colourless grey evening." He is "slender and firm, as if the
setting sun had given him to her." He tells her why he is upset
about the broken umbrella: Lawrence in this version deepens
the emotional texture of the scene by explaining that Miriam
realizes with shame that the umbrella had been damaged not
by Paul but by her brother Geoffrey. In *Paul Morel B,*[1] Lawrence wrote a paragraph about Miriam's later reflections, in
which she was aware of Paul's essential loneliness; Jessie Chambers crossed out several of his sentences in this passage, particularly statements trying to interpret her feelings about him, such
as her inability to understand his sadness. In *Sons and Lovers*
Lawrence omitted all further reference to the incident except
one sentence stating that Miriam "always regarded that sudden
coming upon him as a revelation."

9. In the transition passage between the Good Friday and
Easter Monday excursions, Lawrence in *Paul Morel B* [1] has Paul
from time to time outrage "the family feeling at Willey Farm,"
by becoming suddenly angry at one of Miriam's brothers, and
Miriam ("much distressed") takes Paul's part against the family.
Jessie pencilled out this entire passage and wrote at the end of

it, "This was not my meaning," indicating once again that *Paul Morel B* [1] was possibly based on passages originally written by Jessie Chambers, such as those in the first part of the Miriam Papers. Lawrence included this passage, only slightly modified, in *Sons and Lovers*; this is one of the few times he overruled Jessie's objections. The descriptions of Miriam's dreams, which he wedges into the "family feeling" paragraph in *Sons and Lovers*, he incorporates with little change—it was a separate paragraph in *Paul Morel B* [1]—but he omits the original last sentence, which had stated that Miriam "knew she and Paul were woven together unconsciously"; Jessie noted that Miriam did not realize this "until Paul insisted upon it." She also makes several changes in the account of Easter Monday excursion which, nevertheless, is taken into *Sons and Lovers* very much as it stood in *Paul Morel B*.[1] As usual, the material is enriched in the later version. One of the passages Jessie Chambers crossed out occurred at the end of the paragraph which describes Paul putting his hand over Miriam's hand as she carries her bag by its strings. In *Paul Morel B*,[1] Lawrence remarks that Paul rarely touched her, and that she failed to understand how she could so intensify "his already fierce virginity." Jessie Chambers wrote above these lines she had crossed out that there was no question of Paul's touching her "at that time." Lawrence, as usual, omitted the passages Jessie had crossed out. Her other significant comments on this sequence occur toward the end of it, when Paul is tired at the end of the day; in *Sons and Lovers* Lawrence merely indicates that Miriam understands his fatigue and is gentle with him. In *Paul Morel B*,[1] Lawrence had written that Miriam did not dare speak to Paul, who might have spoken sharply to her. Jessie Chambers drew pencil marks through this passage and added that such a statement was not true as applied "to that time"—she was "not yet unbalanced" by the strife that later caused her to be thrown "into extravaganza etc." This Easter Monday sequence, incidentally, is different from the "Easter Monday" fragment in the first part of the Miriam Papers; they are Easter Mondays of different years, occurring in different chapters in *Sons and Lovers*. The one just discussed is chronologically earlier and occurs in Chapter VII of the published novel, the other in Chapter IX of the novel.

10. The passage describing the blowing of Miriam's skirt is a part of the narrative of the Easter Monday excursion. As Miriam climbs the stone stairway to the ruin of Wingfield Manor, the wind blows her skirt up, so that she is "ashamed"; Paul takes hold of the hem of her dress, holding it down, "chattering naturally all the while." Jessie Chambers, in striking out the last phrase, wrote that "there was no need" for Paul "to chat" while committing this "act of the purest intimacy." She cautioned him: "Do not degrade it." In *Sons and Lovers* this scene stands out, like that of the broken umbrella, as one of the important "human touches" in the book; there are many of them, and they are among the elements that contribute to the book's power. In the novel, Lawrence tells of Paul's catching the hem of Miriam's dress and holding it down, and he ends the passage with telling effectiveness: "He did it perfectly simply, as he would have picked up her glove. She remembered this always."

One more document remains to be examined: the last section of these Miriam Papers is a four-page commentary, in pencil, entitled "Chapter IX." . . . The "Chapter IX" section refers chiefly to what became Chapter VII in *Paul Morel C*, the final draft of *Sons and Lovers*; as previously pointed out, Jessie Chambers refers to this chapter, in her "Chapter IX" section, as "First Love," corresponding to the "Lad-And-Girl Love" title of Chapter VII of *Sons and Lovers*. This chapter begins with an account of Paul's frequent visits to Miriam's farm which, Lawrence explains, had been a laborer's cottage. The kitchen is "irregular" and quite small, but Paul loves it, even the "old and battered furniture." Jessie Chambers' first note in her "Chapter IX" comments is a protest against Lawrence's "cruel and unnecessary" description of the furniture and of the family mealtimes; since the first part of Lawrence's holograph of *Paul Morel B*[1] is missing, we cannot tell how much he may have modified his "unnecessary cruelty" in the final draft.

Jessie accused Lawrence, in these comments, of writing the chapter "from the standpoint of twenty-six instead of that of seventeen." Her questioning of his passage about Nietzsche, Schopenhauer, and Spencer has already been mentioned; here she complains that a boy of seventeen and a girl of sixteen would find these authors "hard stuff." Another hand has scrawled something below this which may be a large NO: it is apparently the same hand (Lawrence's) that wrote a number of such NO's on a manuscript Bertrand Russell sent Lawrence. . . .

Another commentary by Jessie Chambers concerns the episode of the rose tree in Sequence 7 of the *Paul Morel B* [1] fragment; Jessie Chambers reiterated that there was no sexual instinct awake in either Miriam or Paul at that time, and that to suggest that such an instinct was awake in Miriam "destroys the purity of the whole incident," which was as spiritual to her as it was to him. She spoke again of the broken-umbrella episode as "a spiritual awakening" that revealed Paul's inner quality to her and "set her wondering and eternally seeking."

Jessie Chambers protested against p. 220 of Lawrence's holograph; this page has already been discussed in reference to Sequence 7, the Good Friday excursion—Lawrence had written that Miriam knew Paul loved her, but wanted him to acknowledge this, and that Paul had spoken of love engendering love; Jessie had written over this passage that Miriam had been the stronger of the two then, before her love for Paul got beyond control. In her "Chapter IX" commentary she complained that Paul tries to stand aloof in the passage just mentioned, but that in life he (Lawrence) was a part of the situation. Jessie explained that their relationship had been "of the spirit of God, as I lived it and as I gave it to you in my writing"—another indication that all of the *Paul Morel B* [1] chapter was possibly drafted from original manuscripts Jessie Chambers wrote after reading *Paul Morel A*. She asked, in her comments on p. 20 of the *B* [1] holograph, if what she felt for Lawrence could have lasted "till now" had it not been "a fine rare robust thing." Jessie wrote this before she heard of Frieda; possibly just before, rather than after, Lawrence had met Frieda.

Jessie Chambers concluded her notes with a critique of the entire chapter, which she felt was inadequately and unsympathetically conceived; it contained facts but lacked interpretation. Miriam, Jessie felt, should have been more impersonally presented (it might be pointed out that Jessie's presentation of the girl's case is at the remotest extreme from the impersonal). She told Lawrence, in further comment, that since love is so great a miracle, Miriam's "complete" love for Paul should have been treated as something more than a weakness, to be "laughed at a little." She pointed out that Miriam and Paul were in unconscious sympathy at this stage, with no thought of distinguishing between body and spirit "because each was perfectly pure" ("each" probably refers to Paul and Miriam rather than body or soul). Jessie insisted that the idea of purity should dominate the chapter, for Miriam had no thought of kisses; she was proud and delighted that there was between her and Paul "no constraint of sex"; Paul could not have been more virginal than the girl—and this assertion is underlined. The chapter should be "white," she said, unsmudged by sex, which at seventeen would "be rather smudgy." And "all that" (the smudginess of sex?) came largely from the Lawrence family's strife; "my own folk were generous to a fault." The misery and the constraint in Lawrence's and Jessie's relationship came from "interference from outside: with all the inexplicable things of sex dragged in train." Her comments end with the statement that the chapter "First Love" must stand or fall "on Miriam's absolute purity of motive."

All this is the cry of a broken heart—and of a broken Victorian heart. And despite the fact that Jessie Chambers felt betrayed because "in *Sons and Lovers* Lawrence handed his mother the laurels of victory," we must once again remember that Lawrence was writing fiction, not biography; that despite his personal involvement in the subject matter he saw it with the eye of the artist. And at the last he wrote without sentimentalism or self-pity, but with tenderness and with artistic truth.

6 · A Postscript

by Harry T. Moore

Through the kindness of Professor Mark Schorer of the University of California, which has purchased the manuscript of the final version, a matter which has puzzled many readers of *Sons and Lovers* has been cleared up. The end of the last section of the novel contains the sentence, " 'Mother!' he whimpered—'mother!' " In several current editions, the word *whispered* appears instead of *whimpered*. In answer to an inquiry, Professor Schorer helpfully checked the manuscript that went to the printer, and reported that it (regrettably) reads *whimpered*. Since the proofsheets are apparently lost, it is possible that Lawrence changed the word to *whispered* at a later stage, but this is not probable since *whimpered* occurs both in Lawrence's final manuscript and in the first and several other editions of the book published in his lifetime.

Another *Sons and Lovers* item of great interest is now the property of the Humanities Research Center at the University of Texas: this is an earlier version, or parts of two earlier versions, dating from the time when Lawrence was calling the book *Paul Morel*. Acknowledgments are due to Professor Warren Roberts, Director of the Humanities Research Center, and to Mrs. Mary Hirth, Librarian of the University of Texas, for permission to quote here from the *Paul Morel* material at Austin.

These *Paul Morel* manuscripts comprise two fragments of apparently different holograph drafts, numbering respectively

Written *especially* for this book, so that special thanks are due Professor Moore.

pages 1–254 and 115–165; in these sequences, various inter-mediate pages are missing. *Paul Morel* opens in somewhat the same fashion as *Sons and Lovers*; the former begins, " 'The Breach' took the place of Hell Row." Here Lawrence was draw-ing upon fact; the place in question was actually called The Breach, while in *Sons and Lovers* he named it The Bottoms. And, throughout this opening passage of *Paul Morel*, Lawrence gives actual names (the only one repeated in the first paragraph of *Sons and Lovers* is Greenhill Lane); on the first page of *Paul Morel* he speaks of the Nottingham, Derby, and Mansfield Roads. In the opening passage (and elsewhere) in *Sons and Lovers*, he wrote of Eastwood as Bestwood; in the earlier version it appears, in all its actuality, as Eastwood.

In *Paul Morel*, the mining countryside and Sherwood Forest are thoroughly described. The quarrels between Paul's parents occur very much as in *Sons and Lovers*, though with some notable differences. In *Paul Morel*, " 'Lord, let my father not drink,' Paul prayed, time after time, each night, for twenty years, adding occasionally, 'or let him be killed at pit.' " In *Sons and Lovers*, this last phrase becomes, " 'Let him not be killed at pit,' he prayed when, after tea, the father did not come home from work." Later, Paul has met Miriam and, over her protests, tor-ments the rabbit Adolphus, foreshadowing the "Rabbity" chap-ter in *Women in Love*. A Miss May enters the story; a governess, she prefigures the one in *The Lost Girl*. She and Paul and Miriam once see Paul's father involved in a public brawl. Paul is tutored by a man named Revell, who has resigned from the ministry; Paul studies languages, and in turn teaches French to his friend Alec, "a ginger boy" who sometimes has the surname of Greenhalgh and sometimes of Richards. "The two boys, the one [Alec] lusty, big-limbed, clever but unimaginative, the other delicately made and delicate of growth, wonderfully perceptive, remained firm friends. At first, Alec was controller and patroniser, since his was the superior strength and physical energy and enterprise. To all of which Paul submitted, which he even encouraged. But gradually the balance shifted. Alec abased himself without knowing it. He resigned his leadership. Instead of: 'We are going for a swim this morning,' it was, 'Shall you go for a swim, Paul, or don't you want to?' "

In many ways this version follows *Sons and Lovers*. Paul finishes school at thirteen and goes to work for Mr. Jordan in Nottingham; the hunchback girl Fannie also works in the factory, as in the published version of the novel. There is a difference in Miriam's family circumstances, however; when she is fourteen (and Paul fifteen), her mother, Mrs. Staynes, dies; after staying with her father for a while, Miriam goes to live with the Revells; the former clergyman has married Miss May. Soon, as in *Sons and Lovers*, Paul and his mother clash over Miriam: "But the dumb, unconscious part of Paul [*loved* is scratched out] was his mother's." Miriam feels, however, that she will win because Mrs. Morel "is old."

The version numbering pages 115–165, which is perhaps an earlier draft, has some of the same characters besides Paul who, like Miriam, is here a child. He is slightly injured when a sleigh in which he is riding turns over: "Paul Morel had an attack of bronchitis after his adventure on the ice." Miriam's mother, Mrs. Staynes, is described as "a prominent Christian." And: "Mr. Staynes had inherited from his father a large grocery business and had acquired with his wife the old established pharmacy store in Eberwich."

The *Paul Morel* fragments are too sketchy to warrant much critical comment, except it may be said that the scenes—often the seeds for later development in the final version of the novel—rarely come to life. They are not organically arranged, and the people lack the vitality of those in *Sons and Lovers*. Apparently it was not until after Lawrence had met Frieda Weekley-Richthofen, and went away to live with her in Germany and Italy, that he coud see his past experience in perspective and at last make *Sons and Lovers* the coherent—and great—novel which Duckworth published in 1913. But the stages by which he arrived at his final draft are fascinating to study, unfortunately incomplete though they are.

7·A Report on the Final Manuscript

by E. W. Tedlock, Jr.

As Frieda Lawrence told the story in *Not I But the Wind* . . . , she first visited the Kiowa Ranch near Taos in 1923 with Mabel Luhan and said, "This is the loveliest place I have ever seen," and was given it. Lawrence objected to accepting such a present from anybody; but that day she had received word from her sister that the manuscript of *Sons and Lovers* had just been sent, and she gave it to Mrs. Luhan for the ranch. In 1928 Lawrence inquired of Dorothy Brett if Mrs. Luhan had sold the manuscript. It found its way into the possession of the psychoanalyst, Dr. A. A. Brill, the story being that Mrs. Luhan had in turn paid him with it. At any rate, it dropped from sight until 1963 when it was purchased from Dr. Brill's heirs by the Library of the University of California at Berkeley. Through the generosity and courtesy of Mark Schorer, who was instrumental in the purchase of this important record of Lawrence's art, and the Library, I was given the opportunity to examine a photocopy of the manuscript and make a brief report in this book.

The manuscript constitutes the copy used by the printers of the first, Duckworth edition; it bears their names where they began and ended their individual stints. It is, of course, in Lawrence's characteristically graceful, beautifully legible hand, with the familar handsome effect produced when he revised extensively between the lines. These revisions were of great interest in themselves, and no doubt will be studied. What interested me for the purposes of this book was the possibility that

Edward Garnett had an exceptionally, significantly free and extensive hand in cutting and otherwise preparing the manuscript for the printers.

The record of the letters suggested this. As always, there was the problem of impropriety, including the unofficial censorship of publisher and editor—"The British public will stone me if ever it catches sight. . . ." And Lawrence reported that William Heinemann refused the novel "on grounds of its indecency," though, he added, his real motive was his being cross because Lawrence had now committed himself to Duckworth, and Edward Garnett. There was Garnett's insistence on form, and the work of pruning and shaping and filling in that Lawrence defended to him in the letter of November 14, 1912. In the same letter, Lawrence asked if "those naked scenes" were now "tame enough," and told Garnett to cut them if he liked. On December 19th, he was glad that Garnett didn't mind cutting. A few days later, writing to Ernest Collings, he was cross with "damned old stagers" who wanted him to have "*their* pernicious ossiferous skin-and-grief form." But again, December 29th, he told Garnett he didn't "much mind" what Garnett decided to "squash out." In January, 1913, he felt that he "couldn't have done any more at that novel"—"trim and garnish it"—and it fretted him to think of Garnett "pedgilling away" at it. He felt that though Garnett's sympathies were with his own generation, he was the only man "willing to let a new generation come in," and wanted to dedicate the novel to him. On February 18, 1913, after correcting the first batch of proofs, Lawrence thanked Garnett for having done "the pruning jolly well," and wished he "weren't so profuse—or prolix, or whatever it is." There may have been a late crisis, since on March 11th Lawrence exclaimed that, since he had to live, he didn't mind if Duckworth crossed out "a hundred shady pages." At last, on May 19th, he was happy with the copy that had just arrived, and reckoned *Sons and Lovers* was "quite a great book."

The cutting in the manuscript is extensive—some 88 passages, varying in length from three or four lines to eighty-nine, and occasionally amounting to several pages. It is heaviest in Part I—fifty-five times in the six chapters, to thirty-three times in the remaining eight chapters: I, 13; II, 10; III, 10; IV, 4; V,

10; VI, 8; VII, 10; VIII, 3; IX, 11; X, 3; XI, 2; XII, 3; XIII, 0; XIV, 1. There are two methods of indicating cuts—one a simple horizontal line resembling Lawrence's usual practice, the other a diagonal crossing out of the passage with a bracket and a deletion mark in the margin. The latter is by far the predominant one.

David Garnett, Edward's son, who was lecturing in this country, kindly consented to look at the manuscript, and went to Berkeley from Davis, where he then was, for that purpose. His findings and critical opinion follow:

I have noted erasures by Edward Garnett and sometimes the word *stet* restoring the text, on the following pages of the M. S.

3, 5 (2 places), 14, 19, 22, 26, 27, 31, 32, 33, 34, 35, 38, 43 (stets), 44 (stets), 52, 56, 70, 79, 80, 81, 85, 87, 88, 89, 90, 91, 92, 93, 94, 95, 96, 97, 98 (stets), 99, 117, 118, 137, 139, 140, 142, 146, 149, 150, 161, 163, 164, 165 (top line), 166, 176, 177, 178, 183, 187, 188, 190, 192, 220, 222, 224, 227, 228, 229, 230, 241, 242, 249, 251, 252, 277 (bottom of page), 278, 286, 289, 291 (bottom of page, I think is E. G.), 293 (not certain, probably E. G.), 314, 315, 318, 326, 326A (unnumbered sheet of M. S.), 349, 351, 353, 354, 355 (top of page only), 373, 374, 382, 383, 391, 395, 423, 424, 474.
. . . There is no doubt as all the diagonal excisions are in the same hand, the deletion marks look exactly like my father's and the stets are undoubtedly his and in some places he has stetted a deletion which he couldn't possibly have done if the excisions were D. H. L.'s. Actually there is no doubt whatever except for two passages I have indicated. Obviously it would be interesting to have the entire text published. The reason for the excisions is that the novel was far too long and I suspect they improve it, but then I am a prejudiced critic.

Some of the deleted passages in the early chapters have to do with the quarrels between Mr. and Mrs. Morel, and other aspects of the family discord, but plenty of that remains. Some nine passages having to do with William's nature and role as "lover" are deleted. One deletion in particular, of passages dealing with his excitement over wearing a Highlander's costume, his pride in his physique, and his attractiveness to girls, might be regretted. The family contre-temps when William brings Lily Western home is also altered. A four-page scene in which Paul waits for Miriam at the town library, and is scolded by the mother when he returns home late that evening, is deleted; but it would be difficult to argue that the loss is of something essential. The letter to Miriam in Chapter IX is much revised and cut; one would expect the wording of this crucial, involved decision to have given Lawrence trouble, and might wish to have all of it. In connection with Lawrence's fears of the censorious, there is little or no cutting of the sexual encounters between Paul and Miriam, and Paul and Clara. One that might be regarded as severe occurs in the scene between Paul and Clara before the hearth in her mother's house. Here a paragraph is omitted, though not all of it is marked "delete," describing his kissing her breasts and knees; and one wonders if this could have been a printer's decision. The very last cut, in Chapter XIV, involves Paul's seeking out Miriam and, so late in his break with her, asking her to take him, and being refused, as well he might. A rational view of behavior might well have demanded the passage's removal.

Edward Garnett's purpose in making these final deletions was primarily to bring the novel to a length the publishers of the day found economically feasible. David Garnett, in conversation, has recalled his father's sighing unhappily over this necessity of his editorial task. As Mr. Garnett remarks in his report on the manuscript, it would be interesting to have the entire text published. There would also be a belated kind of freedom for and justice to both the author and the editor in that.

II. Freudian Connections and Approaches

When Lawrence changed the title from *Paul Morel*, with its suggestion of traditional hero-centered, picaresquely plotted narrative, he made it easier for the intellectual *avant garde* to connect his "psychological" development with Sigmund Freud's analysis of the causes of divided, troubled sexual behavior. Later critics looking for explicit evidence of this connection could find it in Frieda Weekley's having discussed Freudian theory with him during his final revision of the novel. As it turned out, what was more Lawrencean in spirit than her at best eclectic knowledge was her having been profoundly shaken and, in a sense, liberated by her affair with an Austrian doctor who had studied under Freud and who believed with a romantic, religious fervor that the new psychology could create a new, harmonious era of relationships.[1] Not only the generality of intellectuals but psychoanalysts, expert in the dialectic and the mysteries, hailed Lawrence's novel as a vindication by art of the truth of the master's scientific analysis.

This view is represented here by Alfred Booth Kuttner's essay from *The Psychoanalytic Review* for July, 1916. Through a methodical, detailed exposition first of the novel, then of Freudian theory and the parallels, he concluded that *Sons and Lovers* had not only attested the truth of the theory but that the artist, "sick with the problems of his generation," had cured himself "by expression in his art," a view of the function of art

1 See his letters to her in *Frieda Lawrence: The Memoirs and Correspondence*, edited by E. W. Tedlock, Jr. (Alfred A. Knopf, 1964).

that is remarkably parallel to Lawrence's statement in the letter to A. D. McLeod in 1913 that "one sheds one's sicknesses in books." But by the time of the letter to Barbara Low in September, 1916, Lawrence could object, in what seems to be a reference to Kuttner's article, that the *Psychoanalytic Review* had reduced the "fairly complete truth" of his art to a "half lie." His more formal and intellectual disagreements with psychoanalysis were in the making. These, and the extent and nature of his knowledge of Freud, are the subject of Frederick J. Hoffman's "Lawrence's Quarrel with Freud," a portion of which, most relevant to *Sons and Lovers*, follows Kuttner's essay in this section.

Kuttner's method of identifying Freudian parallels in literature has, of course, been highly refined and subtleized by later psychologically oriented critics. For them, what may appear to be quite literal fact to the author as well as the reader has a place in an unconscious projection of meaning. Even when they mean to praise the complex candor of the art, they tend to reduce the artist to the role, at best, of psychological medium, at worst, of predestinated case history. An example of such an approach that contains insights and intends not to denigrate Lawrence but to demonstrate his sensitive rigorousness, par excellence, and even to trace his maturation, is Daniel A. Weiss's *Oedipus in Nottingham*, of which the chapter, "The Mother in the Mind," is presented here. The range of relationships and feelings in the novel, realized by Lawrence, is reduced because the approach tends to deny him ordinary, or in this case, extraordinary conscious control of his material and medium. And the seriousness and thematic efficacy of his vitalistic "solution" to his predicament, embryonic and contradictory though it may be in this novel, is neglected. At the same time, the essay is a corrective of oversimplification of the son-lover pattern and unawareness of its full implications.

Finally, in this section, Frank O'Connor's rather eclectic essay discusses the pressures of the special Midlands environment and their relevance, then turns to the difficulties and the homosexual implications, noted also by Weiss, of the relationships in the second part of the novel and applies the Freudian frame of reference to the question of the normalcy and fairness of the portraits of Miriam and Clara. It ends, as it began, with the question of why Lawrence, like other significant writers of our time, found normal, heterosexual relations so difficult. Thus O'Connor raises the ultimate question of literary and cultural history—the why of so strange and troubling a direction.

8 · A Freudian Appreciation

by Alfred Booth Kuttner

I

Poets and novelists often strive for impressiveness in their crea-
tions by dealing in strange plots and adventures or in monstrous
and unnatural loves. The advantages gained may well be called
in question: to be grotesque is hardly ever to be great and the
bizarre may survive as a demerit after it is exhausted as a sensation. The great literature of life is after all built around the
commonplace. *The Odyssey* treats of a bad case of homesickness,
a thing which we all understand perfectly. The drama of Œdipus
depicts an incestuous relationship, and we do not have to be
told that it is horrible. What distinguishes enduring literature is
not novelty, but freshness of feeling, and that pointed insight
into life which reveals a vivid personality keenly alive. *Sons and
Lovers* has the great distinction of being very solidly based upon
a veritable commonplace of our emotional life; it deals with a
son who loved his mother too dearly, and with a mother who
lavished all her affection upon her son.

Neither this distinction nor its undeniable freshness and
often amazing style would of itself entitle Mr. D. H. Lawrence's
novel to anything beyond an appreciative book review. But it
sometimes happens that a piece of literature acquires an added
significance by virtue of the support it gives to the scientific

Reprinted from The Psychoanalytic Review, Volume 3, No. 3, July,
1916, *through the courtesy of the Editors and the publisher, National Psychological Association for Psychoanalysis, Inc.*

study of human motives. Literary records have the advantage of being the fixed and classic expression of human emotions which in the living individual are usually too fluid and elusive for deliberate study. The average man, subjected to what seems to him a kind of psychological vivisection, is apt to grow reticent, and mankind must often be convicted through its literature of impulses which under direct scrutiny it would acknowledge only with the greatest reluctance or else deny altogether. Literature thus becomes an invaluable accessory to the psychologist, who usually does well to regard with suspicion any new generalization from his researches for which the whole range of literary expression yields no corroboration. But if he can succeed in finding support there his position is immensely strengthened. For a new truth about ourselves, which may seem altogether grotesque and impossible when presented to us as an arid theory, often gains unexpected confirmation when presented to us in a powerful work of literature as an authentic piece of life. When at last we recognize ourselves we like the thrill of having made a discovery.

Sons and Lovers possesses this double quality to a high degree. It ranks high, very high as a piece of literature and at the same time it embodies a theory which it illustrates and exemplifies with a completeness that is nothing less than astonishing. Fortunately there can be no doubt as to the authenticity of the author's inspiration. For it would be fatal if the novel had been written with the express purpose of illustrating a theory: it would, by that very admission, be worthless as a proof of that theory. But it happens that Mr. Lawrence has already produced notable work, mainly some early and evidently autobiographical poems, which show his preoccupation with the identical theme. *Sons and Lovers* is thus truly creative, in that it is built up internally—as any masterpiece must be—out of the psychic conflicts of the author, and any testimony which it may bear to the truth of the theory involved will therefore be first hand.

The theory to which I have been referring is Professor Sigmund Freud's theory of the psychological evolution of the emotion of love as finally expressed by a man or a woman towards a member of the other sex, and the problem which Mr. Lawrence voices is the struggle of a man to emancipate himself from his maternal allegiance and to transfer his affections to a woman who stands outside of his family circle. What the poet has seen as a personal problem the scientist has formulated as a theory. I shall outline the problem first and then relate it to the theory. If the theory can succeed in generalizing the truth which Mr. Lawrence's novel presents the reader will realize with fresh force that fiction, to be great art, must be based upon human verities.

II

First we shall see how it happened that the mother in this story came to lavish all her affections upon her son. In the opening chapter Mrs. Morel, the wife of a Derbyshire coal miner, is expecting her third child, the boy Paul, who is to become the central figure of the story. Her life with her husband has already turned out to be a complete fiasco. He is a drunkard and a bully, a man with whom she shares neither intellectual, moral or religious sympathies. What strikes her most about Morel is that he presents a striking contrast to her father, who was to her *"the type of all men."* For he had been a harsh, puritan type, given to theology and ignoring "all sensuous pleasure," while Morel is the very opposite; warm, sensuous and indulgent, with a "rich ringing laugh" and a "red, moist mouth." It is this sensuous quality in Morel which overwhelms and confounds her; she goes down before the sheer, impersonal male in him. After the sex illusion has worn off somewhat Mrs. Morel makes an attempt to draw nearer to her husband. But the clash of personalities is stronger than the transitory tie of their poetized passion and Morel's habitual drunkenness, his indulgent and shiftless ways, and his temperamental dishonesty are mercilessly flayed by his almost fanatically moral and religious wife. It is very easy for her to loathe him. At the time of the birth of her third child the breach is already irreparable. Mrs. Morel dreads the coming of another child, conceived unwillingly out of a loveless relation, and at the sight of it a sense of guilt steals over her. She will atone: *"With all her force, with all her soul she would make up to it for having brought it into the world unloved. She would love it all the more now it was hers; carry it in her love."* Towards

Paul she feels, as to none of the other children, that she must make up to him for an injury or a sin committed by her and that he must recompense her for all that she has missed in her shattered love for her husband.

All the early formative influences in Paul's life radiate from his mother. Physically he is more delicate than the other children so that his illnesses tend to further her concentration upon him still more. Paul is a "pale, quiet child" who seems *"old for his years"* and *"very conscious of what other people felt, particularly his mother. When she fretted he understood, and could have no peace. His soul seemed always attentive to her."* His mother and for a time his sister Annie are his only real companions. His brother William is too old to be his playmate and other children play no rôle in his early childhood. One vicious bond of sympathy unites all the Morel children; their common hate and contempt for their father. This feeling poisons the whole family life. Often, of a windy night in their creaking house, the children lie awake listening in terror for his drunken return, his banging fists and the muffled voice of their mother. The strain is greatest upon Paul. Towards evening he grows restless and stays near his mother, waiting for his father's coming and the usual scene of abuse and violence. Already at an early age these hostile feelings take definite shape. He often prays: *"Lord, let my father die."* And then, with a kind of guilty conscience: *"Let him not be killed at pit."* One incident in particular stands out in his memory. Morel has just blackened his wife's eyes and William, then already a tall and muscular youth, threatens to beat him. Paul aches to have him do it; it is his own wish which he cannot carry out. Later, when he is older, he almost does it himself, but for his mother's fainting, and his physical encounters with other men are tinged with a deadly animosity, as if the memory of that earlier hate had lingered on in him. We must remember that Paul had been born into an atmosphere of parental violence; when still a baby his father hurled a drawer at his mother so that the blood had trickled down upon the child's head. Indelible among his earliest impressions must have been that gross and terrifying figure, threatening his life and that of his mother, whose convulsive movements to protect him must have aroused an answering quiver in the child.

The early relations between mother and child are full of a delicate and poetic charm. Paul's admiration for his mother knows no bounds; her presence is always absorbing. Often, at the sight of her, *"his heart contracts with love."* Everything he does is for her, the flowers he picks as well as the prizes he wins at school. His mother is his intimate and his confidante, he has no other chums. When Morel is confined to the hospital through an accident in the mine, Paul joyfully plays the husband, *"I'm the man in the house now."* He is happiest when alone with her. By this time the interaction between mother and son is complete; she lives in him and he in her. In fact his whole attitude towards her is but the answer which she gradually evokes from him as her whole life finds expression in her son. *"In the end she shared everything with him without knowing. . . . She waited for his coming home in the evening, and then she unburdened herself of all she had pondered, or of all that had occurred to her during the day. He sat and listened with his earnestness. The two shared lives."* The emotional correspondence between them is striking, *"his heart contracted with pain of love of her"* just as from the very beginning she has always *"felt a mixture of anguish in her love for him."* Mother and son are one; the husband is completely effaced and the father exists merely as a rival.

But now Paul is to strike out for himself. He takes up an occupation and finds himself attracted to women. His mother's whole emphasis has always been towards making Paul interested in some other occupation than his father's dirty digging, as a protest against the sordidness of the life that she herself has been compelled to lead with him. She therefore encourages the boy's liking for pretty things, for flowers and sunsets and fancy stuffs, and is delighted when his slender artistic endowment begins to express itself in pencil and paint. Her emotional revolt against her husband here takes an esthetic turn, as people are often driven to beauty by their loathing of the ugly, and it is interesting to note that Mrs. Morel's tendencies to estheticize Paul and to effeminate him go hand in hand, as if the two sprang from a common root. Paul never becomes a real artist. He uses his painting to please his mother and to court his women, but in the crises of his life his art means nothing to him either as a consolation or as a satisfying expression. As his painting is essentially dilettante and unremunerative, his mother apprentices him in a shop for surgical appliances where the process of effeminization goes on through his contact with the girls and women with whom he works. He himself has no ambition. All that he wants is *"quietly to earn his thirty or thirty-five shillings a week somewhere near home, and then, when his father died, have a cottage with his mother, paint and go out as he liked, and live happy ever after."* Not, like any normal boy, to strike out for himself, to adventure, to emulate and surpass his father, but to go on living with his mother forever! That is the real seed of Paul's undoing. We shall now trace the various attempts on his part to emancipate himself from his mother by centering his affections upon some other woman.

The first woman to attract Paul is Miriam Leiver, a shy, exalted and romantic girl who leads a rather lonely life with her parents and brothers on a neighboring farm. Paul's approach is characteristically indirect; he begins by avoiding the girl and cultivating her mother. Meanwhile Miriam, piqued by the neglect of this well-mannered boy, who seems so gentle and superior, has fallen in love with him. Paul is fascinated but uneasy and fights shy of personal intimacy with her. The intensity of her emotions frightens him and impresses him as unwholesome. He finds her growing absorption in him strangely discomfitting: *"Always something in his breast shrank from these close, intimate, dazzled looks of hers."* His feminine attitude towards her tends to reverse the usual method of courtship; it is Miriam who has to seek him out, to call for him and make sure of his coming again. Paul tries to approach her in two ways; through his art and as her teacher. Both methods are really self-defensive, they are barriers that he erects against Miriam to prevent anything too personal from arising between them, to keep his real self, as it were, inviolate. For as a painter he distracts her attention from himself to his work and as her instructor he wields an authority with which he can keep her emotions in check by overawing her. Something about her is always putting him on edge, he loses his temper at her very easily and feels a dawning impulse of cruelty. *"It made his blood rouse to see her there, as it were, at his mercy."* Sometimes he feels an actual hatred for her. And immediately he thinks of his mother: *"He was thankful in his heart and soul that he had his mother, so sane and wholesome."*

Paul resists every intimation that he is falling in love with Miriam. He indignantly repudiates his mother's insinuation that he is courting and hastens to assure Miriam: *"We aren't lovers, we are friends."* And Miriam, who has already gone so far, tries to fortify herself with a prayer. *"O Lord, let me not love Paul Morel. Keep me from loving him, if I ought not to love him."* But her love breaks through again and her healthier instincts triumph. Henceforth Paul can do with her as he will. But he can do nothing with her love because he cannot return it. Love seems to him like a *"very terrible thing."* The honest and more impersonal passion that he feels for her frightens him. *"He was afraid of her. The fact that he might want her as a man wants a woman had in him been suppressed into a shame."* He cannot even kiss her. And he hates her again because she makes him despise himself. They gradually move to the edge of a quarrel.

And now Mrs. Morel makes her appeal. Almost from the first she has mistrusted Miriam. She fears that Miriam will absorb him and take him away from her. *"She is one of those who will want to suck a man's soul out till he has none of his own left."* Her jealousy revels in the exaggerated simile of the vampire. *"She exults—she exults as she carries him off from me. . . . She's not like an ordinary woman . . . she wants to absorb him . . . she will suck him up."* So she throws down the gauntlet to her rival. She makes Paul feel wretched, as only a mother can make a son feel, whenever he has been with Miriam. Her comments grow spiteful and satiric; she no longer takes the trouble to hide her jealousy and plagues him like a cast woman. *"Is there nobody else to talk to? . . . Yes, I know it well—I am old. And therefore I may stand aside; I have nothing more to do with you. You only want me to wait on you—the rest is for Miriam."* It sounds like a wife's bitter reproach to her husband. Paul writhes under her words and hates Miriam for it. But Mrs. Morel does not stop there. She makes the final, ruthless, cowardly appeal.

"And I've never—you know, Paul—I've never had a husband —not—really—"

He stroked his mother's hair, and his mouth was on her throat.

"Well, I don't love her, mother," he murmured, bowing his head and hiding his eyes on her shoulder in misery. His mother kissed him, a long, fervent kiss.

"My boy!" she said, in a voice trembling with passionate love.

Without knowing, he gently stroked her face. Thus she wins him back. He will continue to console her for her husband. There follows the scene where Paul almost thrashes his drunken father and implores his mother not to share the same bed with him. It is a crisis in his life: ". . . *he was at peace because he still loved his mother best. It was the bitter peace of resignation."*

But there is some resistance in him still. For a time he stands divided between his two loves. "*And he felt dreary and hopeless between the two.*" In church, sitting between them, he feels at peace: "*uniting his two loves under the spell of the place of worship.*" But most of the time he is torn between the two women. He does not understand his feelings. "*And why did he hate Miriam and feel so cruel towards her at the thought of his mother?*" His emotions towards Miriam are constantly changing. Sometimes his passion tries to break through. But it cannot free itself. "*I'm so damned spiritual with* you *always!*" He blames her for the humiliating sense of impotence which he feels. It is all her fault. He transfers all his inhibitions to her and consciously echoes his mother's accusations. "*You absorb, absorb, as if you must fill yourself up with love, because you've got a shortage somewhere.*" When her love for him flames out to confound him he takes refuge by talking about his work. There at least some freedom is left for them both. "*All his passion, all his wild blood, went into this intercourse with her, when he talked and conceived his work.*" But at last he tells her that he does not love her, that he cannot love her physically. "*I can only give friendship—it's all I'm capable of—it's a flaw in my make-up. . . . Let us have done.*" And finally he writes: "*In all our relations no body enters. I do not talk to you through*

the senses—*rather through the spirit. That is why we cannot
love in common sense. Ours is not an everyday affection.*" Thus
he tries to spiritualize their relations out of existence. He would
persuade himself of his own impotence.

Paul's whole experience with Miriam has thrown him back
upon his mother; he gets away from Miriam by returning to
her. "*He had come back to his mother. Hers was the strongest
tie in life. When he thought round, Miriam shrank away. There
was a vague, unreal feeling about her. . . . And in his soul
there was a feeling of the satisfaction of self-sacrifice because he
was faithful to her*" (his mother). "*She loved him first; he loved
her first.*" He is her child again and for a time he feels content.
They go off on a charming excursion to Lincoln Cathedral. He
behaves like a lover out with his girl, buying her flowers and
treating her. Suddenly there surges up in him a childhood
memory of the time when his mother was young and fair, before
life wrung her dry and withered her. If only he had been her
eldest son so that his memory of her could be still more youthful! "*What are you old for!*" he said, mad with his own impotence. "*Why can't you walk, why can't you come with me to
places?*" He does not like to have such an old sweetheart.

At the same time his whole outlook upon life also grows
childish again. When his sister Annie marries he tries to console
his mother. "*But I shan't marry, mother. I shall live with you,
and we'll have a servant.*" She doubts him and he proceeds to
figure it out. "*I'll give you till seventy-five. There you are, I'm
fat and forty-four. Then I'll marry a staid body. See! . . . And
we'll have a pretty house, you and me, and a servant, and it'll
be just all right.*" His plans for the future have not changed.
He thinks at twenty-two as he thought at fourteen, like a child
that goes on living a fairy-tale. But it is a false contentment and
he pays the penalty for it. In resigning the natural impulse to
love he also resigns the impulse to live. Life cannot expand in
him, it is turned back upon itself and becomes the impulse to
die. Paul makes the great refusal. "*What is happiness!*" he cried.
"*It's nothing to me! How* AM *I to be happy? . . . He had that
poignant carelessness about himself, his own suffering, his own
life, which is a form of slow suicide.*" Mrs. Morel sees the danger
and divines the remedy. "*At this rate she knew he would not*

live. . . . *She wished she knew some nice woman—she did not know what she wished, but left it vague."* But now she knows that she can no longer hold her son to her exclusively.

At this point Paul begins to turn to another woman, Clara Dawes, a friend of Miriam. She is married, but lives separated from her husband. Paul has known her for some time before becoming intimate with her. She exerts a frankly sensual attraction upon him without having any of that mystical unattainableness about her which he felt so strongly with Miriam. Her presence has had the effect of gradually seducing him away from Miriam without his knowing it. There would be less difficulty with her. She is a married woman and is unhappy with her husband, like his mother. To love her would not be so momentous a thing, he would be less unfaithful to his mother if he had an affair with a woman who already belonged to someone else. Their relations threaten to become typical of the young man and the woman of thirty. *"She was to him extraordinarily provocative, because of the knowledge she seemed to possess, and gathered fruit of experience."* The question of marriage would hardly enter; he could go on loving his mother. But still he is inhibited. *"Sex had become so complicated in him that he would have denied that he ever could want Clara or Miriam or any woman whom he knew. Sex desire was a sort of detached thing, that did not belong to a woman."* Clara's first service to him is to talk to him like a woman of the world and thus correct his self-delusion about Miriam: *". . . she doesn't want any of your soul communion. That's your own imagination. She wants you."* He objects. *" 'You've never tried,' she answered."* Thus she gives him courage to do what he never could have done of his own accord.

The force which drives him back to Miriam is nothing but the sheer, pent-up sexual desire that has alternately been provoked and repressed in him. Now indeed it is a completely detached thing which does not belong to any woman. He has almost entirely succeeded in de-personalizing it. That is why he feels that he can let it run its course. But not in any personal way. *"He did not feel that he wanted marriage with Miriam. He wished he did. He would have given his head to have felt a joyous desire to marry her and have her. Then why couldn't he bring it off? There was some obstacle; and what was the obstacle?*

*It lay in the physical bondage. He shrank from the physical con-
tact. But why? With her he felt bound up inside himself. He
could not go out to her. Something struggled in him, but he
could not get to her. Why?"* And Miriam does not insist upon
marriage, she is willing to try out their feelings for each other.
Theirs is a pitiful love-making. He cannot bear the blaze of love
in her eyes; it is as if he must first draw a veil over her face and
forget her. *"If he were really with her, he had to put aside himself and his desire. If he would have her, he had to put her
aside."* Love brings him only a sense of death: *"He was a youth
no longer. But why had he the dull pain in his soul? Why did
the thought of death, the after-life, seem so sweet and consoling?"* Love has brought them no satisfaction, only bitterness and
disillusion. He turns back to his men friends and to Clara's
company and the old quarrel between him and Miriam breaks
out afresh. He decides to break off his relations with her. But at
last he is to hear the truth about himself from Miriam. *" 'Always
—it has been so!' she cried. 'It has been one long battle between us—you fighting away from me.' "* He tries to tell her that
they have had some perfect hours. But she knows that these do
not make up the healthy continuity of life. *"Always, from the
very beginning—always the same!"* She has called him a child
of four. It is the truth, and it goes to the heart of his vanity.
She has treated him as a mother treats a perverse child. He cannot stand it. *"He hated her. All these years she had treated him
as if he were a hero, and thought of him secretly as an infant, a
foolish child. Then why had she left the foolish child to his
folly? His heart was hard against her."*

The full flood of his passion, freed of some of its incubus
through his experience with Miriam, now turns to Clara. He tries
to wear it out on her in the same impersonal way, and for a time
lives in sheer physical ecstasy. With her at least he has had some
solace, some relief. His mother has not stood so much between
them. But it is only temporary, he cannot give himself to Clara
any more than he could give himself to Miriam. Clara loves him
or would love him if he could only rise above the mere passion
that threw them together. *" 'I feel,' she continued slowly, 'as if
I hadn't got you, as if all of you weren't there, and as if it
weren't* ME *you were taking—' 'Who then?' 'Something just for*

*yourself. It has been fine, so that I daren't think of it. But is it
me you want, or is it I₸?'* . . . *'He again felt guilty. Did he leave
Clara out of count and take simply woman? But he thought that
was splitting a hair."* They begin to drift apart. He rehearses his
old difficulties with his mother. *"I feel sometimes as if I wronged
my women, mother."* But he doesn't know why. *"I even love
Clara, and I did Miriam; but to give myself to them in marriage
I couldn't. I couldn't belong to them. They seem to want* ME,
and I can't even give it them."

"You haven't met the right woman."

"And I shall never meet the right woman while you live."

His relations with Clara have brought about a marked
change in Paul's attitude towards his mother. It is as if he
realized at last that she is destroying his life's happiness. *"Then
sometimes he hated her, and pulled at her bondage. His life
wanted to free itself of her. It was like a circle where life wanted
to turn back upon itself, and got no further. She bore him, loved
him, kept him, and his love turned back into her, so that he
could not be free to go forward with his own life, really love
another woman."* But his realization, as far as it goes, brings no
new initiative. He is twenty-four years old now but he still
sums up his ambition as before: *"Go somewhere in a pretty
house near London with my mother."*

The book now rounds out with the death of Paul's mother.
Mrs. Morel gradually wastes away with a slow and changeful illness; it is an incurable tumor, with great pain. Paul takes charge
and never leaves his mother until the end. Their intimacy is
occasionally disturbed by the clumsy intrusion of Morel, whose
presence merely serves to irritate his wife. Paul and she commune with the old tenderness. *"Her blue eyes smiled straight
into his, like a girl's—warm, laughing with tender love. It made
him pant with terror, agony, and love."* Their reserve drops before the imminence of death, it seems as if they would be frank
at last. But there is also the old constraint. *"They were both
afraid of the veils that were ripping between them."* He suffers
intensely. *"He felt as if his life were being destroyed, piece by
piece, within him."* But mingled with his love and his anguish
at her suffering there now enters a new feeling: the wish that
she should die. Something in him wants her to die; seeing that

she cannot live he would free both her and himself by hastening her death. So he gradually cuts down her nourishment and increases the deadliness of her medicine. Here again he approaches close to the source of his trouble; he dimly realizes that he has never lived outside of his mother and therfore has never really lived. The feeling that he cannot live without her and the feeling that he cannot live a life of his own as long as she is alive, here run side by side. But when the death which he himself has hastened overtakes her, he cries with a lover's anguish: " *'My love—my love—oh, my love!' he whispered again and again. 'My love—oh, my love!' * "

But death has not freed Paul from his mother. It has completed his allegiance to her. For death has merely removed the last earthly obstacle to their ideal union; now he can love her as Dante loved his Beatrice. He avows his faithfulness to her by breaking off with the only two other women who have meant anything to him. He is completely resigned, life and death are no longer distinguished in his thinking. Life for him is only where his mother is and she is dead. So why live? He cannot answer, life has become contradictory. *"There seemed no reason why people should go along the street, and houses pile up in the daylight. There seemed no reason why these things should occupy space, instead of leaving it empty. . . . He wanted everything to stand still, so that he could be with her again."* But life in him is just a hair stronger than death. *"He would not say it. He would not admit that he wanted to die, to have done. He would not own that life had beaten him, or that death had beaten him."*

The last chapter of the book is called "Derelict." The title emphasizes Mr. Lawrence's already unmistakable meaning. Paul is adrift now; with the death of his mother he has lost his only mooring in life. There is no need to follow him further; when he is through despairing he will hope again and when he has compared one woman to his mother and found her wanting, he will go on to another, in endless repetition. The author's final picture of Paul's state of mind is full of seductive eloquence: *"There was no Time, only Space. Who could say that his mother had lived and did not live? She had been in one place and was in another; that was all. And his soul could not leave* her, wherever she was. Now she was gone abroad in the night, and he was with her still. They were together. And yet there was his body, his chest, that leaned against the stile, his hands on the wooden bar. They seemed something. Where was he?— one tiny upright speck of flesh, less than an ear of wheat lost in the field. He could not bear it. On every side the immense dark silence seemed pressing him, so tiny a spark, into extinction, and yet, almost nothing, he could not be extinct. Night, in which everything was lost, went reaching out, beyond stars and sun. Stars and sun, a few bright grains, went spinning round for terror, and holding each other in embrace, there in a darkness that outpassed them all, and left them tiny and daunted. So much, and himself, infinitesimal, at the core of nothingness, and yet not nothing."

" 'Mother!' he whimpered—'mother!' "

III

Such is the condensed account of Paul's love-life. Textual testimony could hardly go further to show that Paul loved his mother too dearly. And shall we now say that it was *because* Mrs. Morel lavished all her affection upon her son? But then, most mothers lavish a good deal of affection upon their sons and it is only natural for sons to love their mothers dearly. Why should an excess of these sacred sentiments produce such devastating results? For it is undoubtedly the intention of the author to show us Paul as a wreck and a ruin, a man damned out of all happiness at the age of twenty-five, who has barely the strength left to will not to die. And why should we accept as a type this man who seems to bear so many ear-marks of degeneracy and abnormal impulse, who is alternately a ruthless egotist and a vicious weakling in his dealings with women, and who in the end stoops to shorten the life of his own mother? Surely the thing is deeper and due to profounder causes. But of these the author gives us no indication. Let us therefore assume for the moment that Paul is by no means a degenerate, but merely an exaggeration of the normal, unhealthily nursed into morbid manifestations by an abnormal environment. If that can be established it may very well be that the story of

Paul's love-life simply throws into high relief an intimate and constant relation between parent and child the significance of which has hitherto escaped general observation. Perhaps all men have something of Paul in them. In that case their instinctive recognition of their kinship with the hero of the book would go a great way towards explaining the potency of "Sons and Lovers." We are fond of saying something like that about Hamlet.

The theory which would enable us to assume such a point of view is at once concrete, humanly understandable, and capable of personal verification. For Freud holds that the love instinct, whose sudden efflorescence after the age of puberty is invested with so much poetic charm, is not a belated endowment, but comes as the result of a gradual development which we can trace step by step from our earliest childhood. In fact, according to Freud, the evolution of the mature love instinct begins as soon as the child has sufficiently developed a sense of the otherness of its surroundings to single out its mother as the object of its affections. At first this is entirely instinctive and unconscious and comes as the natural result of the child's dependence upon its mother for food, warmth and comfort. We come preciously close to being born lovers. The mother is the one overwhelming presence of those earliest days, the source from which all good things flow, so that childhood is full of the sense of the mother's omnipotence. From her we first learn how to express affection, and the maternal caresses and the intimate feeling of oneness which we get from her form the easy analogies to love when we feel a conscious passion for another individual of the opposite sex. Our mother is, in a very real sense of the word, our first love.

As soon as the child is capable of making comparisons with other people it proceeds to celebrate the superiorities of its mother. She is the most beautiful, the most accomplished, the most powerful, and no other child's mother can equal her. But meanwhile the influence of the father, that other major constellation of our childhood, is also felt. Though not so gracious, he too is mighty, mightier than the mother, since he dominates her. His presence brings about a striking change in the attitude of the child, according to its sex. The boy, seeing that the mother loves the father, strives to be like him, in order to draw the mother's affection to himself. He takes his father as an ideal and sets about to imitate his masculine qualities. And the girl, becoming aware of the father's love for the mother, tries to attract some of his love to herself by imitating the mother. This is the process of self-identification which is already conditioned by the natural physical similarity where parent and child are of the same sex. Father and son, and mother and daughter, now have a common object of affection. But to the child this means at the same time an active rivalry, for the child is an unbridled egotist, intent upon nothing less than the exclusive possession of the affection of the beloved parent. It therefore manifests unmistakable signs of jealousy, even of frank hostility. So strong is this feeling that a careful examination of the unconscious childhood memories of thousands of individuals, such as is possible with the Freudian method of psychoanalysis, has yet to reveal an infancy in which a death phantasy about the rival parent has not played a part. The childish wish is ruthlessly realized in imagination; the boy suddenly dreams of living in a cottage with his mother after the father, let us say, has been devoured by the lion of last week's circus, while the girl revels in the thought of keeping house for her father after the mother has been conveniently removed. We may feel, then, that we were fellow conspirators with Paul when he prayed to God to have his father slain. For we have had the same wish in common: to eliminate the rival and celebrate a childish marriage with the parent of our choice.

From this naïve attitude the child is normally weaned by the maturing influences of education and by the absolute barriers which its childish wish encounters. It is a slow and gradual process of transference, which continues through childhood and puberty. The child is tenaciously rooted in its parents and does not easily relinquish its hold upon them. Even after it has acquired a dawning sense of the meaning of sex it continues to interweave its immature phantasies of procreation with its former ideal adoration of the parent. Thus the girl, having had a glimmering that the father has had something essential to do with her birth, may assign to him a similar function in regard to her dolls, which of course are her children. And the boy, similarly aware that his father has played a mysterious part with regard to the mother when she suddenly introduces another child into the nursery, is likely to usurp the exercise of this function to himself. Both substitutions are merely more sophisticated ways of eliminating the rival parent by making him unnecessary. It must be remembered, of course, that the child can have none of our reservations as to the direction which the erotic impulse may take, and therefore quite innocently directs its crude and imperfect erotic feelings towards its parent, from whom they must then be deflected. This is most favorably accomplished when there are other children in the family. The girl is quick to see the father in her brother and the boy transfers his worship of the mother to his sister. The father's manly qualities are used by the girl to embellish the brother when she sets him up as a love ideal. From him again she slowly extends her love phantasies to other boys of his and her acquaintance. The boy on his part, dowers his sister with the borrowed attributes of his mother and then passes from her to other girls who in turn are selected on the basis of their similarity to the sister and to the mother. In default of brothers or sisters other playmates have to serve the same purpose. The enforced quest of a love object other than the parent thus becomes the great incentive of our social radiation towards other individuals and to the world at large.

This process of deflection and transference, which is one of the main psychic labors of childhood, is facilitated by a parallel process that constantly represses a part of our thoughts to the unconscious. The mechanism of repression, as the Freudian psychology describes it, does not become operative until the age of about four or five, for at first the child does not repress at all and therefore has no unconscious. But the function of education consists largely in imposing innumerable taboos upon the child and in teaching it to respect the thou-shalt-nots. Thoughts and feelings such as the cruder egotistical impulses and the associations with bodily functions, which seem quite natural to the child's primitive and necessarily unmoral mind, gradually fall under the cultural ban proclaimed by parents and educators, so that the unconscious becomes a receptacle for all the thoughts that are rendered painful and disagreeable by the slowly developing sense of shame and of moral and ethical behavior. We

"put away childish things" by putting them into the unconscious. Our germinating sexual ideas and our naïve erotic
attitude towards our parents become particularly "impermissible" and we therefore draw an especially heavy veil of forgetfulness over this part of our childhood. But though we can
forget, we cannot obliterate, and the result of this early fixation
upon our parents is to leave in our mind an indelible imprint, or
"imago," of both our mother and our father. Our parents are
always with us in our unconscious. They become our ultimate
criterion by which we judge men and women, and exercise the
most potent influence upon our love choice. The imago of them
that holds us to our unconscious allegiance is a picture, not as
we know them later, old and declining, but as we saw them first,
young and radiant, and dowered, as it seemed to us then, with
godlike gifts. We cannot go on loving them so we do the next
best thing; the boy chooses a woman who resembles his mother
as closely as possible, and the girl mates with the man who
reminds her most of her father.

Such, according to Freud, is the psychological genesis of
the emotion of love. The normal evolution of love from the first
maternal caress is finally accomplished when the individual
definitely transfers his allegiance to a self-chosen mate and
thereby steps out of the charmed family circle in which he has
been held from infancy. That this is difficult even under normal
circumstance seems already to have been recognized in the
Bible, where Christ says with so much solemnity: "For this
cause shall a man leave father and mother"; as if only so
weighty a reason could induce a child to leave its parents.
Freud, in postulating the above development as the norm,
proceeds to attach grave and far-reaching consequences to any
deviations from this standard. The effect of any disturbance in
the balanced and harmonious influence of both parents upon
the child, or of any abnormal pressure of circumstances or wilful
action that forces the child into a specialized attitude toward
either parent, is subtly and unerringly reproduced in the later
love-life. The reader himself will probably recall from his own
observation, a large number of cases where the love-life has
been thwarted, or stunted, or never expressed. He will think of
those old bachelors whose warm attachment to their mother has

so much superficial charm, as well as of those old maids who so self-effacingly devote themselves to their fathers. He will also recall that almost typical man whose love interest persistently goes where marriage is impossible, preferably to a woman already preempted by another man or to a much older woman, so that his love can never come to rest in its object; he will wonder whether this man too is not preserving his ideal allegiance to his mother by avoiding that final detachment from her which marriage would bring. He will notice a class of men and women who, even though their parents are dead, seem to have resigned marriage and live in a kind of small contentment with a constantly narrowing horizon. Or he may know of actual marriages that are unhappy because the memory of one of the parents has not been sufficiently laid to rest, and the joke about the mother-in-law or the pie that mother used to make, will acquire a new significance for him. And to all these cases thousands must still be added where neurotic and hysteric patients reveal with unmistakable clearness that the ghosts of the parents still walk about in the troubled psyches of these unfortunates, influencing life and happiness with paralyzing effect. These are all manifestations which the reader hitherto has observed only as results, without knowing the causes or trying to ascertain them. With the aid of the Freudian theory such examples may now help him to see, as perhaps he has already begun to see in Paul, the tremendous rôle that the abnormal fixation upon the parent plays in the psychic development of the individual. And in so doing he may perhaps also gain some insight into the part that his own parents have played in his normal psychic growth, just as disease gives us a clearer understanding of health or as Madame Montessori's study of subnormal children has enabled her to formulate general laws of education.

IV

We can now return to *Sons and Lovers* with a new understanding. Why has the attitude of the son to his mother here had such a devastating effect upon his whole life? Why could he not overcome this obstacle like other children and ultimately attain some measure of manhood? Why, in short, was the surrender so complete? In Paul's case the abnormal fixation upon the mother is most obviously conditioned by the father, whose unnatural position in the family is responsible for the distortion of the normal attitude of the child towards its parents. The father ideal simply does not exist for Paul; where there should have been an attractive standard of masculinity to imitate, he can only fear and despise. The child's normal dependence upon the mother is perpetuated because there is no counter-influence to detach it from her. But there is another distortion, equally obvious, which fatally influences the natural development. Paul's early fixation upon his mother is met and enhanced by Mrs. Morel's abnormally concentrated affection for her son. Her unappeased love, which can no longer go out towards her husband, turns to Paul for consolation; she *makes* him love her too well. Her love becomes a veritable Pandora's box of evil. For Paul is now hemmed in on all sides by too much love and too much hate.

If now we compare Paul's boyhood and adolescence with, let us say, the reader's own, we find that the difference is, to a great extent, one of consciousness and unconsciousness. All those psychic processes which are usually unconscious or at least heavily veiled in the normal psycho-sexual development lie close to consciousness in Paul and break through into his waking thoughts at every favorable opportunity. Everything is raw and exposed in him and remains so, kept quick to the touch by the pressure of an abnormal environment which instead of moulding, misshapes him. The normal hostility towards the father which is conditioned in every boy by a natural jealousy of the mother's affection, is nursed in him to a conscious hate through Morel's actual brutality and his mother's undisguised bitterness and contempt. And the normal love for the mother which ordinarily serves as a model for the man's love for other women is in him perverted into abnormal expression almost at his mother's breast, so that he is always conscious of his infatuation with his mother and can never free his love-making from that paralyzing influence. These powerful determinants of the love-life which we acquire from our parents would be too overwhelming in every case were it not for the process of submersion or repression already referred to. This repression usually sets in at an early stage of childhood and acts biologically as a protective mechanism by allowing us to develop a slowly expanding sense of selfhood through which we gradually differentiate ourselves from our parents. In this way the fateful dominance of the parents is broken, though their influence remains in the unconscious as a formative and directing impulse.

In Paul this salutary process never takes place because he cannot free himself from the incubus of his parents long enough to come to some sense of himself. He remains enslaved by his parent complex instead of being moulded and guided by it. One turns back to that astonishing scene at Lincoln Cathedral. Here Paul goes to the roots of his mother's hold upon him. For his passionate reproaches hurled at his mother because she has lost her youth, prove that the mother-imago, in all its pristine magic, has never diminished its sway over him; he has never been able to forget or to subordinate that first helpless infatuation. If only she could be young again so that he could remain her child-lover! With that thought and wish so conscious in him nothing else in life can become really desirable, and all initiative is dried up at the source. Paul cannot expand towards the universe in normal activity and form an independent sex interest because for him his mother has become the universe; she stands between him and life and the other woman. There is a kind of bottomless childishness about him; life in a pretty house with his mother— the iteration sounds like a childish prattle. Miriam feels it when she calls him a child of four which she can no longer nurse. Nor can Clara help him by becoming a wanton substitute for his mother. Only the one impossible ideal holds him, and that means the constant turning in upon himself which is death. Paul goes to pieces because he can never make the mature sexual decision away from his mother, he can never accomplish the physical and emotional transfer.

If now this striking book, taken as it stands, bears such unexpected witness to the truth of Freud's remarkable psychosexual theory, it is at least presumable that the author himself and the rest of his work also stand in some very definite relation to this theory. The feeling that Sons and Lovers must be autobiographical is considerably strengthened by the somewhat meager personal detail which Mr. Edwin Björkman supplies in an introduction to Mr. Lawrence's first play. Mr. Lawrence was himself the son of a collier in the Derbyshire coal-mining district and his mother seems to have occupied an exceptional position in the family, showing herself to be a woman of great fortitude and initiative, who evidently dominated the household. Mr. Björkman is silent concerning the father, but gives us the interesting information that *Sons and Lovers* was written not long after the mother's death. This information is not sufficient, however, to warrant our inquiry going beyond the author's writings, a step for which, in any case, it would be necessary to have both his permission and his coöperation. We must therefore limit ourselves to the testimony of Mr. Lawrence's work. This consists of two additional novels, a volume of poems, and a play. What is truly astonishing is that all of these, in various disguises and transparent elaborations, hark back to the same problem: the direct and indirect effects of an excessive maternal allegiance and the attempt to become emancipated from it.

Reference has already been made to the poems. This is the way the author ends a love poem:

> What else—it is perfect enough,
> It is perfectly complete,
> You and I,
> What more—?
> *Strange, how we suffer in spite of this!*

Why, it may well be asked, should the perfection of love bring suffering? Certainly the love poems of adolescence are not as a rule colored with the feeling of suffering as unmotivated as this. But there is a second poem, entitled "End of Another Home-holiday" which in the short space of three pages states Paul's whole problem with unmistakable precision. The poet tells how dearly he loves his home and then continues as follows:

> The light has gone out from under my mother's door.
> That she should love me so,
> She, so lonely, greying now,
> And I leaving her,
> Bent on my pursuits!

How curiously that last line comes in, "Bent on my pursuits!" as if he felt that he ought to stay at home. Here we have again the son who cannot leave his mother; the mere thought of doing so fills him with self-reproach. In the next few lines the reproach deepens:

> Forever, ever by my shoulder pitiful Love will linger,
> Crouching as little houses crouch under the mist when I turn.
> Forever, out of the mist the church lifts up her reproachful
>   finger,
> Pointing my eyes in wretched defiance where love hides
>   her face to mourn.

Even inanimate things point the finger of reproach at him. A little later in the same poem the mother becomes a symbolic figure, following the son through life like a Norn, as she begs for his love.

> While ever at my side,
>   Frail and sad, with grey bowed head,
>   The beggar-woman, the yearning-eyed
>   Inexorable love goes lagging.

. . . .

> But when I draw the scanty cloak of silence over my eyes,
> Piteous Love comes peering under the hood.
> Touches the clasp with trembling fingers, and tries
> To put her ear to the painful sob of my blood,
> While her tears soak through to my breast,
>   Where they burn and cauterize.

The poem ends with the call of the corncrake in the poet's ear, crying monotonously:

> With a piteous, unalterable plaint, that deadens
>   My confident activity:
> With a hoarse, insistent request that falls
>   Unweariedly, unweariedly,
>   Asking something more of me,
>   Yet more of me!

An interesting, tell-tale clew in these last lines shows how thoroughly this poem is Paul's and to how great an extent Paul and the author are one and the same. For the careful reader will remember that Paul too, coming home over the fields after visiting Miriam is strongly depressed by the call of this same little bird and immediately goes in to his mother to tell her that he still loves her best and that he has broken off with Miriam.

Has not his mother too, "deadened his confident activity." Her influence could hardly be better described in a single phrase. The whole poem is a protest against the terrible allegiance that the mother exacts, just as Paul, towards the end of the book, reproaches his mother for the failure of his life. It can hardly be doubted that a vital part of the lyricist has gone into Paul.

In reading the two remaining novels and the play our attention is immediately struck by a curious sameness and limitation of motif that underlies them all. In each there is a deadly father or husband hate, a poignant sense of death, and a picture of marriage or love that does not satisfy. Siegmund, the husband in *The Trespasser*, is exposed to a hate so withering that he collapses before it. He is a kind and gentle musician, too effeminate for a man, and entirely devoid of initiative. The hatred of his wife and children is practically unmotivated, we are simply asked to assume it in order to follow him in his affair with Helena. This brings him no solace, he cannot come to rest in her, his love for her simply brings him the sense of death. It is the psychology of Paul transferred to a man of forty, and Helena's struggle to make his love for her real is much like Miriam's. In the play, *The Widowing of Mrs. Holroyd*, the wife seeks to escape from a brutal and drunken husband by eloping with another man. The death of her husband in a mining accident intervenes and brings her a sense of pity and remorse because she never tried to win and hold her husband's love. She had married him without love. Her son hates his father and wishes him dead. Blackmore, the man with whom she wanted to elope, has much of Paul in him; his belief that love can bring happiness is never more than half-hearted. The sense of guilt that the death of the husband brings to both of them, makes the elopement impossible. Death always supervenes upon the impermissible with Mr. Lawrence.

In *The White Peacock* the background is again a ruthless hate for the husband and father. One of the daughters says: *"There is always a sense of death in this house. I believe my mother hated my father before I was born. That was death in her veins for me before I was born. It makes a difference."* We get a picture of women who marry meaningless husbands and men who marry unsatisfying wives. Lettie marries Leslie because

George, whom she really loves, lacks the initiative to claim her, and George marries Meg after his abortive love for Lettie has made him despair of life. Neither he nor she come to any emotional satisfaction; Lettie consoles herself for her aimlessly empty husband by living in her children, and George ends his "Liebestod" in drink. Lettie's brother, who tells the story, is almost sexless except towards his sister, whom he admires like a lover. One gradually gets a sense of monotony; happiness in love is always impossible in this fictional world of Mr. Lawrence, and hate for the parent or husband is the master passion. The motivation is often indistinct or inadequate in all three stories, and the artistry is inferior. They were evidently only preludes to *Sons and Lovers*.

In the story of Paul the author has reached the final expression of a problem which haunts his every effort. The creative labor of self-realization which makes *Sons and Lovers* such a priceless commentary on the love-life of to-day, accomplished itself but slowly in Mr. Lawrence, waiting, no doubt, for his artistic maturity and the final clarity which the death of his mother must have brought. And if, as I have tried to show, he has been able, though unknowingly, to attest the truth of what is perhaps the most far-reaching psychological theory ever propounded, he has also given us an illuminating insight into the mystery of artistic creation. For Mr. Lawrence has escaped the destructive fate that dogs the hapless Paul by the grace of expression: out of the dark struggles of his own soul he has emerged as a triumphant artist. In very epoch the soul of the artist is sick with the problems of his generation. He cures himself by expression in his art. And by producing a catharsis in the spectator through the enjoyment of his art he also heals his fellow beings. His artistic stature is measured by the universality of the problem which his art has transfigured.

9 · Lawrence's Quarrel with Freud

by Frederick J. Hoffman

I

In May, 1913, when *Sons and Lovers* was published by Duckworth of London, Lawrence was pointed out as a novelist with exceptional insight into such psychoanalytic problems as incest-horror and the oedipus complex. Yet that novel was written before Lawrence had any real acquaintance with Freud, and before he mentions Freud in any of his letters. Such Freudian criticisms of *Sons and Lovers* were at best exaggerated. *Sons and Lovers* demonstrates that Lawrence needed no theory except his own to aid him in his analysis of character. Most important, *all* of Lawrence's work bears ultimate reference to his own experience, no matter how many suggestions of "alien theory" it may contain.

When we examine Lawrence's habits of reading, we find him either enthusiastic or bitter over the literary offerings of his contemporaries; we discover that his reading interests are based upon what books he has available at any given moment of his life and upon what his particular mood happens to be. He was opposed to intellectual analysis at all times, though especially so in his early life, the life described in *Sons and Lovers*, and "E. T.'s" *A Personal Record*. The intellectual experience of the early years, as described by "E. T." moves from one position to

Reprinted from "Lawrence's Quarrel with Freud," by Frederick J. Hoffman, from The Achievement of D. H. Lawrence, *by Frederick J. Hoffman, Harry T. Moore, and others. Copyright 1953 by the University of Oklahoma Press.*

another—from T. H. Huxley and Haeckel, to Kant, Schopen-hauer, and Nietzsche: "In all his reading he seemed to be grop-ing for something that he could lay hold of as a guiding principle in his own life. There was never the least touch of the academic or the scholastic in his approach." (pp. 112–13)

Lawrence's reading was sporadic, by reason both of his habit of traveling to the ends of the earth, and therefore having to rely on anything he could get, and of his habit of measuring all influ-ences by his emotions rather than by his intellect. To say that Lawrence was superficial is to neglect certain important personal determinants of his thought. His *distrust* of the intellect, of its cynicism and "whimpering futility," gave him his sole basis for an attack upon the "academic chairs of virtue." But in this repudiation not only the strictly skeptical, or the rigidly logical minds suffered; those who seemed to have something to say to him, or who spoke along the same lines, were also rejected. Bergson, for example, bored him: "He feels a bit thin." [1]

He would seem, therefore, the most thoroughgoing anti-intellectual of his time. But one must speak in paradoxes about this paradoxical figure. With the statement, "Lawrence rejected everything," must be linked the judgment, "Lawrence rejected nothing." He *never gave anything up.* He assumed a critical ambivalence of acceptance-rejection in all his reactions to the intellectual world around him. It was through no ordinary fickle-ness of mind that he responded to any influence in this way. It is a mistake, therefore, to say that Lawrence was influenced by Freud, or Bergson, or Nietzsche; one can only say that "Law-rence was influenced by Lawrence." Another point ought to be made, in order to clarify the problem of influence: he often used reading as a test of his emotional state; likewise, he frequently resorted to writing to "clear his mind." Horace Gregory points out that Lawrence's two essays on psychoanalysis were motivated in this manner: "the writing of such essays offered him the means of checking-back results of his convictions, and . . . by this process he was enabled to unroll himself like a map and

[1] Letter to A. D. McLeod, April 26, 1913, in *The Letters of D. H. Lawrence*, p. 121.

thus review (in the only way he knew how) the existing worth of his beliefs." [2]

Lawrence's reading was never impersonal. He measured books as he did persons; for him there was little if any distinction between them. Hence, his evaluation of John Middleton Murry, for example, was not in terms of Murry's mind, nor in terms of his literary or critical talents, but almost entirely in terms of Murry's ability to "get along" with him—that is, to enter sympathetically into Lawrence's emotional life. The difference between their minds is important. The sensitivity of Lawrence was dynamic: the difference was one between an angry mood and a sulking introversion. Murry held tenaciously to critical categories which had been tested and found satisfactory to his taste; Lawrence had from the beginning insisted upon a dynamically personal and subjective tribunal at which ideas—*any* ideas—were to be tried. Hence Murry from the beginning admits that he cannot understand Lawrence: "Lawrence's ideas are rather difficult for me to get hold of, because he uses all kinds of words in a curious symbolic sense to which I have no clue." [3]

So far as we can determine, Lawrence's interest in Freud came at the same time as his whirlwind courtship of Frieda. Frieda has explained her own interest in Freud, which began just before she met Lawrence: "I had just met a remarkable disciple of Freud and was full of undigested theories. This friend did a lot for me. I was living like a somnambulist in a conventional set life and he awakened the consciousness of my own proper self." [4] Lawrence caught Frieda's enthusiasm for "things German" almost immediately; and, in his trip to Germany, soon afterward (1912), he found time to explore both the language and the literature of her native land. How much of Frieda's own personality went into the revision of *Sons and Lovers*, one can only guess; but it is sufficient to say that the "Miriam" of that novel lost her hold upon Lawrence; and that the novel was altered in

2 Horace Gregory, *Pilgrim of the Apocalypse*, p. 58.

3 John Middleton Murry, "Reminiscences of D. H. Lawrence," *New Adelphi*, Vol. 3 (1930), 270.

4 Frieda Lawrence, *Not I but the Wind* (New York, Viking, 1934), p. 3.

detail and in point of view as a result.[5] Before the final draft was ready for the publishers, perhaps during the time of revision, Lawrence was listening to Frieda's explanations of Freud and arguing with her about Freud's contribution to modern thought. "Yes, Lawrence knew about Freud before he wrote the final draft of *Sons and Lovers*," Frieda tells me in a letter of November 21, 1942. "I don't remember whether he had read Freud or heard of him before we met in 1912. But I was a great Freud admirer; we had long arguments and Lawrence's conclusion was more or less that Freud looked on sex too much from the doctor's point of view, that Freud's 'sex' and 'libido' were too limited and mechanical and that the root was deeper."

These arguments and discussions may have affected the final structure of *Sons and Lovers* in one way at least: Lawrence may have increased the emphasis in the novel upon the mother-son relationship, to the neglect of other matters, and given it the striking clarity which it enjoys in the published book. But the relationship was there long before Lawrence's final revision; and he did not allow any clinical or psychological commentary to interfere with the literary excellence of the novel as a whole. It is doubtful that the revision of *Sons and Lovers* was more than superficially affected by Lawrence's introduction to psychoanalysis; Freudianism belongs to a later period in Lawrence's development. The influence of Lawrence on the psychoanalysts was another matter altogether. They hailed *Sons and Lovers* as the most penetrating study of the oedipus complex yet to be found in English literature. Lawrence was at first pleased and amused, then became interested in psychoanalysis—as though he had anticipated it and therefore expected it to clarify his own mind. Dr. David Eder began to attend the "Lawrence evenings" and to undertake a serious discussion of Freudian theory, especially as it influenced the reading of *Sons and Lovers*. Lawrence studied psychoanalysis with his usual intense interest, but was soon disappointed with its "odor of the laboratory." He objected to its habits of analysis, which never "let one's feelings alone"; he complained that the psychoanalysts

5 *Ibid.*, p. 56. The final draft was written in Gargnano, Italy, with "Frieda helping."

"can only help you more completely to *make your own feelings.*
They can never let you *have* any real feelings."

II

The excitement caused by *Sons and Lovers* in psychoanalytic
circles did not, therefore, lead to any wholehearted acceptance by
Lawrence of Freud, but it did give him some cause for reflection.
He was anxious at first to point to the experience described in
Sons and Lovers as "normal," but he gave the psychoanalysts
careful attention—perhaps waiting for some way of proving them
false. This opportunity seems to have come at the same time that
he was himself formulating his "theory of being" in two essays,
Psychoanalysis and the Unconscious (1921), and *Fantasia of the
Unconscious* (1922). Here he has apparently subdued psychoanalysis and given it the disparaging label *scientific,* but he does
not let psychoanalysis rest; his letters and book reviews refer to
the new psychology almost until the time of his death. After
the writing of *Fantasia,* he justifies his rejection of psychoanalysis on two grounds: (a) that it is just a "fad," unworthy of
serious consideration, and (b) that it does not account for the
problems of group-association, but fastens the physician's ego to
the patient's in an unequal struggle for dominance.

As a support for his first objection, his letters to Mabel
Dodge Luhan are most illuminating. He writes the much-
analyzed Mrs. Luhan: "I rather hate therapy altogether—
doctors, healers, and all the rest. I believe that a real neurotic
is a half devil, but a cured neurotic is a perfect devil. . . . I
would prefer that neurotics died." [6] When Lawrence hears of
her interest in Jung, he is resentful; she reports his indignation
in the following manner: "More attempts to know and to understand! More systems and more consciousness! All he wanted was
the *flow* and not the knowing about it!" [7] He is sufficiently
astute to recognize the real reason for Mrs. Luhan's interest in
psychoanalysis—her restless search for "new" experience: "It
all seems to me a false working-up, and an inducement to
hysteria and insanity. I know what lies back of it all: the same

6 Letter, December 4, 1921, in Luhan's *Lorenzo in Taos* (New York,
Knopf, 1932), pp. 13–14.
7 *Ibid.,* p. 138.

indecent desire to have everything in the *will* and the *head*. Life itself comes from elsewhere." [8]

Lawrence did seem interested in one version of psychoanalysis—the un-Freudian analysis of Trigant Burrow, a New York psychologist. Burrow's theory of "group images" he reads with great interest and considers the only one of any value. Lawrence believes he shares with Burrow a distaste for science and the scientific method: "your criticism of psychoanalysis as practised is to the quick. . . . But do you know, I think you are really more a philosopher, or artist, than a scientist—and that you have a deep natural resistance to this scientific jargonizing." [9] The book to which Lawrence refers is Burrow's *The Social Basis of Consciousness*. In a review of it, he applauds Burrow again for his criticism of practising psychoanalysts. Therapy is simply an artificial conflict between the analyst and the patient; Burrow has discovered the artificiality of his position as an analyst; he "found, in his clinical experiences, that he was always applying a *theory*. . . . The mind could not be open, because the patient's neurosis, all the patient's experience, *had* to be fitted to the Freudian theory of the inevitable incest-motive." The analyst's intentions are good; he wants to set the patient free; but he merely substitutes one image for another, "the fixed motive of the incest-complex. . . . While the Freudian theory of the unconscious and of the incest-motive is valuable as a *description* of our psychological condition, the moment you begin to *apply* it, and make it master of the living situation, you have begun to substitute one mechanistic or unconscious illusion for another." [10]

These remarks to and about Trigant Burrow have the value of showing us Lawrence's attitude toward psychoanalysis near the end of his creative career. He is still interested in the psychology, but has long since convicted it on the counts of its scientific nature and its inadequacy as a psychological guide for living. The inert, dead mass of clinical material did not interest Lawrence in the slightest; but he always credited psychoanalysis

8 *Ibid.*, p. 151.
9 *Letters*, p. 695; cf. pp. 643, 693.
10 D. H. Lawrence, "A New Theory of Neuroses," *Bookman*, Vol. 66 (1927), 314; reprinted in *Phoenix: The Posthumous Papers of D. H. Lawrence*, ed. Edward D. McDonald (New York, Viking, 1936), pp. 377, 378.

with value as a descriptive science. Similarly, he distrusted the analytic situation; it placed too much emphasis upon complete submission on the part of the patient. Lawrence was unwilling to have any one person submit entirely to another; such a condition would destroy the organic individuality which gives life to so many of Lawrence's fictional heroes. The spark which kept alive a person's original self was in itself kept alive by clashes of personality, and not by submission.

Lawrence did agree with Freud in at least one particular—that the normal sex life of man had been disastrously repressed and neglected. Even here the differences between the two men are marked. Whereas Freud suggested that the source of most mental illness was repression of normal sex development, Lawrence argued that full expression of the personalities of both man and woman involved a genuine sex relationship, which went far beyond the mere "understanding" that modernists offered as the clue to sex happiness. These are not at all the same attitudes: Freud's is, in a sense, a negative approach; it is to *remove illness* that he is forced to emphasize sex. Lawrence, however, considers the sex experience (and all of its implications for family life) as basic to initial health and happiness. Sex experience is a part of Lawrence's "religion"—an important expression of the self in its search for vital mysteries. Hence, many of his characters find their most vital happiness or their most bitter disillusionments during and after such experience.

Lawrence believed that sex is is the ultimate expression of a person's individuality. The "mass mind," as Lawrence saw it in operation during the First World War, or as he viewed it in the industrial centers of England and America, had sacrificed much to the principle of collective action. Under such conditions, sexual experience degenerates to insect lust (*Letters*, p. 231). Modern man had debased sex by looking at it in one of two ways: (a) as an interesting thing, which can be "known" and "experimented with" (or, thought about); (b) as lust, which shows no consideration for either self or object. Lawrence was in many respects a Puritan; he abhorred mere lust, which, he felt, lacked the emotional concomitants of joy and was merely the perversion of the life instinct: "There is a brief time for sex, and a long time when sex is out of place. But when it is out of place as an activity there still should be the large and quiet space in the consciousness where it lives quiescent" (*Letters*, p. 781). For this reason he is horrified by Aldous Huxley's *Point Counter Point*, though he has to admit that Huxley has "shown the truth, perhaps the last truth," about his generation, and "with really fine courage" (*Letters*, p. 765). He is opposed to sex censorship as much as he is to sex looseness; they are two sides of the same coin. The "censor-moron" hates nothing so much as truly vital and essential living. His prudery threatens "our developing and extending consciousness" (*Letters*, p. 769). But the modernist of the twenties repels him as thoroughly; the American woman especially, who "intellectualizes" sex: "The one woman who *never* gives herself is our free woman, who is always giving herself. America affects me like that" (*Letters*, p. 559).

Lady Chatterley's Lover contains Lawrence's most complete statement about sex. The novel argues for complete freedom, not from restraint, but from false prudery. Lady Chatterley is placed in an impossible situation—tied by bonds of sympathy and memory to a gentleman who has been paralyzed by a war injury but who insists upon holding her. "*Il n'a pas de quoi.*" In her first attempt to escape from her marriage, she meets with a representative modernist, one who regards sex as an interesting and pleasant pastime, and flattering to his ego, but who has never really experienced it in the manner of which Lawrence approves: "it is in the passional secret places of life, above all, that the tide of sensitive awareness needs to ebb and flow, cleansing and freshening." [11] Lady Chatterley was destined to find these passional secret sources of life; in submitting to them, she threw aside all of her possessions—not only the husband she despised but all of his wealth. This theme of repudiation is necessary to Lawrence's life-view; for it involves condemnation of industrial society as one of the principal causes of life failure.[12] Mellors, the complete Lawrencean man, furnishes the

[11] D. H. Lawrence, *Lady Chatterley's Lover* (Florence, Italy, Orioli, 1928), p. 118.

[12] Clifford's wealth has been inherited, and it depends on the work of the mines. While Lady Chatterley has her secret affair with Mellors, Clifford is busy improving the collieries in a way which is to plunge the workers into deeper automatism. Cf. Gerald Crich's similar plans, *Women in Love* (New York, Modern Library, n.d.; first published, 1920), pp. 240–65. Lawrence believed that the only true equality lay in the uninterrupted spiritual development of man; the machine imposed another type of equality upon this, and the result was chaos. (F.J.H.)

key to her final understanding of sex as a living thing; for he has kept aloof both from the repressive forces of modern industrialism and from the petty intellectualism of Clifford's tribe.

In the controversy over *Lady Chatterley's Lover* Lawrence engaged willingly and with enthusiasm. He tried to redefine the terms *pornography* and *obscenity*. The first term does not refer merely to a representation of sex: it is "the attempt to insult sex, to do dirt on it."

> In the degraded human being the deep instincts have gone dead. . . . It happens when the psyche deteriorates, and the profound controlling instincts collapse. Then sex is dirt and dirt is sex, and sexual excitement becomes a playing with dirt, and any sign of sex in a woman becomes a show of her dirt. This is the condition of the common, vulgar human being whose name is legion, and who lifts his voice and it is the *Vox populi, vox Dei*. And this is the source of all pornography.[13]

During the First World War, Lawrence had thought deeply of these matters, and he came to the conclusion that Christianity had misunderstood love throughout its history. Near the end of his life (1927), he published the short novel, *The Man Who Died*; if the life of Christ had come to an end as Lawrence describes it, instead of in the manner of the gospels, the problem of Christianity and sex might have been solved. The body of Jesus has been taken down and laid into the tomb; but he has not really died—or, rather, the life of the gospel accounts has been killed within him and he is free to find the true source of human vitality and happiness. Death has saved him from his own salvation. He has neglected his own body in pursuance of a spiritual mission. In a temple of Isis he meets the fulfillment for which he has been seeking, and he understands why he has been put to death: "I asked them all to serve me with the corpse of their love. And in the end I offered them only the corpse of my love. . . . If I had kissed Judas with live love, perhaps he would never have kissed me with death." [14]

The proper sex relationship is best demonstrated in an ideal marriage. As ever, Lawrence draws chiefly from his own experience for his statement of marital harmony. Contrary to the impression given in most contemporary accounts, Lawrence was

13 Lawrence, "Pornography and Obscenity," in *Phoenix*, p. 176.
14 *The Man Who Died* (London, Secker, 1931), pp. 137–38.

supremely happy only with Frieda. The violent quarrels were an important part of their relationship. His friends saw often that the tie with Frieda was indissoluble. Frieda herself never lost her conviction that the marriage was suitable: "I think the greatest pleasure and satisfaction for a woman is to live with a creative man, when he goes ahead and fights—I found it so. . . . Often before he conceived a new idea he was irritable and disagreeable, but when it had come, the new vision, he could go ahead, and was eager and absorbed." [15]

Lawrence's happiest years, when he was enjoying the first full realization of Frieda's love, inspired him to make a number of statements about the importance of man's love for woman: "I think the only resourcing of art, revivifying it, is to make it more the joint work of man and woman. I think the *one* thing to do, is for men to have courage to draw nearer to women, expose themselves to them, and be altered by them; and for women to accept and admit men" (*Letters*, 198). He believed in marriage because he was happily married. But marriage was not complete unless it involved a violent clashing of supplementary natures. Man must surmount an initial objection to woman in order to realize her fundamental nature. Being kind, or benevolent, or liberal merely serves to overemphasize this objection. Lawrence sees the failure of all liberalism—the "twentieth-century enlightenment," founded upon philanthropy and improved sewage disposal—as the tendency to break away from essential physical values, which have always seemed a little disagreeable to civilized man. In modern literature the repulsiveness of man was finally being investigated—especially in the novels of Joyce, Huxley, and Gide. "For a long time, the *social* belief and benevolence of man towards man keeps pace with the secret physical repulsion of man away from man. But ultimately, inevitably, the one outstrips the other. The benevolence exhausts itself, the repulsion only deepens. The benevolence is external and extra-individual. But the revulsion is inward and personal." [16]

15 Frieda Lawrence, *Not I but the Wind*, p. 194.
16 Introduction to Dahlberg's *Bottom Dogs*, in *Phoenix*, p. 270. Cf. Freud, *Civilization and Its Discontents*, trans. Joan Riviere (New York, J. Cape and H. Smith, 1930), pp. 66–67, n. 1.

Lawrence's criticism of modern sex attitudes is addressed to their failure to recognize the deep sources of vital experience, their tendency to prevent a complete and satisfactory sex experience. In this respect, both the "censor-moron" and the modern "free woman" err alike: the one in considering sex itself unwholesome; the other, in fearing its consequences. Neither is entirely honest; neither wishes life to be fully charged with elements of danger and beauty. In this indictment Lawrence includes all of modern science; scientists do not instinctively or intuitively grasp what they outwardly assert. They count, tabulate, announce results in bewildering figures, or in hesitant semi-conclusions. This is true, as well, of Freudianism, which substitutes the "intellectual-psychological" for the "intuitive-psychological."

. . . .

10 · The Mother in the Mind

by Daniel A. Weiss

Gertrude Morel moves through *Sons and Lovers* like a cry of pain. Her truth is valid only as she is an expression of her son's anguish—and this both in spite of and because of the clinical verisimilitude with which Lawrence images her as the Jocasta par excellence. Of the other characters it can be said that Lawrence is truly their creator, since they live in obedience to their own laws. But of Gertrude Morel he is merely the undertaker, responsible for her careful embalming. Her likeness is a magnificent death mask. Around her cluster the metaphors of queenliness, and virginity, and youth, the mechanically collated evidence of the Oedipal relationship. Her son William was "like her knight who wore *her* favor in the battle." When she goes into town with Paul, they feel "the excitement of lovers having an adventure together." "She was gay like a sweetheart. . . . As he saw her hands in their old black gloves getting the silver out of the worn purse, his heart contracted with pain of love for her."

The inevitable wish of the child that his mother remain young becomes the conscious theme of Paul's outbursts:

"Why can't a man have a *young* mother? What is she old for? . . . And why wasn't I the oldest son? Look—they say the young ones have the advantage—but look, *they* had the young mother. You should have had me for your eldest son."

"I didn't arrange it," she remonstrated. "Come to consider you're as much to blame as me." He turned on her, white, his eyes furious.

Reprinted from Oedipus in Nottingham: D. H. Lawrence, *by Daniel A. Weiss. Copyright 1962 by the University of Washington Press.*

Here the subtle disguise Paul's wish wears is the important thing. His real desire is to be even more than the "oldest son," is not even that his mother remain young, but that they be equal in age no matter what it is.

Lawrence completely idealizes Gertrude's maternal role as the mother of the infant Paul. She is Rachel, the virginal mother.

> Mrs. Morel watched the sun sink from the glistening sky, leaving a soft, flower-blue overhead. . . . A few shocks of corn in a corner of the fallow stood up as if alive; she imagined them bowing; perhaps her son would be a Joseph. In the east a mirrored sunset floated pink opposite the west's scarlet. The big haystacks on the hillside that butted into the glare went cold.
>
> In her arms lay the delicate baby. . . . She no longer loved her husband. She had not wanted this child to come, and there it lay in her arms and pulled at her heart. . . . She would make up for having brought it into the world unloved. She would love it all the more now it was here; carry it in her love.

Gertrude's virginal quality expresses itself chiefly in floral arrangements. She soothes herself with "the scent of flowers"; she is Flora, never Ceres, having long ago chosen between her son's moss rose and Walter Morel's unhappy, hairy coconut.

The necessity for this purity rests, not with Gertrude, but with Paul. It is his wish that she remain pure. Freud suggests that "the grown man's conscious mind likes to regard the mother as the personification of impeccable moral purity" out of an unconscious jealousy of the father and a horror of adult sexuality. And E. T., writing of Lawrence's disgust at hearing "commercial travellers" talking on a train, remembers "that the whole question of sex had for him the fascination of horror, and also that in his repudiation of any possibility of a sex relation between us he felt that he paid me a deep and subtle compliment." The nature of the compliment will be taken up in connection with a discussion of Miriam.

Yet through the mask of Lawrence's mother there emerge occasionally the living signs of the deathly relationship between Paul and Gertrude Morel. Gertrude's careful distinction between the mind and the body, made originally in her relations with William when she refuses to acknowledge his manhood and its needs, leads, in her life with Paul, to a love affair of the spirit. And with Paul she is freer to lead it, for it is with his complicity. When Paul's picture wins a prize at the Castle, Mrs. Morel cries, "Hurrah my boy! I knew we should do it!" as if it were a child they had borne between them.

Confronted with Paul's mistresses she directs most of her bitterness against the one who most resembles herself, Miriam, the one whom Paul likewise recognizes as his mother's rival. Her judgments of Miriam are true for both of them: " 'She is one of those who will want to suck a man's soul out till he has none of his own left,' she said to herself; 'and he is just such a baby as to let himself be absorbed. She will never let him become a man; she never will.' "

In the scene leading up to the discovery by Walter Morel of Paul and Gertrude embracing, that point after which, I have suggested, the real nature of the relationship becomes intolerable, Paul, Miriam, and Gertrude are involved in almost a fairy-tale situation. Paul is tending his mother's bread, setting the loaves to bake. Miriam is there, and a hoydenish, sensual girl named Beatrice. It is Beatrice who teases him and plays with him sexually, and Miriam, prudish and as disapproving as his mother would have been, who reminds him that the loaves are burning. Quickly he takes the loaf from the oven, scrapes it, and sets it aside. When he returns from having seen Miriam home, he finds his mother, pale and blue-lipped with the beginnings of her illness, the charred loaf on the table in front of her. "I suppose it's my heart," is her explanation of her illness, but her mental concern is that she supposes Paul to have been too engrossed in Miriam to mind the loaf. And the loaf itself, like the giant's egg in the fairy tale, becomes the external repository of Gertrude's heart.

The little story seems to contain within it the irony of identities failing to recognize one another. Mrs. Morel does not realize that it is not through Miriam that her grasp on Paul will be destroyed, but through the more wholesome sensuality of a Beatrice. When we consider Clara Dawes we find Lawrence attributing to Gertrude a preference for her rather than for Miriam. It is the expression of a wish whose fulfillment would preserve the spiritual nexus in which Paul and Gertrude meet as lovers. The addition of Clara (who, as we shall see, did not exist but had to be invented) to the relationship would provide a *modus vivendi* for both mother and son. Gertrude is made to see this:

> Mrs. Morel considered. She would have been glad now for her son to fall in love with some woman who would—she did not know what. But he fretted so, got so furious suddenly, and again was melancholic. She wished he knew some nice woman —She did not know what she wished, but left it vague.

For Clara represents the dancing side of the relationship, which neither she nor Miriam could provide. And both Gertrude and Miriam give Clara to him in order to purge his spiritual nature of its fleshly dress and to have him back refined and virginal. But it is important to remember that it is Paul who is the unconscious seeker, and the one, ultimately, who realizes the need Clara can satisfy in him. Mrs. Morel's compliance with the idea of Clara is the compliance of a woman putting her child out to wet-nurse. For Paul the sexuality Clara offers is feasible incest, just as his relationship with Miriam, although consummated, is not; and both relationships are determined by the root Oedipal relationship.

The death of Lawrence's mother came about as the result of natural causes; the death of Mrs. Morel has the tragic inevitability of Clytemnestra's murder or Jocasta's suicide. It is the sequel to revelation, which presents two equally horrid alternatives to the protagonist: either the conscious continuation of an unnatural relationship, or the cessation by death of any such possibility. I have suggested that the artist of *Sons and Lovers* brought the passional side of his affair with his mother to a halt when it threatened to become an enormity. Symptomatic of that enormity were the recognition by the father of the "mischief" Paul and his mother were up to and the subsequent beginnings of a real physical struggle between father and son. It is the mother's fainting, not her death but the simulacral prefiguring of her death, that brings about Paul's search in the ensuing chapters of the novel for a mother substitute, if not a way out completely. The enfeebling of Gertrude puts her beyond being desirable as a sexual object, the girl who could race up a hill and who attracted Walter Morel. More and more, fuller and deeper complexities of "terror, agony, and love" are injected into the descriptions of Paul's love for his mother: "His life wanted to free itself of her. It was like a circle where life turned back on itself, and got no further." It is at this point that he is sexually involved, for the first time with some success, with Clara, the younger rival in a new triangle. His open, terrible, revealing fight with Baxter Dawes is followed, as his narrowly avoided fight with Walter Morel is followed, by another failure in Gertrude's health, this time a fatal one.

The recognition, as Lawrence consciously indicates it, is now complete. And his task, as before, is to render its consummation impossible. Now, in accord with the old myth, following the parricide and the achieved marriage (with both Clara and Miriam), the mother must be destroyed. "He and his mother seemed almost to avoid each other. There was some secret between them which they could not bear. He was not aware of it. He only knew that his life seemed unbalanced, as if it were going to smash into pieces." Gertrude's cancer comes as a relief to this stalemate, like the diabolical fulfillment of an oracle. For at the heart of Paul's anguish lies an unconscious awareness of the secondary advantage to be gained from her death—she will be preserved to him. One of his great wishes has been that she remain young and uncorrupted, virginal. As the terminator of life, death is also the preserver of life, a bitter truism that suicides must intuitively grasp, pinching their lives off to anticipate destruction. Gertrude, dying, gathers to herself the imagery of youth:

> He sat down by the bed, miserably. She had a way of curling and lying on her side, like a child. The grey and brown hair was loose over her ear.
> "Doesn't it tickle you?" he said, gently putting it back.
> "It does," she replied.
> His face was near hers. Her blue eyes smiled straight into his, like a girl's—warm, laughing with tender love. It made him pant with terror, agony, and love.

And with her death the transformation is complete. She becomes the fulfillment of his wish: "She lay like a maiden asleep. With his candle in his hand, he bent over her. She lay like a girl asleep and dreaming of her love. . . . She was young again. . . . She would wake up. She would lift her eyelids. She was with him still."

Paul's other great wish is that he himself may die. When Lawrence writes about Paul, his artistic ego, he continually offers himself, like Dostoevsky, "as a victim to fate." The flow of pity between Gertrude and Paul is continually being reciprocated, each one anguished at the other's doomed quality, each one guilty because he cannot alter fate.

> She listened to the small, restless noise the boy made in his throat as she worked. Again rose in her heart the old, almost weary feeling towards him. She had never expected him to live. And yet he had a great vitality in his young body. Perhaps it would have been a little relief to her if he had died. She always felt a mixture of anguish in her love for him.

Gertrude's anguish is related to her thought of the "relief" it might have brought her if Paul had died, and similarly Paul's anguish and wish to die find their source in his open hostility and death wish toward his father, and in his repressed death wish toward his mother when her love threatens his manhood.

Gertrude's death gives rise in Paul to a very dangerous line of thought: that in dying he will be with his mother, just as the minister promises Gertrude that she will be with her son William. "Sometimes they looked into each other's eyes. Then they almost seemed to make an agreement. It was almost as if he were agreeing to die also." Paul waters her milk to weaken her, and finally he administers an overdose of morphia to her— all as if he were sending her ahead to an assignation.

> "What are you doing?" said Annie.
> "I s'll put 'em in her night milk."
> Then they both laughed together like two conspiring children. On top of all their horror flickered this little sanity.

What gives the death of Gertrude its special intensity and importance—Paul's reaction to it is the point on which the novel resolves itself—is the unwritten confusion in the artist's mind. Gertrude's death is at once a real death and a sexual death. Never is she described with such amorous concern as when she is on her deathbed, dreaming her young dream. She is, for the first time in the novel, sexually desirable and seemingly available to the son. His only rival skulks below stairs and will not even look at her. Walter Morel is afraid of her. Only Paul is her lover. "They all stood back. He kneeled down and put his face to hers and his arms round her: 'My love—my love—oh, my love!' he whispered again and again. 'My love—oh, my love.' " But the agent that brings about both these deaths, Death itself, is Fate, God, the father in his destructive phase. Paul's speeding of Gertrude's death is simply one more attempt to interpose himself between his father and his mother. Even when she first becomes sick, his attempt to save her is halfhearted. He knows she must die.

And finally, when he kisses her "passionately" and feels a "coldness against his mouth," he is brought to a last realization and choice. Like Baxter with Clara, he cannot get "at her." He must, as he does with Baxter Dawes, return her to the father, or else, in a continuation to the end of the closed circle, follow his mother into death for the sake of her embrace. William, Paul's brother, of whom he was "unconsciously jealous," faced the same choice earlier in the novel. Preoccupied, like Paul, with death, he anticipates his mother and prepares a place in the grave before her. Like Gertrude's death, William's death *really* happened to Lawrence's brother Ernest; what is more important, as in Gertrude's death, is that William's death *must* happen in *Sons and Lovers* to justify William's part in the novel. William's is the way not taken, the negation of Paul's choice. William's way is consciously rejected, at the end of the novel, by Paul: " 'Mater, my dear—' he began, with the whole force of his soul. Then he stopped. He would not say it. He would not admit that he wanted to die, to have done. He would not own that life had beaten him, or that death had beaten him."

. . . .

Freud postulates the unconscious "conditions of love" that govern the objects of the affections of certain men. The more urgent of these conditions Freud terms "the need for an injured third party," that is, the Oedipal man's choice of woman will require that she be attached to someone else, lover or husband, who has some "right of possession" over her. The second condition, operating as a corollary to the first, requires that the woman be in some way "sexually discredited," the subject of gossip, "loose," or openly promiscuous. With the fulfillment of these conditions the lover conceives of his role as being that of rescuer, rescuing the woman he loves from moral, economic, or social ruin.

The etiology of these strange patterns of choice and response, says Freud, is identical with the normal pattern of love:

> They are derived from the infantile fixation of tender feelings on the mother, and represent one of the consequences of that fixation. In normal love, only a few characteristics survive, which reveal unmistakably the maternal prototype of the object-choice; as, for instance, the preference shown by young men for mature women; the detachment of libido from the mother has been effected relatively swiftly. In our type, on the other hand, the libido has remained attached to the mother for so long, even after the onset of puberty, that the maternal characteristics remain in the love-objects that are chosen later, and all these turn into easily recognizable mother-surrogates.

The "injured third party" is immediately recognizable as the father, in the family situation as the child first conceives of it, with the mother as the sole object of his love. The choice of the "loose" woman seems at first paradoxical, since men tend normally to think of their mothers as being morally impeccable. But the preference derives from the unstable amalgam the son must construct from things as he wants them and things as they are. His first response, upon learning about adult sexuality, is to deny his mother's complicity in such an act. And then, when he can no longer cling to the logical absurdity of such a denial, he swings with a "cynical logic" to the identification of his mother with any sexually available woman:

> The enlightening information he has received has in fact awakened the memory-traces of the impressions and wishes of his early infancy, and these have led to a reactivation in him of certain mental impulses. He begins to desire the mother herself in the sense with which he has recently become acquainted, and to hate his father anew as a rival who stands in the way of his wish; he comes, as we say, under the dominance of the Oedipus complex. He does not forgive his mother for having granted the favours of sexual intercourse not to himself but to his father, and he regards it as an act of unfaithfulness. . . . As a result of the constant, combined operation of the two

driving forces, desire and thirst for revenge, phantasies of the
mother's unfaithfulness are by far the most preferred; the lover
with whom she commits her act of infidelity almost always
exhibits the features of the boy's own ego, or more accurately,
of his own idealized personality, grown up and so raised to a
level with his father.

Ernest Jones refers to a similar deviation in object choice when
he discusses Hamlet's sexual revulsion, his cruel abuse of
Ophelia, and his "complex reaction" toward his mother:

> The underlying theme relates ultimately to the splitting of
> the mother image which the infantile consciousness effects into
> two opposite pictures: one of the virginal madonna, an in-
> accessible saint towards whom all sensual approaches are un-
> thinkable, and the other of a sensual creature accessible to
> everyone. . . .
> When sexual repression is highly pronounced, as with
> Hamlet, then both types of women are found to be hostile: the
> pure one out of resentment at her repulses, the sensual one out
> of the temptation she offers to plunge into guiltiness. Misogyny,
> as in the play, is the result.

Miriam's contribution to the composite mother image is
her purity. She is the "virginal madonna," the "virtuous and
reputable woman," the "personification of impeccable moral
purity," that aspect of the mother image that represents the
spiritual, the physically untouchable. Like Gertrude she prefers
the blossom to the fruit. On their first visit to the Spinney
Farm, Paul and Gertrude are in "ecstasy together" over the
gillivers and guelder roses, bluebells and forget-me-nots, a pleasure Miriam shares with them. It is her coarse brothers who tell
Paul that if he picks the apple blossom there will be no apple,
and who tease Miriam for not being able to stand the sharp
peck the hen makes at the corn in her hand. She is afraid of
Paul's painting of pine trees towering in a red sunset. "Paul
took his pitch from her and their intimacy went on in an utterly
blanched and chaste fashion. It never could be mentioned that
the mare was in foal."

Upon Miriam, Lawrence heaps even more extravagant
attributes of purity than upon Gertrude Morel, who has in
some degree "fallen" through her marriage a victim to sexuality.
Miriam is a *religieuse*:

And she was cut off from ordinary life by her religious intensity which made the world for her either a nunnery garden or a
paradise where sin and knowledge were not, or else an ugly
cruel thing.

All the life of Miriam's body was in her eyes, which were usually dark as a dark church, but could flame with light like a
conflagration. . . . She might be one of the women who went
with Mary when Jesus was dead. . . . There was no looseness
or abandon about her.

Her resemblance to Ophelia approaches paraphrase. Paul writes
to Miriam *after* the turning point that follows his passionate
avowal to his mother and fight with his father: " '. . . You see
I can give you a spirit love, I have given it you this long, long
time; but not embodied passion. See, you are a nun. I have
given you what I would give a holy nun—as a mystic monk to a
holy nun.' " Again this is a symbol based on actuality. E. T.
records a letter Lawrence sent her: " 'Look, you are a nun. I give
you what I would give a holy nun. You must let me marry a
woman I can kiss and embrace and make the mother of my
children.' "

Having raised Miriam to the status of the virgin mother,
Paul, because of his sexual repression, is full of "resentment
at her repulses." Jones defines the same situation in *Hamlet*:

His resentment against women is still further inflamed by the
hypocritical prudishness with which Ophelia follows her father
and brother in seeing evil in his natural affection, an attitude
which poisons his love in exactly the same way that the love of
his childhood, like that of all children must have been poisoned.

Miriam follows her Father in heaven, her religiosity, and
her mother, for whom sex is "always dreadful, but you have
to bear it." But the result, Paul's Hamlet-like, disproportionate
outbursts of rage against her, is the same. In the following most
notable passage the naturalism of the act is fused with the
phallic symbolism of the things described and the action itself.
Miriam is slow to learn (ignorance is the intellectual abstract of
virginity), and Paul, who is trying to teach her algebra, becomes
impatient with her:

She never reproached him or was angry with him. He was
often cruelly ashamed. But still again his anger burst like a
bubble surcharged; and still, when he saw her eager, silent, as

it were, blind face, he felt he wanted to throw the pencil in it; and still, when he saw her hand trembling and her mouth parted with suffering, his heart was scalded with pain for her. And because of the intensity to which she roused him, he sought her.

The cause for this emotional schism is more apparent immediately following the clarifying scene between Paul and Gertrude and Walter Morel. The chapter "Defeat of Miriam" begins:

> Paul was dissatisfied with himself and with everything. [Man delights me not, no, nor woman neither.] The deepest of his love belonged to his mother. When he felt he had hurt her, or wounded his love for her, he could not bear it. Now it was spring and there was battle between him and Miriam.

The juxtaposition here of a consciously made choice of a loved object, Paul's mother, with whom only an attenuated spiritual communion would be possible, and a resolution to do "battle" with another loved object, with whom more than this communion would eventually be possible, suggests an identification of the two. In Paul's mind Miriam has become too firmly established as a mother surrogate. He must shake her loose. His final desperate suggestion to her that they become lovers represents the attempt to dislodge his mother from Miriam, the young girl, "full-breasted and luxuriantly formed." But even this wish, when it is granted, fails, and Paul remains, with her, Oedipus, doomed perpetually to stand on the steps of the palace and abide his incest.

From the very beginning Lawrence assigns to Miriam the maternal attributes that so embittered the real woman behind her. He makes her love Paul because he has been ill:

> Then he was so ill, and she felt he would be weak. Then she would be stronger than he. Then she could love him. If she could be mistress of him in his weakness, take care of him, if he could depend on her, if she could, as it were, have him in her arms, how she could love him.

She is referred to as the "threshing floor" of his ideas. Like Gertrude, who triumphs with him over his winning of a prize, Miriam is his means of conceiving. But all these births are virgin births; the real encounter, gross and physical, is beyond him. In terms of the conditions Freud sets up for the Oedipal type, Paul, torn between a repressed hostility and identification with his father, actually "rescues" Miriam from himself.

What points first to the "rescue" situation is Paul's peculiar rebelliousness toward his mother's values as his sexual drives increase in intensity. He becomes, for example, the champion of the common people, his father's class, because from them one gets "life itself, warmth, you feel their hates and loves." And Mrs. Morel retorts, "Why don't you go and talk to your father's pals?" It is from this man that Paul must save Miriam.

In a sociological excursus Lawrence describes Paul as a type:

> Being the sons of mothers whose husbands had blundered rather brutally through their feminine sanctities, they were themselves too diffident and shy. They could easier deny themselves than incur any reproach from a woman; for a woman was like their mother, and they were full of the sense of their mother.

Paul's entire relationship with Miriam is the unconscious purgation of his own attitude toward her, accomplished by attributing to her that same attitude, which accurately describes his infantile need for love. Needing her love, yet unable to accept it, he accuses her of the same thing Gertrude Morel accused her of, of "sucking" the soul out of him:

> "You don't want to love—your eternal and abnormal craving is to be loved. You aren't positive, you're negative. You absorb, absorb, as if you must fill yourself up with love, because you've got a shortage somewhere." She was stunned by his cruelty.

What is actually tormenting him in Miriam is the exact opposite of this accusation. It is that for the first time in his life he is facing a mature relationship between himself and another woman, *not* his mother, and that a different mode of love is being demanded from him. It is Miriam's refusal to allow him to regress to the Nirvana, the paradisal state of the infant, her insistence that he recognize her, that fills him with anguish. His further accusation of Miriam clarifies this. Paul makes his plea for the impersonality of passion, which Miriam denies him:

Never any relaxing, never any leaving himself to the great hunger and impersonality of passion; he must be brought back to a deliberate, reflective creature. As if from a swoon of passion she called him back to the littleness of the personal relationship. He could not bear it. "Leave me alone—leave me alone!" he wanted to cry; but she wanted him to look at her with eyes full of love. His eyes full of the dark impersonal fire of desire, did not belong to her.

"To be rid of our individuality, which is our will, which is our effort—to live effortless, a kind of conscious sleep—that is very beautiful, I think; that is our afterlife—our immortality."

Here in these few sentences is an adumbration of that "drift toward death" as Lawrence sublimated it into the passional relationship par excellence between men and women. But implicit in it here is the ultimate regression to the child's status with its mother. In his final achievement of a sexual union between them, Paul, more strongly than ever, identifies Miriam with his mother—but not his mother alive, in spite of the fact that her death is still remote; that identification would be too painful. Just as his mother's lips were cold to his passionate kiss, he realizes, after his orgasm, that Miriam "had not been with him all the time, that her soul had stood apart in a sort of horror." But still with this virginal woman there is a pleasure:

He, as he lay on his face on the dead pine leaves, felt extraordinarily quiet. He did not mind if the raindrops came on him: he would have lain and got wet through: he felt as if nothing mattered, as if his living were smeared away into the beyond, near and quite lovable. This strange reaching out to death was new to him. . . .

To him now, life seemed a shadow, day a white shadow; night, and day, and stillness and inaction, this seemed like *being*. To be alive, to be urgent and insistent—that was *not-to-be*. The highest of all was to melt out into the darkness and sway there, identified with the great Being.

The pleasure is deadly: the road to Thebes again, which for a moment he agrees to take, and which, in the end, he will not take. In the end the same wish is distasteful to him, and described in a tone of horror, after his mother's death: ". . . the tear in the veil, through which his life seemed to drift slowly, as if he were drawn toward death. He wanted someone of their own free initiative to help him." But in his first intercourse with Miriam he seems to be insisting that she be a mother before she has a name. The artist seems unconsciously to be trying, with his mother's death, to find some sexual substitute for it, describing in Miriam's frigidity the more tolerable mask of a repressed necrophilia, a desire to be at any cost with his mother. Because these things are latent in his relationship with Miriam, it is imperative that Paul cast her off. As with his own mother, Paul cannot get "at her" either in life or death.

The curiously withering, deathlike nature of Paul's pleasure after Miriam's defloration will continue to echo through Lawrence's works. Freud offers an interesting insight into the reactions of an artist whose young manhood was spent in an atmosphere of such virginal purity. Freud speaks of the primitive taboos of virginity as deriving from the ambivalent nature of the act of defloration—the inflicting of pain instead of pleasure upon the woman one marries—and so incurring in a love object emotions of hostility and the desire to return evil for evil by destroying the man:

> Perhaps this dread is based on the fact that woman is different from man, for ever incomprehensible and mysterious, strange, and therefore apparently hostile. The man is afraid of being weakened by the woman, infected with her femininity, and of then showing himself incapable. The effect which coitus has of discharging tensions and causing flaccidity may be the prototype of what the man fears; and realization of the influence which the woman gains over him through sexual intercourse, the consideration she thereby forces from him, may justify the extension of the fear. In all this there is nothing obsolete, nothing which is not still alive among ourselves.

With his growing tendency in his sexual relations to equate himself with his father, Paul has in the example of his mother not only the woman who took his father's strength from him and made him "paltry and insignificant," but the additional threat of the cold, puritanical woman, the virgin, who does not experience the "flaccidity" of the father, and who emerges from their "acts of violence" the moral victor. Of both these virginal qualities Miriam is the obvious continuation. Her purity triumphs hatefully over his weakness, nor will she permit him the escape advantage of regression into "impersonality."

Paul misses in Miriam-as-mother the presence of the "injured third party" and tries, as he tried to shift his own emotional passivity, to thrust Miriam into the maternal situation. His attempts follow, as we can almost predict they will follow, the "recognition" scene with his parents. The offering of the role is disguised as a tender concern, the wish that Miriam would become interested in someone else, for fear her family would insist upon a formal engagement. "Do you think—if I didn't come up so much—you might get to like somebody else—another man?" The attempts fail, and with the failure the relationship, in Freudian terms, loses one of its most important underpinnings.

While Miriam cannot produce an "injured third party" to satisfy Paul's unconscious need for a rival, she is capable of fulfilling the mother-love role in another way, which is an even more striking insight into the true nature of Paul's relationships with all three women. Throughout *Sons and Lovers* we notice a chiasmus of "giving," on the parts of the women, with varying shades of approval and disapproval. The first woman to give is of course Gertrude. She "gives" William's girls to Walter Morel by purposely confusing the father and son. In the repressed phantasy of the son the act appears to be a diverting of the father that leaves the mother free for the son. Later, with great reluctance she gives William up to the girl he is engaged to. But the results are fatal.

Miriam's act of giving coincides exactly with Gertrude Morel's approval of Clara for Paul, as something he needs, as something neither of them can give him. Gertrude, considering Clara, refuses to define her approval: "She did not know what she wished, but left it vague. At any rate she was not hostile to the idea of Clara." Miriam's recognition disguises itself as a struggle between higher and lower natures:

> So in May she asked him to come to Willey Farm and meet Mrs. Dawes. There was something he hankered after. She saw him, whenever they spoke of Clara Dawes, rouse and get slightly angry. He said he did not like her. Yet he was keen to know about her. Well, he should put himself to the test. She believed that there were in him desires for higher things, and desires for lower, and that the desires for the higher would conquer. At any rate, he should try.

It is a recapitulation of Gertrude Morel's reluctant giving of William to Lily, which constitutes in effect the necessary condition for such a union—the acceptance from the mother's hand of her successor.

When Paul and Clara and Miriam are together, Miriam falls into the role of the Gertrude who disapproves of dancing and of sexual desires. And Paul, treating Miriam exactly as if she were his mother, pantomimically makes his escape: "He was utterly unfaithful to her even in her own presence; then he was ashamed, then repentant; then he hated her, and went off again. Those were the ever-recurring conditions."

But Clara, too, is a surrogate mother, the opposite of Gertrude and Miriam, the "harlot," the possession of another. It is from her hands that Paul receives, not the virginal Miriam, but the sexually obtainable Miriam. Before she sleeps with Paul, Clara symbolically introduces Paul to sex. She tells him, in effect, what the real relations between his parents are. Paul insists that Miriam wants only a "soul union."

> "How do you know what she is?"
> "I do! I know she wants a sort of soul union."
> "But how do you know what she wants?"
> "I've been with her for seven years."
> "And you haven't found out the first thing about her."
> "What's that?"
> "That she doesn't want any of your soul communion.
> That's your imagination. She wants you."
> He pondered over this. Perhaps he was wrong.
> "But she seems—" he began.
> "You've never tried," she answered.

"With the spring came again the old madness and battle," starts the next chapter, called "The Test on Miriam." It is full of the imagery of the impenetrable hymen, against which Paul, armed with knowledge, must force himself. There is an "obstacle," "physical bondage," virginity as a "positive force," so "hard to overcome," something Paul must "deliberately break through." Paul fears the "sacrifice" of himself in marriage as "degrading." In giving Paul to Miriam, before taking him herself, Clara is like Queen Gertrude, and Paul like Hamlet. Clara's sexual knowledgeableness inspires Paul to talk to the "nunlike" Miriam of "country matters" for the first time, suggesting that they become lovers. " 'Sometime you will have me?' he murmured [note the passivity of the speaker], hiding his face on her shoulder. It was so difficult." And when the affair is disastrous, and the "dead" Miriam gives Paul back to Clara, Clara strews Miriam's grave with contempt. She agrees with Gertrude Morel about her. "What I hate is the bloodhound quality in Miriam," she tells Paul's mother, and Paul, angry, yet in agreement with her, buries Miriam forever.

The shift from Miriam to Clara is the shift from *mater urania* to *mater pandemos*. Miriam is the incomplete metamorphosis of the real mother to her unconsciously idealized form. Miriam resembles Gertrude in purity and intellectuality and protectiveness. With Clara the metamorphosis is complete; we can no longer refer her maternal qualities to some real person, but must look to some elemental concept of maternity and orgiastic sexuality as one sees it in the chthonic goddesses, Cybele, Ishtar, Hertha. The transition from Miriam to Clara is rendered florally. Paul walks in the garden. The madonna lilies, the flowers that consoled his mother, call to him with their scents, but he ignores them:

> Behind him the great flowers leaned as if they were calling. And then, like a shock, he caught another perfume, something raw and coarse. Hunting round, he found the purple iris, touched their fleshy throats and their dark, grasping hands. At any rate, he had found something. They stood stiff in the darkness. Their scent was brutal. The moon was melting down upon the crest of the hill. It was gone; all was dark. The corncrake called still.

Paul's relationship with Miriam fails because his repressed image of the beloved is fundamentally denied him. Like Ophelia she is sexually desirable, or should be, but her virginity is a supreme article of her desirability. With her as with his mother, Paul cannot act out the desired incest. His relationship with Clara, on the other hand, succeeds and fails in turn because his repressed image of the beloved mother is realized in every essential. With Miriam, who was an actual person, the life situation as it might have been appeals to conscious experience. Clara, whom E. T. describes as a "clever adaptation of elements from three people. The events related had no foundation in fact," speaks to the artist's unconscious wishes. Hence the almost rigidly determined nature of Paul's relationship with her.

Clara fulfills all the conditions Freud describes as proper to her being chosen by Paul. She is the possession of another man, the "injured third party," Baxter Dawes, from whom it seems desirable that Paul "rescue" her. Paul suddenly realizes her vulnerability when they first meet, her need to be rescued: "Suddenly looking at her, he saw that the upward lifting of her face was misery and not scorn. His heart grew tender for everybody. He turned and was gentle with Miriam whom he had neglected till then." In the perfect grasp he has of this sudden reaction there is implicit the further desire by Paul that Clara be a fallen woman, Magdalen, the "harlot." Before this he has recognized her sensual appeal to him. " 'Look at her mouth—made for passion and the very setback of her throat'—He threw his head back in Clara's definite manner."

When Paul visits Clara and sees the shabbiness of her life he is unconsciously excited by the notion of "rescue":

> He experienced a thrill of joy, thinking she might need his help. She seemed denied and deprived of so much. And her arm moved mechanically, that should never have been subdued to a mechanism, and her head was bowed to the lace that never should have been bowed. She seemed to be stranded there among the refuse that life has thrown away, doing her jennying. . . . Her grey eyes at last met his. They looked dumb with humiliation, pleading with a kind of captive misery. He was shaken and at a loss. He had thought her high and mighty.

Seated at her lacework she seems to Paul a Penelope, waiting. The image is apt, for it is again the waiting mother in need of a rescue, to which Telemachus dedicates himself. Paul sees her also as a "Juno dethroned," a comparison that introduces another remarkable series of descriptive terms applied to Clara. One infallible sign of a divinity, either male or female, according to Greek religious belief, was the slightly larger than human size of the visitant. According to Freudian theory the giants of the world's mythologies originated in the infantile phantasies concerning adults, parents especially, the memories of a time when certain human beings were regularly huge and terrifyingly capable of lifting one up bodily. Shakespeare's Venus—

> Over one arm the lusty courser's rein,
> Under the other was the tender boy—

is the love-enthralled Titan with Adonis. To Clara, Lawrence applies the images of giantism. Paul sees under her clothes "her strong form that seemed to slumber with power." He sees her hand, "large, to match her large limbs," in contrast to his own smaller, delicate hands. He feels her heavy shoulder upon him, her "white, heavy arms." "There was no himself. The grey and black eyes of Clara, her bosom coming down on him. . . . Then he felt himself small and helpless, her towering in her force above him." So in this "composite" imaginary woman Lawrence gathers the attributes of the Great Mother par excellence, "her bosom coming down on him"; what Freud calls "the memory picture of his mother as it has dominated him since the beginning of childhood."

In their sexual intercourse Lawrence carries on the idealizing process, "the way of phantasies." It is a kind of intercourse the real Miriam would not allow him to have, the paradisal situation (Paradise is mentioned) in which there is no consciousness:

> To know their own nothingness, to know the tremendous living flood which carried them always, gave them rest within themselves. If so great a magnificent power could overwhelm them, identify them altogether with itself, so that they knew they were only grains in the tremendous heave that lifted every grass blade its little height, and every tree, and living thing, then why fret about themselves? They could let themselves be carried by life. . . .

But underneath the stock vitalism there lurks the same passive yielding that characterized his intercourse with Miriam. The difference lies in the role Clara plays as the "harlot" of phantasy. Freud expands the harlot theme in another essay to explain the phenomenon of psychical impotence in terms of the "incest-barrier" and steps taken to overcome it. One step is to separate the lust object from the love object, i.e., the harlot from the madonna:

> The whole sphere of love in such people remains divided in the two directions personified in art as sacred and profane (or animal) love. Where they love they do not desire and where

they desire they cannot love. They seek objects which they do
not need to love, in order to keep their sensuality away from
the objects they love; and, in accordance with the laws of the
"complexive sensitiveness" and of the return of the repressed,
the strange failure shown in psychical impotence makes its
appearance whenever an object which has been chosen with
the aim of avoiding incest recalls the prohibited object through
some feature, often an inconspicuous one.

The main protective measure against such a disturbance
which men have recourse to in this split in their love consists
in a physical *debasement* of the sexual object, the overvalua-
tion that normally attaches to the sexual object being reserved
for the incestuous object and its representatives. As soon as
the condition of debasement is fulfilled, sensuality can be
freely expressed, and important sexual capacities and a high
degree of sexual pleasure can develop. There is a further factor
which contributes to this result. People in whom there has not
been a proper confluence of the affectionate and the sensual
currents do not usually show much refinement in their modes
of behaviour in love; they have retained perverse sexual aims
whose nonfulfillment is felt as a serious loss of pleasure, and
whose fulfillment on the other hand seems possible only with
a debased and despised sexual object.

We can now understand the motives behind the . . .
phantasies . . . which degrade the mother to the level of a
prostitute. They are efforts to bridge the gulf between the two
currents in love, at any rate in phantasy, and by debasing the
mother to acquire her as an object of sensuality. . . . I do
not hesitate to make the two factors at work in psychical impotence in the strict sense—the factors of intense incestuous
fixation in childhood and the frustration by reality in adolescence—responsible too, for this extremely common characteristic of the love of civilized men.

In terms of the above-quoted pasage Paul's affair with Clara
falls within a predictable pattern of behavior, compatible with
the other actions of the protagonist. Relieved for the moment,
with this beautful "composite," of the incestuous identification,
Paul lapses into the very pleasurable but extremely regressive
pleasure of the "nothingness" passion can reduce him to, closely
related to the "reaching out to death" of his affair with Miriam.
Then, because Clara is, even more than Miriam, the product of
an incestuous synthesis, the "return of the repressed" reasserts
itself:

Their loving grew more mechanical, without the marvellous glamour. Gradually they began to introduce novelties to get back some of the feeling of satisfaction. . . . And afterward each of them was rather ashamed, and these things caused a distance between the two of them. He began to despise her a little, as if she had merited it!

Part of the "debasement" of the object involves, I believe, an element of self-debasement or, if debasement is not the exact term, an attempt to achieve a callousness of sensibility which will make the woman's debasement acceptable. In this case, the refined, sensitive Paul, in the very beginning, which is the most exciting phase of his affair with Clara, lapses into his father's Midland dialect after he has been with Clara on the raw, red, clay bank of the Trent in flood, as if this gross, sexual act had been the *rite de passage* that put him on terms of equality with his father. The brutal natural surroundings, so unlike the soft meadow and pine forest of Miriam's defloration, and the scattered red petals of the carnation, a dream symbol of the menses, speak for the degradation both of the woman into adultery and of the man into the coarser, less sensitive state of manhood. But afterward, as if to reassert his status as the son, Paul, just as he did with Gertrude, insists upon cleaning Clara's boots. The harlot-mother identification is completed. " 'And now I'll clean thy boots and make thee fit for respectable folk,' he said." Paul had cleaned his mother's boots "with as much reverence as if they had been flowers." Not that his mother's shoes needed cleaning. "Mrs. Morel was one of those naturally exquisite people who can walk in mud without dirtying their shoes." In the light of this comparison the boot cleaning becomes a ritual, like the raising of Magdalen to the level of Mary. Gertrude's sexual "shoes" (compare the removal of shoes as a sign of refusal to marry in the Bible in Deuteronomy 25:6) are not dirty, even though she has borne children. Clara's shoes, after her intercourse with Paul, must be cleaned. The act raises her to the status of mother as well as mistress. Freud points out the fetichism connected with the foot as a very primitive sexual symbol and notes the aptness of the shoe as a symbol for the female genitals.

Similarly, Lawrence places a peculiar emphasis on the tak-

ing off of collars. In *Sons and Lovers* the phallic significance of
the collar is connected with Gertrude Morel's hold upon her
husband and her children. Walter Morel's shame before her,
after he has fought with her and locked her out, is an acknowledgment of moral superiority and her mastery of him. When she
enters the house he takes flight: ". . . she saw him almost run-
ning through the door to the stairs. He had ripped his collar off
his neck in his haste to be gone ere she came in, and there it
lay with bursten button holes. It made her angry."

William, her first favorite, loves his collar:

> She liked to do things for him; she liked to put a cup for his
> tea and to iron his collar, of which he was so proud. It was a
> joy to her to have him proud of his collars. There was no
> laundry. So she used to rub away at them with her little con-
> vex iron, to polish them till they shone from the sheer pressure
> of her arm.

The collar figures in his death:

> On the Sunday morning as he was putting his collar on:
> "Look," he said to his mother, holding up his chin, "What
> a rash my collar's made under my chin!"
> Just at the junction of chin and throat was a big red in-
> flammation.

It is the lesion of the disease that kills him.

In the scene between Paul and his mother that ends in his
fight with his father, Gertrude openly expresses her jealousy of
Miriam, and Paul insists to her that he does not love her:

> "No, mother—I really *don't* love her. I talk to her, but I
> want to come home to you."
> He had taken off his collar and tie, and rose, bare-throated,
> to go to bed. As he stooped to kiss his mother, she threw her
> arms round his neck, hid her face on his shoulder, and cried
> in a whimpering voice, so unlike her own that he writhed in
> agony.

Now the collar has become Gertrude. (In *Aaron's Rod*, Aaron
tears himself away from the sexual bondage of his wife Lotte.
In one struggle between them he escapes, leaving his torn collar
behind in her hand.)

With the dying of Paul's mother, Paul's sexuality begins to
equate itself more and more with actual death. Like Dostoevsky's

epileptic seizures, whose psychogenic origin Freud founds in a pantomine of his father's death, Paul's orgasm in Clara's arms is a little death.

> When he had her then, there was something in it that made her shrink away from him—something unnatural. She grew to dread him. He was so quiet, yet so strange. She was afraid of the man who was not there with her, whom she could feel behind this make-belief lover; somebody sinister, that filled her with horror. She began to have a kind of horror of him. It was almost as if he were a criminal. He wanted her—he had her—and it made her feel as if death itself had her in its grip. She lay in horror.

With Paul's last embrace of a living woman all three women are finally joined and identified as one, the mother. When she dies, the regressive, incestuous phantasies her life had fed sicken and die with her. The pleasantly deathly consummation with Miriam and the Nirvana-like "impersonality of passion" with Clara resolve themselves in Paul's horror at the coldness of his mother's lips, a horror he inverts and feels in Clara when he lies with her. Gertrude's death releases both Clara and Miriam from their functions as mother surrogates. They do not die for Paul; it is he, finally, who samples death, first pantomiming it in Clara's arms and, at the last, feeling it on his mother's mouth. Clara's horror of him is based on this: that Paul is trying to "die" on her.

In the end Paul rejects death; *Sons and Lovers* is a comedy of the Oedipus complex. He is not Oedipus standing on the steps of his stricken house—he is journeying forth. Even the blindness is touched upon. Paul is described as turning "blindly." "He dared not meet his own eyes in the mirror. He never looked at himself." But the rejection of death is positive and absolute, and in its rejection, perverse as it may seem, is the implicit rejection, valid in unconscious terms, of the women to whom he might have turned after the long night of his childhood was past. By rejecting Miriam and Clara, Paul dramatically represents to himself the profound change that has come over him. Fiction is invoked to dispel what in real life might have been an attenuating relationship, and to put in its place a more dramatic *hic incipit vita nova*.

When Miriam, out of compassion, asks him to marry her,

his reply shows the extent of his knowledge of what has happened. "But—you love me so much, you want to put me in your pocket. And I should die there, smother." The unconscious formulation of the reply is rather an expression on Paul's part of his refusal to be tempted to crawl into another pocket, now that the one he has been in for so long has worn out and left him free.

It is Paul's walk, on the last page of *Sons and Lovers*, toward the "faintly humming, glowing town" that sounds the note of positive choice. And the choice is, in psychoanalytic terms, a classically important one. In choosing the town Paul is accepting his father, an idealized image, like Hamlet's father, a "man," with all the expansive attributes the generic term allows. Turning his back upon his home place he is rejecting, or at least modifying, his acceptance of the mother. I think the process can be decribed as an inversion, a turning over to find a new center of gravity, long withheld. Whereas before Paul had, in the mother, loved an idealized image, capable of dangerous extensions into mother surrogates like Miriam and Clara, he had, in the father, hated (with that curious ambivalence, already noted) an identity, with a local habitation and a name. With Baxter Dawes, the process begins to reverse itself. The father's identity begins to be idealized and lose its historical boundaries in Walter Morel, while Gertrude Morel is forced, by the exigencies of Paul's insistence upon becoming a man, into mere motherhood; and with this her surrogates lose their vitality and fall away.

From the very beginning the town stands in polar hostility to Gertrude, as the world of men, of deflowered countryside. It is to the town that Walter Morel and Jerry Purdy take their pub-crawling walk. The "wakes" is a part of town life, the first sounds, for young William Morel, of the outside world: "the braying of a merry-go-round and the tooting of a horn." Gertrude hates the wakes, and Lawrence describes William, crucified by a choice, who "stood watching her, cut to the heart to let her go, and yet unable to leave the wakes." For Paul in his turn the town exercises its attraction: "From the train going home at night he used to watch the lights of the town, sprinkled thick on the hills, fusing together in a blaze in the valleys. He felt rich in life and happy." Like the "stars and sun, a few bright grains . . . holding each other in embrace," the town defies the dark, sometimes horrible, onetime appeal of the maternal invitation to be still and passive. It is, like all the towers, citadels, mountaintops, and Beautiful Cities of literature, the place to which one fights his way through the seas and jungles of world or mind.

In the end of *Sons and Lovers* is implicit an acceptance of the father's values. Oedipus says, in what is the essential irony of the play: "In doing right by Laius I protected myself, for whoever slew Laius might turn a hand against me." Paul Morel is categorically rejecting all the elements of his Oedipal involvement. Having restored the Player King, Baxter Dawes, to his Player Queen, Clara, he enters the town, a man both driven and drawn across the threshold into manhood. In ratifying finally the bents and needs of the father, he "protects" himself.

11·D. H. *Lawrence:* Sons and Lovers

by Frank O'Connor

When we look at the last complete period of the novel, we find such names as Marcel Proust, James Joyce, André Gide, D. H. Lawrence, E. M. Forster, Thomas Mann, and Virginia Woolf.

And we are at once pulled up because at least four of the principal figures did not write novels at all. They wrote autobiography more or less thinly disguised as fiction. Another characteristic of this quartet is that none of them seems to have been sexually normal. All fell deeply under the influence of their mothers; Gide and Proust remainded homosexual for their entire lives; Lawrence showed strongly marked homosexual tendencies, while Joyce's work covers practically every known form of sexual deviation. The only subject that none of them could apparently treat was normal heterosexual love.

Now, this can scarcely be a coincidence, and when we examine their work and find that even the types of deviation resemble one another, we are forced to the conclusion that there must be a common element that makes their authors react in this particular way.

Let us look first at Lawrence's *Sons and Lovers,* which is particularly interesting because, though it ends as a novel of the modern type, it begins as one of the classical kind, made familiar to us by nineteenth-century novelists.

To begin with, we have to notice that it is the work of one

of the New Men who are largely a creation of the Education Act of 1870. Besides, we must note that it comes from the English Midlands, the industrial area. Naturally, the two facts are linked, and they represent a cultural shift not only from the middle to the working classes, but also from the area of wealth to the area of industry. The young people in the book are full of literary allusions that are not merely the self-conscious showing off of a young literary man, but represent the whole struggle of the working classes for culture. There is the same atmosphere in C. P. Snow's *Strangers and Brothers*, and for a similar reason.

It indicates too the dangers of such a shift of attitudes, for the Midlands, at least to a foreigner like myself, seem to be a different country altogether from the South of England, and even at times to resemble Ireland more than England. They are dissenting in religion, socialist in politics, and with a way of life which—again to a foreigner—seems full of dignity and even beauty. And, again, it is worth remembering that one of Lawrence's best stories, *Odour of Chrysanthemums*, which describes a miner's death, is not only quite unlike any other English story: though the critics have failed to notice it, it is also a very careful pastiche of Synge's *Riders to the Sea*. It suggests that young people of Lawrence's period did apparently recognize that in some ways their life was closer to Irish than to English ways, and that if it was to be given its full dignity, it had to be approached from an Irish standpoint.

But—and this is Lawrence's tragedy—it reminds us too that, unlike Ireland, the Midlands have no cultural capital, and that a young man of genius is necessarily driven to London, where he may learn only too quickly to despise the standards of his own people. This is not true of everybody, but of Lawrence it certainly is true. London acquaintances thought him something of a bounder and a cad. The family described under the name of Leivers in *Sons and Lovers* certainly did not think him either. It is the tragedy of William in the same novel. In later years Lawrence is the homeless, rootless man of letters drifting from country to country, continent to continent, writing with unfailing energy and brilliance, but never with the intensity displayed in *Sons and Lovers* and some of his early stories.

The break with his roots occurred during the writing of the

novel, and it is plain for anyone who will take the trouble to read it carefully. Absolutely, the opening half is the greatest thing in English fiction. It has all the brilliance of *Pride and Prejudice* and the opening of *Middlemarch* with the tragic power of certain scenes in *The Last Chronicle*. Put in its simplest form, it is the dilemma of a sensitive boy between the conflicting claims of mother and sweetheart. This adds a new element of tragedy to the novel, for, despite the universal quality of the theme, it is an element that could only have come from the New Men and the industrial areas, for it is only in those surroundings that a boy is forced to recognize the spiritual achievement of motherhood. A hundred pounds a year would have been sufficient to mask the whole achievement and tragedy of Mrs. Morel. Even a difference in class would have done so, for, greatly as Mrs. Crawley is drawn by Trollope, her struggle is presented as it appeared to a member of the upper classes: a sordid, unnecessary, *imposed* ordeal. In Lawrence, poverty is treated as a necessary condition of life, and it is by means of the explicit exiguous budgets that we are made to appreciate the full significance of Mrs. Morel's attempts to create order and beauty about her, and the delight and anguish these could bring to a sensitive boy. We *respect* Mrs. Crawley's struggle to find necessities for her family; we *rejoice* in the glorious scene in which Mrs. Morel gives rein to her wicked extravagance and comes home clutching a pot that cost her fivepence and a bunch of pansies and daisies that cost her fourpence.

Again it is the Midland backgound that gives significance to Miriam's passion for culture, this, too, a struggle toward the light, though of a different kind. As we are made to feel the weight of Morel's physical violence and the brutality of the mines crushing us down like a leaden sky, so too we feel with almost agonizing intensity the upward movement in chapel, school, and home, the passion of desire to "build Jerusalem in England's green and pleasant land." Nature is not, as in Hardy, a dark background to a gloomy fate, but an upward surging like music, poetry, religion. No other novel is so filled with flowers. When in a novel for the leisured classes someone talks of Rilke, or a Picasso print, or carnations, one's tendency is to groan: "Holy Smoke, he's off again!" But we rejoice in Mrs.

Morel's little triumph over the potman, in Miriam's algebra lesson, in Mrs. Morel's three little bulbs under the hedge. These are no longer the negatives of dandyism or the neutrals of an educated class, but the positive achievements of a life with a sense of purpose and direction, lived by people who are complete moral entities. Joyce, too, had known the same thing, and in the terrible little scene in *Ulysses* when Dedalus's ragged sister covets the secondhand French grammar, he makes us feel it, but we feel it rather as an icy clutch on our hearts than as a moment of rejoicing in man's passionate desire to transcend himself. Joyce's Dublin was a place without signposts. Again, his poverty is pathetic rather than tragic.

It is hard to criticize this matchless book, yet there *is* something wrong with it, and, whatever it may be, it is the same thing that is wrong with Lawrence himself and that turns him into a homeless man of letters, and it is here, under our eyes, that the smash occurs if only we could see what it is. What I mean is not a literary fault, or is so only in a secondary sense. It would be only natural that a young man's book should contain shifting planes, particularly when all the significant scenes are written with such explosive power that it is a miracle when he recovers any sense of direction at all. No, the smash is a psychological one and inherent in the situation that he describes rather than in the technique he uses to describe it. It is inherent in the situation of the young man torn between his mother and Miriam, both of whom want the same thing from him.

There is almost certainly a false note in the chapters describing Miriam as Paul Morel's mistress. I do not know if in real life Lawrence was actually the lover of the girl he describes as Miriam, nor am I greatly concerned about the question. But the situation of the novel implies that they could never have been lovers, and that this was in fact the thing that drove Paul to Clara. The trouble with the Œdipal relationship is that it specializes the sexual instinct. Sexual contact is the only thing lacking between the boy and his mother, and he tends to seek this in a form where it implies nothing else, where it does not produce an actual feeling of betrayal of the mother—in Gogol in the form of self-abuse, in Proust in the form of homosexuality. Human love—the type represented by Miriam—is bound to represent a betrayal of the mother, because the love is identical except for this one slight specialized thing. Miriam is his mother's rival because the love that she offers is human love; Clara is not because the love that she offers is in fact a non-human love.

Clara is non-human in the same way as every single woman whom Lawrence described after the writing of this book is non-human. None of them is allowed to challenge the image of his mother in humanity. And this is where we come to the really pathological streak in the book. Clara is a married woman whose husband is a smith in the surgical-appliance store where Paul is employed, and immediately she appears in the novel her husband appears also. He hates Paul long before Paul becomes the lover of his wife. When Paul and she become friendly, Paul presses her with questions about her relations with Dawes. He even has a fight with Dawes, and later goes to visit him in the the hospital and makes friends with him. The two men have a peculiar relationship centered on their common possession of Clara, and finally Paul brings about the reunion of husband and wife.

Now, these chapters, which occupy a considerable part of the last half of the book, have nothing whatever to do with the subject of the novel—at least on the surface. They might easily belong to an entirely different novel. Indeed, they might be about different characters, for from this point onward Paul is referred to as "Morel," a name which has so far been associated only with his father, so that we even get superficially confused in our reading. Lawrence's original intention is fairly clear. It was to present Miriam not as a type of human love, but as a type of spiritual love, Clara as a type of sensual love, neither of which can satisfy the heart of the young man who loves his mother. This design has been obscured by the irrelevant physical relations with Miriam on the one hand, and on the other by the emphasis laid on Clara's husband as opposed to Clara herself. But that is only part of the trouble. The real trouble is that Paul Morel is not in love with Clara, but with Dawes. Subject and object have again changed places, and we are back with the old extraordinary theme of *The Eternal Husband*. That this is not merely a personal and perverse reading of the strained melodrama imposed on a young man of genius by his lack of experience will be clear to anyone who knows his Lawrence, for the theme occurs again and again in his later work. The most interesting example is an early story, *The Shades of Spring*, in which the girl we have come to know as Miriam is shown after her young man's desertion of her. She has now become engaged to a second man, and the story describes the odd attraction that the first feels for him. It is most explicit in *Jimmy and the Desperate Woman*, where Lawrence recognizes in the person of another man of slightly effeminate tastes the attraction of a physically powerful husband transmitted through the wife. The biographers tell us that the hero of the story is Middleton Murry, which merely indicates how incapable Lawrence became of drawing any character objectively: he can only attribute to him his own peculiar weakness. The whole passage is worth considering again in context.

> And, as he sat in the taxi, a perverse but intense desire for her came over him, making him almost helpless. He could feel, so strongly, the presence of that other man about her, and this went to his head like neat spirits. That other man! In some subtle, inexplicable way he was actually bodily present, the husband. The woman moved in his aura. She was hopelessly married to him.
>
> And this went to Jimmy's head like neat whiskey. Which of the two would fall before him with a greater fall—the woman, or the man, her husband?

It is hard to know what the real origin of this perverse attraction in Lawrence represents. That it existed in him in real life we may safely deduce from Murry's remark—made in all innocence of the meaning of the texts I have quoted—that Lawrence was attracted to Frieda's husband almost as much as to Frieda. Obviously the attraction is homosexual, but that word is so loosely and coarsely abused that it can scarcely be applied without misgivings to a noble and refined personality like Lawrence's. It is certainly linked with his adoration of his mother, and it seems as though the link must be a specialized form of sexuality which excludes the spiritual element merely because it would then become a rival to mother love. At the same time, the figure of the father, consciously excluded by the boy, would seem to return in an unrecognizable, unconscious form and take its place in the relationship with the woman. If one accepts this reading of it (and it is as tentative as any reading of an analogical situation must be), Dawes is really Paul's father, and Paul, through his relationship with Clara, which gives him the opportunity of probing Dawes's relations with his wife, is not only able to repeat the offense against his father by robbing him of his wife, but is also, in the manner of a fairy tale, able to undo the wrong by reconciling them. It is a beautiful example of the dual function of such analogical relationships.

Whatever the origin of the situation, it is the key to Lawrence's later work. His rejection of Miriam is a rejection of masculinity in himself, and after it he is condemned to write only of those things which the feminine side of his character permits him to write of. He is an intuitive writer by sheer necessity. To Edward Garnett he defended his new, non-human form of writing by the pretense that the old sort of realistic writing which Garnett understood was out of date, but that his own choice of his sort of writing took place only after *Sons and Lovers* is clearly untrue. The choice was made during the actual writing, and the result is the Clara-Dawes section, the end of the old Lawrence and the beginning of the new.

Not that he may not have felt the necessity, for all over Europe the old human conception of character was breaking down. Character in Turgenev and Trollope exists as an extension, by virtue of its predictability. All their great characters have been lived with. They are regarded, rightly or wrongly, as being essentially knowable. When Joyce uses the word "epiphany," "a showing forth," for the themes of his own stories, he indicates already that the temporal, objective conception of character no longer exists, and that it can be apprehended only in moments when it unconsciously betrays itself. Virginia Woolf, too, insists on this moment of revelation, and, like Joyce, she writes the typical one-day novel of the period. The day itself is regarded as an epiphany. Proust's characters are all perceived in such moments, and nothing that we have learned about them at one moment gives us the least indication of what they may be like in another. It is, of course, a view, deeply influenced by Freud's theories, which make the character unknowable except to the analyst; it is even, in many of the writers of

III. Technique and Values

The essays in this section, with perhaps the exception of the first and the last, by John Middleton Murry and Alfred Kazin, discuss the novel in terms of technique and values, hand in hand. They furnish the reader with the stages of concern with unity, and increasing critical attention to Lawrence's kind of symbolism as constituting the nearest thing to technical innovation he made, and as furnishing the most reliable clue to the kind of characterization, relationships, and values he explored. In a continuum, the critics refer to their predecessors, and make their disagreements, modifications, and extensions.

Murry is not so interested in understanding the art as he is the man. He was intimately and painfully involved with Lawrence personally, both as potential greatest friend and as a quite serious rival for Frieda. Having both disagreed with Lawrence on values, and stood aside in love, he here raises thoroughgoing doubts about what might be called, following Mark Spilka, the love ethic operating in the novel. Lawrence was a great artist, but he is not to be judged as a pure artist. Murry is on Jessie Chambers' ("Miriam's") side, like her, charging Lawrence ("Paul Morel") with shirking the issue between his mother and the other women in his life, seeking only sexual love from these because he was unable, or perhaps unwilling, to give them also the spiritual, and sympathetic, love his mother had commanded. Love in that sense revealed itself only in such an encounter as that with George Saxton in *The White Peacock*.[1]

1 No one in this section deals more than passingly with the question of a homosexual transfer of feeling. Lawrence's essays and fiction from about 1923 forward contain his countercharges that Murry was a moral weakling and betrayer.

It was Mark Schorer who first, or at least most cogently and with the greatest command of attention, suggested a connection between the failure of Paul Morel to be fair to Miriam and a failure of technique. Lawrence the artist could not detach himself from Lawrence the man and rise free of the latter's involvement and confusion, a position resembling the old conundrum of which came first, the chicken or the egg—the technique or the discovery.

When Dorothy Van Ghent turned her attention to the technique of the novel, which in many ways seems quite traditional, or even old-fashioned, hardly the work of a major writer, she located the innovation and the power in "a structure rigorously controlled by an idea." She anticipates Spilka, and others, including the editor,[2] by locating this idea, and its accompanying vitalistic ethic, primarily in the imagery and the concreteness of the symbolism—the book's poetic logic. This approach, as it does for others using it, tends to range the characters according to life-or-death-directed principles. She differentiates Lawrence's approach to nature from those of such predecessors as Fielding, Jane Austen, George Eliot, Emily Brontë, and Hardy. Unlike Murry and Schorer, and later in this section, Louis Fraiberg, she does not find Lawrence's technical deployment of this idea in conflict with other ideas, and ethical positions, involved in the novel.

Mark Spilka's essays follow similar lines of study of the relationship of technique and values (what he calls in the book from which they are taken "the love ethic"). As in Lawrence's later novels, the logic is poetic rather than narrative, depending on image and, paradoxically, a symbol rendered concrete and literal by the vitalistic correspondences. Since an ethic is "discovered" through this symbolism, he disagrees with Schorer's position that the technique failed. He does, however, like Fraiberg, find a mixing of psychologies—Lawrence's and Freud's. The novel is "mainly an exploration of destructive or counterfeit loves—with a garbled Freudian 'split' imposed upon it." In terms of the Lawrencean psychology and ethic, the responsibility for the difficulty between Paul and Miriam belongs with

2 In *D. H. Lawrence: Artist and Rebel* (University of New Mexico Press, 1963).

her. Spilka sees Paul's interest in Dawes not as obliquely homosexual but as a matter of making vital restitution to him, by
reconciling him with Clara. He argues also that the crucial
scene in which Paul, ill, takes ease of his mother, is a legitimate
communion, not as oedipal as it seems. She is the most vital
woman in the novel, and there is a healthy side to Paul's love for
her.

For Louis Fraiberg, there are two frames of reference for
behavior, not harmoniously interwoven—an oversimplification of
Freudian ideas involving the notion that "the psychic imprints
of childhood can never be revised," and "Lawrence's mystique
of sexual experience." Paying his respects to both Weiss and
Spilka, Fraiberg finds that the flower symbolism and the
oedipal relationships bind the book together structurally, and
he adds a third means of unity (Spilka's symbolism involves it),
the split between physical and spiritual love. Schorer goes too
far. "Character and ideology do not always work together," but
this is not "to imply any derogation" of the novel's merits.
Rather, "Lawrence was still perfecting his vision and learning
his craft." The chronological plan, and picaresque "outer
shape" do not work because Paul's "character is set and he is
doomed to repeat himself." In Freud's terms, Paul "failed to
establish the childhood conditions for a healthy development
toward an adult selfhood." On Lawrence's terms, he also fails
because Lawrence "has not woven the representations into a
harmonious pattern with the theoretical." Miriam is too virginal "to afford Paul the experience of mutual discovery which
a first love can bring." Thus, in the Miriam debate, Fraiberg
seems to side neither with Jessie Chambers nor Lawrence and
considers the problem an artistic one. But, unlike Van Ghent
or Spilka, he finds Lawrence's view of communion to be obtained through passionate sexuality "inadequate for the achieving of true self-realization." And Paul's mercy-killing of his
mother springs not simply from pity "but likewise from his all-
but-conscious recognition that he was governed forever by the
impulse to deny the rights of others in him, to sever the con-
ventions which might bind him and them to life, and to seek
instead a false union in the greater-than-human universality
which he felt fleetingly in moments of surrender to strong emo-

tion." The reading resembles Murry's but is subtler in distingush-ing causes inherent in tendency and idea.

To close the book, there is Alfred Kazin's essay, designed as an introduction, but perhaps useful here as a broad-ranging summary: the novel's modernity after its nineteenth-century kind of opening; its manifestation of cultural change; its relation to Lawrence's sense of his own authority and powers (Freud's mother's favorite became conqueror); its valuation of love in the mythological sense of a sacred, life-force connection; the question of the treatment of "Miriam" in terms of Lawrence's sense of a problem not to be solved but a subject to be presented, the writer redeeming "the weakness of being too much his mother's son." The perspective is wide in terms of Lawrence's personal necessity and whole career; yet there is much on the novel's power of presentation and heightening of awareness.

12 · Son and Lover

by John Middleton Murry

At the age of thirty-five D. H. Lawrence wrote one of his greatest books—*Fantasia of the Unconscious*. It marks the zenith of his mortal course. . . . In it, he declares a faith, and takes a position, which afterwards he slowly relinquishes. His courage, or rather his simple strength, is not great enough to maintain him in the precarious harmony he has won out of his own conflicting elements. In this halcyon moment, he looks back calmly upon his own life and sees clearly what he is: how compounded, how conditioned, how compelled. And, in essence, *Fantasia of the Unconscious* is the effort, born of this clear self-knowledge, so to change the world of men that in future no child shall be compounded, and conditioned, and compelled as he was.

The relation of marriage between a man and woman, he says in *Fantasia,* is the necessary basis of the new order of society which he desires. In order that this relation should be creative, and not destructive, it is necessary that the man should, at the age of maturity, assume a sacred responsibility for the next purposive step into the future. If this creative responsibility is not undertaken by the man, then the love-craving of the woman will become frenzied and lay waste the family.

The unhappy woman [he goes on] beats about for her insatiable satisfaction, seeking whom she may devour. And usu-

Reprinted from Son of Woman: Being the Life Story of D. H. Lawrence, *by John Middleton Murry, Jonathan Cape, Ltd., 1931, by permission of The Society of Authors as the literary representative of the Estate of the late John Middleton Murry.*

ally, she turns to her child. Here she provokes what she wants. Here, in her own son who belongs to her, she seems to find the last perfect response for which she is craving. He is a medium to her, she provokes from him her own answer. So she throws herself into a last great love for her son, a final and fatal devotion, that which would have been the richness and strength of her husband and is poison to her boy. . . .

"*On revient toujours à son premier amour.*" It sounds like a cynicism to-day. As if we really meant: "*On ne revient jamais à son premier amour.*" But as a matter of fact, a man never leaves his first love, once the love is established. He may leave his first attempt at love. Once a man establishes a full dynamic communication at the deeper and the higher centres, with a woman, this can never be broken. . . . Very often not even death can break it.

The establishment of the upper love and cognition circuit inevitably provokes the lower sex-sensual centres into action, even though there be no correspondence on the sensual plane between the two individuals concerned. Then see what happens. If you want to see the real desirable wife-spirit, look at a mother with her boy of eighteen. How she serves him, how she stimulates him, how her true female self is his, is wife-submissive to him as never, never it could be to a husband. This is the quiescent, flowering love of a mature woman. It is the very flower of a woman's love . . . which a husband should put in his cap as he goes forward into the future in his supreme activity. For the husband, it is a great pledge, and a blossom. For the son also it seems wonderful. The woman now feels for the first time as a true wife might feel. And her feeling is towards her son. . . .

And then what? The son gets on swimmingly for a time, till he is faced with the actual fact of sex necessity. He gleefully inherits his adolescence and the world at large, without an obstacle in his way, mother-supported, mother-loved. Everything comes to him in glamour, he feels he sees wondrous much, understands a whole heaven, mother-stimulated. Think of the power which a mature woman thus infuses into her boy. He flares up like a flame in oxygen. No wonder they say geniuses mostly have great mothers. They mostly have sad fates.

And then?—and then, with this glamourous youth? What is he actually to do with his sensual, sexual self? Bury it? Or make an effort with a stranger. For he is taught, even by his mother, that his manhood must not forego sex. Yet he is linked up in ideal love already, the best he will ever know. . . . You will not easily get a man to believe that his carnal love for the woman he has made his wife is as high a love as that he felt for his mother. . . .

That is Lawrence's history of his own life. It is the history of *Sons and Lovers* told again, eight years later, with the added insight and detachment that come of maturity. If we are to understand the motions of this greatly gifted, greatly tortured man, we must grasp that fundamental history. Everything derives from it. . . .

"The first part of *Sons and Lovers*," Lawrence wrote in an account of himself not many months before he died, "is all autobiography." The direct assurance was hardly necessary. We have only to compare *The White Peacock*, which preceded it, with *Sons and Lovers* to be instantly aware of a new element of immediate veracity. *The White Peacock* is a story, *Sons and Lovers* is the life of a man. Moreover, it easy to see that the experience which is so richly recorded in *Sons and Lovers* had supplied the solid foundation for the imaginative structure of *The White Peacock*.

The White Peacock, then, may fairly be regarded as an effort to reconstruct the fundamental life of Lawrence's youth. His youth ended—he said so himself—with "the great crash," the death of his mother in the winter of 1910. *Sons and Lovers* is the record of that youth. It is a magnificent book: for those who do not care to follow Lawrence in the passionate exploration of life which subsequently engrossed him, it will probably remain his greatest book. If Lawrence is to be judged as the "pure artist," then it is true that he never surpassed, and barely equalled, this rich and moving record of a life. But Lawrence is not to be judged as a "pure artist"; if ever a writer had "an axe to grind" it was he. Set in the perspective—the only relevant perspective—of his own revealed intentions, *Sons and Lovers* appears as the gesture of man who makes the heroic effort to liberate himself from the matrix of his own past. With it he tries to put his youth firmly behind him, and to stand stripped to run his own race. He is the brilliant, jewel-brown horse-chestnut, of his favourite image, newly issued from the burr. He breaks forth from the husk of his youth, from the husk which had been one flesh with him till this emergence, and takes the past into consciousness and cognizance. That knowing is as much a severance, as an acknowledgment. Lawrence therefore tried to make it extraordinarily complete.

Sons and Lovers has a double riches: as the intimate life-history of the youth of a genius, and as a significant act. The significance of the act of writing the book will only be fully apparent when we have considered the life-history which it records.

Lawrence was born on September 11, 1885, the fourth child of a collier father and bourgeoise mother. The father was almost the pure animal, in the good and bad senses of the phrase: warm, quick, careless, irresponsible, living in the moment and a liar. The mother was responsible, and "heroic." In *Sons and Lovers* Lawrence makes a great effort to hold the balance fairly between them. Not being God, he found the task impossible. He would have liked to excuse the father, to make the mother bear some part of the blame for the father's slow disintegration.

> The pity was, she was too much his opposite. She could not be content with the little he might be; she would have him the much that he ought to be So, in seeking to make him nobler than he could be, she destroyed him. She injured and hurt and scarred herself, but she lost none of her worth.

But not to have "destroyed" him in this recondite sense would have meant to be destroyed herself, and not only herself, but her children also. To seek, as she did, "to make him undertake his own responsibilities, to make him fulfil his obligations" was not an encroachment, but a sheer necessity. Had she been less his opposite, she might indeed have suffered less, but the family would have collapsed upon itself. In the last issue, the father was responsible. Lawrence declared it again in the *Fantasia*.

So the mother withdrew from the father. There was no help for it. The essential estrangement had happened before Lawrence was born. She had not desired his coming, as she had desired the coming at least of the first of the two brothers before him. A lovely and tender passage of the book describes the sudden birth of her devouring love for the frail little boy, with blue eyes like her own. . . .

This, if it is wholly imagination—which it is probably not, for there must have been little of her inward history which Lawrence's mother did not eventually confide in him—is an imagination we can trust as truth. The sudden resolve of her heart was fulfilled, and lavishly. She "made it up" in love a hundredfold to the child. He became, as was inevitable in such a case, abnormally sensitive. He expanded preternaturally in this warm atmosphere of love. His capacity for experience was unusually great, so likewise was his shrinking from it. A hungry desire for contact of the same intimate kind as that which he and his mother lavished upon each other was counterpoised by an anguished fear of it. At fourteen, "he was a rather small and rather finely-made boy, with dark brown hair and light blue eyes. His face was becoming . . . rough-featured, almost rugged . . . and it was extraordinarily mobile."

> Usually he looked as if he saw things, was full of life, and warm; then his smile, like his mother's, came suddenly and was very lovable; and then, when there was any clog in his soul's quick running, his face went stupid and ugly. He was the sort of boy that becomes a clown and a lout as soon as he is not understood, or feels himself held cheap; and, again, is adorable at the first touch of warmth. He suffered very much from the first contact with anything. When he was seven, the starting school had been a nightmare and a torture to him. But afterwards he liked it.

Those who knew Lawrence well as a man will recognize immediately the truth of this picture of him as a boy. That *is* the boy who became the man they knew.

He grew with his soul sensitized utterly to the determination and the suffering of his mother in the long, unending struggle with her husband. Fortunately for him, it was not a silent and suppressed struggle such as so often, in a like situation, undermines the inmost being of an uncomprehending child. The antagonism was manifest and violent; more terrifying, but less subtly disintegrating. There were outbursts of drunkenness and downright brutality on the father's part, and they were fearful; but they belonged to a child's world. They were plain and elemental. The father does not come home from the pit: his dinner waits, the potatoes go dry. A hundred to one he has stayed drinking at the public house; but there is the agonising chance that something bad may have happened in the pit. If he comes home with too much beer in him, it will be bad; if he is brought home on a stretcher, or jolted off over the cobbles in the ambulance to the hospital, it will be worse. Or perhaps, if the injury is not too bad, it may be better. For there is the club money, and the ten shillings a week that the men of his stall put aside, which together makes more than the twenty-five shillings he has been giving lately. And, if it is beer, the worst won't happen, for he is in his heart afraid of mother. But then, once or twice, he has done evil things—cut her head open by flinging a drawer at her. There is still the fear. The children listen, with indrawn breath and thumping hearts, to the angry voices contending, one hot, one cold in anger, mingled inextricably and for ever with the shrieking of the ash-tree in the wind.

.   .   .   .

A fearful childhood, judged from one point of view, but from another how rich in the elemental drama that a child could understand and a man never forget! The issue how simple, manifest as the stars! The call upon the children the deepest their souls could sustain. They cleaved like little champions to their mother; they despised their father. And he, who knew that they were right to despise him, who knew that "he had denied the God in him," rotted in his own isolation.

That his father "had denied the God in him" was Lawrence's verdict also in the *Fantasia*; but then it was a still more advised pronouncement. Morel refused to take "the next creative step into the future." It was not an inordinate demand; for Morel the creative step consisted simply in taking responsibility for his children, in being in act, not merely in name, a father, in becoming a man whom his wife must respect and could not despise. He made not even a faint attempt; he slunk away. Inevitably, the mother's starved spirit sought satisfaction through her sons; and two of them, the eldest and the youngest, responded wholly to her call. When the eldest died, evidently on the threshold of a brilliantly successful career, the youngest son became her "man." As his great namesake had said, "Whatever I do, I do it unto the Lord," so Paul Morel could have said, "Whatever I do, I do it unto my mother." She was to live the life of which she had been cheated, through him; he would bring her the spiritual fulfilment she longed for. He had no ambition for himself, but all for her.

Sons and Lovers is the story of Paul Morel's desperate attempts to break away from the tie that was strangling him. All unconsciously, his mother had roused in him the stirrings of sexual desire; she had, by the sheer intensity of her diverted affection made him a man before his time. He felt for his mother what he should have felt for the girl of his choice. Let us be clear, as Lawrence himself tried to be clear in the *Fantasia*. Lawrence was not, so far as we can tell, sexually precocious; he was spiritually precocious. We are told that Paul Morel remained virgin till twenty-three. But his spiritual love for his mother was fully developed long before. What could be more poignant, or in implication more fearful, than the story he tells of the illness which fell upon him at sixteen? (He had told the same story before, in *The Trespasser*; it was a crucial happening in his boyhood.)

> Paul was very ill. His mother lay in bed at nights with him; they could not afford a nurse. He grew worse, and the crisis approached. One night he tossed into consciousness in the ghastly, sickly feeling of dissolution, when all the cells in the body seem in intense irritability to be breaking down, and consciousness makes a last flare of struggle, like madness.
>
> "I s'll die, mother!" he cried, heaving for breath on the pillow.
>
> She lifted him up, crying in a small voice:
>
> "Oh, my son—my son!"
>
> That brought him to. He realized her. His whole will rose up and arrested him. He put his head on her breast, and took ease of her for love.

It is terribly poignant, and terribly wrong. Amost better that a boy should die than have such an effort forced upon him by such means. He is called upon to feel in full consciousness for his mother all that a full-grown man might feel for the wife of his bosom.

In this same year, when Lawrence was sixteen, he met the girl Miriam, whose destiny was to be linked with his own for the next ten years, until his mother's death. He also met the farm and the family of which Miriam was the daughter. It became a second home to him. Beautifully situated in a valley about three miles away from the miner's cottage in Eastwood, the small decaying farm, with its pastures nibbled by rabbits to the quick, gave him the full freedom of that natural life which was always washing to the edge of the mining village. There he found the richness of life without which he wilted. He became as one of the family, and the Leivers' kitchen more dear to him than his own.

.   .   .   .

Miriam was about the same age as himself, perhaps a year younger, when Lawrence met her. She encouraged, stimulated, and appreciated his gifts; she saw in him the wonderful being that he was, and she had fallen in love with him long before he with her. She was free to fall in love; he was not. So that when we say that Lawrence fell in love with Miriam, we mean that had he been free, and not bound, and ever more deliberately and tightly bound, he might have fallen in love with her, as she undoubtedly did with him. He fell in love with her only so far as he was capable of falling in love.

The history is painful. In *Sons and Lovers*, Lawrence tells it as though Miriam failed him; and he tried, even at the end of his life in *Lady Chatterley's Lover*, to tell the story thus.

> I held forth with rapture to her, positively with rapture. I simply went up in smoke. And she adored me. The serpent in the grass was sex. She somehow didn't have any, at least not where it's supposed to be. I got thinner and crazier. Then I said we'd got to be lovers. I talked her into it. So she let me. I was excited, and she never wanted it. She adored me, she loved me to talk to her and kiss her; in that way she had a passion for me. But the other she just didn't want. And there are lots of women like her. And it was just the other that I *did* want. So there we split. I was cruel and left her.

Lawrence at all times needed desperately to convince himself in this matter of Miriam, and to the end he did not succeed. He does not tell the truth in *Sons and Lovers*, still less in *Lady Chatterley*: he comes closest to the truth in the *Fantasia*. Actually, while his mother still lived, he was incapable of giving to another woman the love without which sexual possession must be a kind of violence done: done not to the woman only, but also and equally to the man: above all to a man like Lawrence. All his life long Lawrence laboured to convince himself, and other people, that sexual desire carried with it its own validity: that the spiritual and the sexual were distinct. In fact, he never could believe it. What he did believe was something quite different, and quite true, namely that, in a man and woman who are whole, as he never was whole, the spiritual and the sexual might be one. This he declared in *Fantasia,* and yet again with his latest breath, in *The Escaped Cock.* He believed in a harmony which it was impossible for him personally to achieve, without a physical resurrection.

So saying, we anticipate: but it is essential to grasp as clearly as we can the subtle human tragedy of the affair with Miriam. It was the tragedy of Lawrence's entry into sexual life, and it haunted him all his days. In *Sons and Lovers* he conceals the truth. He cannot endure really to face it in consciousness. The story told there is subtly inconsistent with itself. At one moment comes a gleam of full recognition, as when he says of his mother: "She bore him, loved him, kept him, and his love turned back into her, so that he could not be free to go forward with his own life, really love another woman." But as he tells the story of the passion itself, he represents that it is not himself, but Miriam who is at fault. She is frigid, she shrinks from sexual passion; and this may have been true in part. But the truth was only partial. When later Lawrence came to a woman who was not frigid, the failure, though long drawn out, was more painful still. In representing that the fault was Miriam's, Lawrence wronged her. But we have to remember that *Sons and Lovers* was written after the death of his mother at a moment when Lawrence believed that he had attained sexual fulfilment. If he had not attained it with Miriam, he had some faint excuse for thinking that the fault was hers. He felt that it was not his own fault, and he had good reason for that. Nevertheless, it was his duty in *Sons and Lovers* to put the blame where it lay—if on a person at all, then upon his mother, who had taken from him that to which she had no right, and had used the full weight of her tremendous influence to prevent her son from giving to a woman the love which she so jealously guarded for herself. The fight was between his mother and Miriam, and it was an utterly unequal battle, between a strong and jealous woman and a diffident and unawakened girl.

In the story, Miriam is sacrificed, because Lawrence cannot tell the truth. Probably he could not tell it even to himself. The physical relation with Miriam was impossible. "You will not easily get a man to believe," he wrote in *Fantasia,* "that his carnal love for the woman he has made his wife is as high a love as that he felt for his mother." If Lawrence could write that when he had found his wife, and when his mother had been dead ten years, what did he feel while his mother was still alive, and he was engaged in talking Miriam into being his lover? He might talk and talk, but how could he convince her of what he did not himself believe—namely, that it was good that she should yield herself to him. He was a divided man. His love and his passion were separated. And because his passion was separated from his love, his passion was not true passion; it had but half the man behind, and to his own thinking, the worse half. This was the poisoned sting. He was, in his own eyes, degrading her, and degrading himself by his demand upon her.

What there was between Miriam and himself was an intense spiritual communion, and mutual stimulation of the mind. Whether it would ever, or could ever, have ripened into love on his side, who can say? Whatever it might have been was cankered in the bud. But I do not believe it ever could have ripened; Lawrence's subsequent history makes that plain to me. Happiness in love was not in Lawrence's destiny.

The appeal he made to Miriam was to her charity. He needed the comfort of her body, and she yielded herself to the sacrifice.

> She looked at him and was sorry for him; his eyes were dark with torture. She was sorry for him; it was worse for him to have this deflected love than for herself, who could never be properly mated. He was restless, for ever urging forward and trying to find a way out. He might do as he liked, and have what he liked of her.

Paul did not want her, but, as Mellors says in *Lady Chatterley's Lover*, "he wanted *it*." Miriam did not want him, but she wanted to give him *it*, because he wanted it. The indulgence of their "passion" was disastrous, because it was not passion at all. On both sides it was deliberate, and not passionate. Miriam's charity was passionate, but she had no sexual desire for Paul; Paul's need for the release and rest of sexual communion was passionate, but not his desire for Miriam. Each was a divided and tortured being. Miriam strove to subdue her body to her spirit, Paul strove to subdue his spirit to his body. They hurt themselves, and they hurt each other. Consider Lawrence's own words in *Sons and Lovers:*

> A good many of the nicest men he knew were like himself, bound in by their own virginity, which they could not break out of. They were so sensitive to their women that they would go without them for ever rather than do them a hurt, an injustice. Being the sons of mothers whose husbands had blundered rather brutally through their feminine sanctities, they were themselves too diffident and shy. They could easier deny themselves than incur any reproach from a woman; for a woman was like their mother, and they were full of the sense of their mother.

Yet Paul did the hurt, the injustice, to Miriam, and still more to himself in the process. And the hurt he does her and himself is more delicate than he can acknowledge here. He does not and cannot feel towards her what by his own standards he must feel in order to justify his demand of her. He sacrifices her, or allows her to sacrifice herself, and in so doing, he violates himself. And the consequence is disaster; for their "passion" brings not the release from the torment of inward division which he seeks, but an exasperation of the torment.

From the new torment, new release is sought: and the appeal is always to the woman's charity. Clara Dawes is a married woman, where Miriam was virgin. It is easier for her to give, and easier for Paul to take. But the desire is not for the woman, but for release through the woman; and the woman gives not from desire but from pity.

> He needed her badly. She had him in her arms, and he was miserable. With her warmth she folded him over, loved him. . . . She could not bear the suffering in his voice. She was afraid in her soul. He might have anything of her—anything; but she did not want to *know*. She felt she could not bear it. She wanted him to be soothed upon her—soothed. She stood clasping him and caressing him, and he was something unknown to her—something almost uncanny. She wanted to soothe him into forgetfulness. . . . She knew how stark and alone he was, and she felt it was great that he came to her; and she took him simply because his need was bigger either than her or him. . . . She did this for him in his need.

At the crucial moment, we cannot distinguish between Clara and Miriam. One is married, one is virgin; but their attitude towards him is the same, the appeal he makes to them the same.

One's instinct shrinks from it all. It is all wrong, humanly wrong. This man, we feel, has no business with sex at all. He is born to be a saint: then let him be one, and become a eunuch for the sake of the Kingdom of Heaven. For him, we prophesy, sex must be one long laceration, one long and tortured striving for the unattainable. This feverish effort to become a man turns fatally upon itself; it makes him more a child than before. He struggles frenziedly to escape being child-man to his mother, and he becomes only child-man again to other women, and the first great bond is not broken. If the woman is virgin like Miriam, he breaks her, by communicating to her the agony of his own division; if the woman is married like Clara, she breaks him, by abasing him in his own eyes.

To love a woman, in the simplest and most universal sense of the word, was impossible to Lawrence while his mother lived. Whether it was possible afterwards, the event will show. It will need almost a miracle, if he is to find his sexual salvation; for the fearful phrase of his own later invention fits him. It should fit him. He made it for himself. He is a man who is "crucified into sex," and he will carry the stigmata all his life.

Is it, we ask in pity and wonder, just a destiny? Is it simply that the sin of the father is visited through the mother upon the child? Was no escape possible? There is no answer to these questions; yet they return again and again to the mind. Surely, we say to ourselves, he could have broken that fearful bond that bound him to his mother. Was there not some ultimate weakness in the man that held him back? We may say that it was the terror of inflicting pain upon her. But there is a point at which the rarest and most tender virtue becomes a vice and a weakness; and perhaps to decide where that point lies is not so hard as it seems. When we begin to resent the compulsion of our virtues, they have become vices. Then the necessity of a choice and a decision is upon us: we must either cease to resent, or cease to obey, our virtues. Integrity lies either way. But to continue to obey, and to continue to resent—this means a cleavage which, once past a certain point, can never be healed again. Perhaps the final tragedy of Lawrence—and his life was

finally a bitter tragedy—was that he could never make the choice
on which his own integrity depended. To the end he resented his
virtues, yet in act obeyed them, and in imagination blasphemed
them.

Certainly, while his mother lived, until he himself was
twenty-six, he resented the compulsion of his fear of paining
her more and more deeply, yet he obeyed it. She was determined,
consciously or unconsciously, that no woman save herself should
have her son's love; and he obeyed her. What genuine and un-
hesitating passion there was in Lawrence's life before his
mother's death went to a man, not a woman.

Miriam's eldest brother, the farmer's eldest son, Edgar
Leivers of *Sons and Lovers*, George Saxton of *The White
Peacock*, called forth in Lawrence something far more near to
what most of us understand by passionate love than either
Miriam or Clara. Contact with Miriam made him glow with
a kind of spiritual incandescence; they throbbed together in a
tense vibration of soul, which Paul strove vainly to convert into
a passion of the body. His passion for Clara was from the beginning a physical need. But for the original of George and Edgar
he must have felt something for which the best name is the
simple one of love. In *Sons and Lovers* this friendship is but
lightly touched; in *The White Peacock* the tremor of authenticity is not to be mistaken. Cyril's love for George has more of
reality in it than any of the love affairs in the book; it yields in
convincingness only to the diffused yet passionate affection for
the farm and all its inhabitants which is the real emotional
substance of the story. . . .

13 · Technique as Discovery

by Mark Schorer

Modern criticism, through its exacting scrutiny of literary texts, has demonstrated with finality that in art beauty and truth are indivisible and one. The Keatsian overtones of these terms are mitigated and an old dilemma is solved if for beauty we substitute form, and for truth, content. We may, without risk of loss, narrow them even more, and speak of technique and subject matter. Modern criticism has shown us that to speak of content as such is not to speak of art at all, but of experience; and that it is only when we speak of the *achieved* content, the form, the work of art as a work of art, that we speak as critics. The difference between content, or experience, and achieved content, or art, is technique.

When we speak of technique, then, we speak of nearly everything. For technique is the means by which the writer's experience, which is his subject matter, compels him to attend to it; technique is the only means he has of discovering, exploring, developing his subject, of conveying its meaning, and, finally, of evaluating it. And surely it follows that certain techniques are sharper tools than others, and will discover more; that the writer capable of the most exacting technical scrutiny of his subject matter will produce works with the most satisfy-

Reprinted from The Hudson Review, Vol. I, No. 1 (Spring, 1948) *by permission of the author and* The Hudson Review. *Copyright 1948 by The Hudson Review, Inc. Only the opening statements of critical position, and the portion having to do with Lawrence and* Sons and Lovers *appear here. For Mr. Schorer's full argument concerning the art of fiction, the reader should consult the entire essay.*

ing content, works with thickness and resonance, works which reverberate, works with maximum meaning.[1]

We are no longer able to regard as seriously intended criticism of poetry which does not assume these generalizations; but the case for fiction has not yet been established. The novel is still read as though its content has some value in itself, as though the subject matter of fiction has greater or lesser value in itself, and as though technique were not a primary but a supplementary element, capable perhaps of not unattractive embellishments upon the surface of the subject, but hardly of its essence. Or technique is thought of in blunter terms than those which one associates with poetry, as such relatively obvious matters as the arrangement of events to create plot; or, within plot, of suspense and climax; or as the means of revealing character motivation, relationship, and development; or as the use of point of view, but point of view as some nearly arbitrary device for the heightening of dramatic interest through the narrowing or broadening of perspective upon the material, rather than as a means toward the positive definition of theme. As for the resources of language, these, somehow, we almost never think of as a part of the technique of fiction—language as used to create a certain texture and tone which in themselves state and define themes and meanings; or language, the counters of our ordinary speech, as forced, through conscious manipulation, into all those larger meanings which our ordinary speech almost never intends. Technique in fiction, all this is a way of saying, we somehow continue to regard as merely a means of organizing material which is "given" rather than as the means of exploring and defining the values in an area of experience which, for the first time *then*, are being given.

. . . .

Technique in fiction is, of course, all those obvious forms of it which are usually taken to be the whole of it, and many others; but for the present purposes, let it be thought of in

1 "The best form is that which makes the most of its subject—there is no other definition of the meaning of form in fiction. The well-made book is the book in which the matter is all used up in the form, in which the form expresses all the matter." (*The Craft of Fiction*, by Percy Lubbock. Jonathan Cape: Chas. Scribner's Sons, 1921; Peter Smith, 1947, p. 40.)

two respects particularly: the uses to which language, as language, is put to express the quality of the experience in question; and the uses of point of view not only as a mode of dramatic delimitation, but more particularly, of thematic definition. Technique is really what T. S. Eliot means by "convention"— any selection, structure, or distortion, any form or rhythm imposed upon the world of action; by means of which—it should be added—our apprehension of the world of action is enriched or renewed.[2] In this sense, everything is technique which is not the lump of experience itself, and one cannot properly say that a writer has no technique or that he eschews technique, for, being a writer, he cannot do so. We can speak of good and bad technique, of adequate and inadequate, of technique which serves the novel's purpose, or disserves.

. . . .

To say what one means in art is never easy, and the more intimately one is implicated in one's material, the more difficult it is. If, besides, one commits fiction to a therapeutic function which is to be operative not on the audience but on the author, declaring, as D. H. Lawrence did, that "one sheds one's sicknesses in books, repeats and presents again one's emotions to be master of them," the difficulty is vast. It is an acceptable theory only with the qualification that technique, which objectifies, is under no other circumstances so imperative. For merely to repeat one's emotions, merely to look into one's heart and write, is also merely to repeat the round of emotional bondage. If our books are to be exercises in self-analysis, then technique must—and alone can—take the place of the absent analyst.

Lawrence, in the relatively late Introduction to his *Collected Poems*, made that distinction of the amateur between his "real" poems and his "composed" poems, between the poems which expressed his demon directly and created their own form "willy-nilly," and the poems which, through the hocus pocus of technique, he spuriously put together and could, if necessary, revise. His belief in a "poetry of the immediate present," poetry in which nothing is fixed, static, or final, where

2 See Eliot on "Four Elizabethan Dramatists" in his *Selected Essays* (Harcourt, Brace & Co., 1932), p. 94.

all is shimmeriness and impermanence and vitalistic essence, arose from this mistaken notion of technique. And from this notion, an unsympathetic critic like D. S. Savage can construct a case which shows Lawrence driven "concurrently to the dissolution of personality and the dissolution of art." The argument suggests that Lawrence's early, crucial novel, *Sons and Lovers*, is another example of meanings confused by an impatience with technical resources.

The novel has two themes: the crippling effects of a mother's love on the emotional development of her son; and the "split" between kinds of love, physical and spiritual, which the son develops, the kinds represented by two young women, Clara and Miriam. The two themes should, of course, work together, the second being, actually, the result of the first: this "split" is the "crippling." So one would expect to see the novel developed, and so Lawrence, in his famous letter to Edward Garnett, where he says that Paul is left at the end with the "drift towards death," apparently thought he had developed it. Yet in the last few sentences of the novel, Paul rejects his desire for extinction and turns toward "the faintly humming, glowing town," to life—as nothing in his previous history persuades us that he could unfalteringly do.

The discrepancy suggests that the book may reveal certain confusions between intention and performance.

The first of these is the contradiction between Lawrence's explicit characterizations of the mother and father and his tonal evaluations of them. It is a problem not only of style (of the contradiction between expressed moral epithets and the more general texture of the prose which applies to them) but of point of view. Morel and Lawrence are never separated, which is a way of saying that Lawrence maintains for himself in his book the confused attitude of his character. The mother is a "proud, *honorable* soul," but the father has a "small, *mean* head." This is the sustained contrast; the epithets are characteristic of the whole; and they represent half of Lawrence's feelings. But what is the other half? Which of these characters is given his real sympathy—the hard, self-righteous, aggressive, demanding mother who comes through to us, or the simple, direct, gentle, downright, fumbling, ruined father? There are two attitudes here. Lawrence (and Morel) loves his mother, but he also hates her for compelling his love; and he hates his father with the true Freudian jealousy, but he also loves him for what he is in himself, and he sympathizes more deeply with him because his wholeness has been destroyed by the mother's domination, just as his, Lawrence-Morel's, has been.

This is a psychological tension which disrupts the form of the novel and obscures its meaning, because neither the contradiction in style nor the confusion in point of view is made to right itself. Lawrence is merely repeating his emotions, and he avoids an austerer technical scrutiny of his material because it would compel him to master them. He would not let the artist be stronger than the man.

The result is that, at the same time that the book condemns the mother, it justifies her; at the same time that it shows Paul's failure, it offers rationalizations which place the failure elsewhere. The handling of the girl, Miriam, if viewed closely, is pathetic in what it signifies for Lawrence, both as a man and artist. For Miriam is made the mother's scape-goat, and in a different way from the way that she was in life. The central section of the novel is shot through with alternate statements as to the source of the difficulty: Paul is unable to love Miriam wholly, and Miriam can love only his spirit. The contradictions appear sometimes within single paragraphs, and the point of view is never adequately objectified and sustained to tell us which is true. The material is never seen as material; the writer is caught in it exactly as firmly as he was caught in his experience of it. "That's how women are with me," said Paul. "They want me like mad, but they don't want to belong to me." So he might have said, and believed it; but at the end of the novel, Lawrence is still saying that, and himself believing it.

For the full history of this technical failure, one must read *Sons and Lovers* carefully and then learn the history of the manuscript from the book called *D. H. Lawrence: A Personal Record*, by one E. T., who was Miriam in life. The basic situation is clear enough. The first theme—the crippling effects of the mother's love—is developed right through to the end; and then suddenly, in the last few sentences, turns on itself, and Paul gives himself to life, not death. But all the way through, the insidious rationalizations of the second theme have crept in to destroy the artistic coherence of the work. A "split" would occur in Paul; but as the split is treated, it is superimposed upon rather than developed in support of the first theme. It is a rationalization made from it. If Miriam is made to insist on spiritual love, the meaning and the power of theme one are reduced; yet Paul's weakness is disguised. Lawrence could not separate the investigating analyst, who must be objective, from Lawrence, the subject of the book; and the sickness was not healed, the emotion not mastered, the novel not perfected. All this, and the character of a whole career, would have been altered if Lawrence had allowed his technique to discover the fullest meaning of his subject.

14·*On* Sons and Lovers

by Dorothy Van Ghent

Novels, like other dramatic art, deal with conflicts of one kind or another—conflicts that are, in the work of the major novelists, drawn from life in the sense that they are representative of real problems in life; and the usual urgency in the novelist is to find the technical means which will afford an ideal resolution of the conflict and solution of the living problem—still "ideal" even if tragic. Technique is his art itself, in its procedural aspect; and the validity of his solution of a problem is dependent upon the adequacy of his technique. The more complex and intransigent the problem, the more subtle his technical strategies will evidently need to be, if they are to be effective. The decade of World War I brought into full and terrible view the collapse of values that had prophetically haunted the minds of novelists as far back as Dostoevsky and Flaubert and Dickens, or even farther back, to Balzac and Stendhal. With that decade, and increasingly since, the problems of modern life have appeared intransigent indeed; and, in general, the growth of that intransigence has been reflected in an increasing concern with technique on the part of the artist. D. H. Lawrence's sensitivity to twentieth century chaos was peculiarly intense, and his passion for order was similarly intense; but this sensitivity and this passion did not lead him to concentrate on refinements and

Reprinted from The English Novel: Form and Function, *by Dorothy Van Ghent. Copyright © 1953 by Dorothy Van Ghent. Reprinted by permission of the author and Holt, Rinehart, and Winston, Inc. Minor changes have been made with the author's permission.*

subtleties of novelistic technique in the direction laid out, for instance, by James and Conrad. Hence, as readers first approaching his work, almost inevitably we feel disappointment and even perhaps shock that writing so often "loose" and repetitious and such unrestrained emotionalism over glandular matters should appear in the work of a novelist who is assumed to have an important place in the literary canon. "There is no use," Francis Fergusson says, "trying to appreciate [Lawrence] solely as an artist; he was himself too often impatient of the demands of art, which seemed to him trivial compared with the quest he followed." [1] And Stephen Spender phrases the problem of Lawrence in this way: what interested him "was the tension between art and life, not the complete resolution of the problems of life within the illusion of art. . . . For him literature is a kind of pointer to what is outside literature. . . . This outsideness of reality is for Lawrence the waters of baptism in which man can be reborn." [2] We need to approach Lawrence with a good deal of humility about "art" and a good deal of patience for the disappointments he frequently offers as an artist, for it is only thus that we shall be able to appreciate the innovations he actually made in the novel as well as the importance and profundity of his vision of modern life.

Sons and Lovers appears to have the most conventional chronological organization; it is the kind of organization that a naïve autobiographical novelist would tend to use, with only the thinnest pretense at disguising the personally retrospective nature of the material. We start with the marriage of the parents and the birth of the children. We learn of the daily life of the family while the children are growing up, the work, the small joys, the parental strife. Certain well-defined emotional pressures become apparent: the children are alienated from their father, whose personality degenerates gradually as he feels his exclusion; the mother more and more completely dominates her sons' affections, aspirations, mental habits. Urged by her toward middle-class refinements, they enter white-collar jobs, thus making one

1 "D. H. Lawrence's Sensibility," in *Critiques and Essays in Modern Fiction*, edited by John W. Aldridge (New York: The Ronald Press Company, 1952), p. 328.
2 "The Life of Literature," in *Partisan Review*, December, 1948.

more dissociation between themselves and their proletarian father. As they attempt to orient themselves toward biological adulthood, the old split in the family is manifested in a new form, as an internal schism in the characters of the sons; they cannot reconcile sexual choice with the idealism their mother has inculcated. This inner strain leads to the older son's death. The same motif is repeated in the case of Paul, the younger one. Paul's first girl, Miriam, is a cerebral type, and the mother senses in her an obvious rivalry for domination of Paul's sensibility. The mother is the stronger influence, and Paul withdraws from Miriam; but with her own victory Mrs. Morel begins to realize the discord she has produced in his character, and tries to release her hold on him by unconsciously seeking her own death. Paul finds another girl, Clara, but the damage is already too deeply designed, and at the time of his mother's death he voluntarily gives up Clara, knowing that there is but one direction he can take, and that is to go with his mother. At the end he is left emotionally derelict, with only the "drift toward death."

From this slight sketch, it is clear that the book is organized not merely on a chronological plan showing the habits and vicissitudes of a Nottinghamshire miner's family, but that it has a structure rigorously controlled by an idea: an idea of an organic disturbance in the relationships of men and women—a disturbance of sexual polarities that is first seen in the disaffection of mother and father, then in the mother's attempt to substitute her sons for her husband, finally in the sons' unsuccessful struggle to establish natural manhood. Lawrence's development of the idea has certain major implications: it implies that his characters have transgressed against the natural life-directed condition of the human animal—against the elementary biological rhythms he shares with the rest of biological nature; and it implies that this offense against life has been brought about by a failure to respect the complete and terminal individuality of persons—by a twisted desire to "possess" other persons, as the mother tries to "possess" her husband, then her sons, and as Miriam tries to "possess" Paul. Lawrence saw this offense as a disease of modern life in all its manifestations, from sexual relationships to those broad social and political relationships that have changed people from individuals to anonymous economic properties or to military units or to ideological automatons.

The controlling idea is expressed in the various episodes—the narrative logic of the book. It is also expressed in imagery—the book's poetic logic. Perhaps in no other novelist do we find the image so largely replacing episode and discursive analysis, and taking over the expressive functions of these, as it does in Lawrence. The chief reason for the extraordinary predominance of the image as an absolute expressive medium in Lawrence lies in the character of the idea which is his subject. He must make us aware—sensitively aware, not merely conceptually aware—of the profound life force whose rhythms the natural creature obeys; and he must make us aware of the terminal individuality —the absolute "otherness" or "outsideness"—that is the natural form of things and of the uncorrupted person. We must be made aware of these through the *feelings* of his people, for only in feeling have the biological life force and the sense of identity—either the identity of self or of others—any immediacy of reality. He seeks the objective equivalent of feeling in the image. As Francis Fergusson says, Lawrence's imagination was so concrete that he seems not "to distinguish between the reality and the metaphor or symbol which makes it plain to us." [3] But the most valid symbols are the most concrete realities. Lawrence's great gift for the symbolic image was a function of his sensitivity to and passion for the meaning of real things—for the individual expression that real forms have. In other words, his gift for the image arose directly from his vision of life as infinitely creative of individual identities, each whole and separate and to be reverenced as such.

Let us examine the passage with which the first chapter of *Sons and Lovers* ends—where Mrs. Morel, pregnant with Paul, wanders deliriously in the garden, shut out of the house by Morel in his drunkenness. Mrs. Morel is literally a vessel of the life force that seems to thrust itself at her in nature from all sides, but she is also in rebellion against it and the perfume of the pollen-filled lilies makes her gasp with fear:

3 Fergusson, *op. cit.*, p. 335.

The moon was high and magnificent in the August night. Mrs. Morel, seared with passion, shivered to find herself out there in a great white light, that fell cold on her, and gave a shock to her inflamed soul. She stood for a few moments helplessly staring at the glistening great rhubarb leaves near the door. Then she got the air into her breast. She walked down the garden path, trembling in every limb, while the child boiled within her. . . .

She hurried out of the side garden to the front, where she could stand as if in an immense gulf of white light, the moon streaming high in face of her, the moonlight standing up from the hills in front, and filling the valley where the Bottoms crouched, almost blindingly. There, panting and half weeping in reaction from the stress, she murmured to herself over and over again: "The nuisance! the nuisance!"

She became aware of something about her. With an effort she roused herself to see what it was that penetrated her consciousness. The tall white lilies were reeling in the moonlight, and the air was charged with their perfume, as with a presence. Mrs. Morel gasped slightly in fear. She touched the big, pallid flowers on their petals then shivered. They seemed to be stretching in the moonlight. She put her hand into one white bin: the gold scarcely showed on her fingers by moonlight. She bent down to look at the binful of yellow pollen; but it only appeared dusky. Then she drank a deep draught of the scent. It almost made her dizzy.

Mrs. Morel leaned on the garden gate, looking out, and she lost herself awhile. She did not know what she thought. Except for a slight feeling of sickness, and her consciousness in the child, herself melted out like a scent into the shiny, pale air.

She finally arouses Morel from his drunken sleep and he lets her in. Unfastening her brooch at the bedroom mirror, she sees that her face is smeared with the yellow dust of the lilies.

The imagery of the streaming moonlight is that of a vast torrential force, "magnificent" and inhuman, and it equates not only with that phallic power of which Mrs. Morel is the rebellious vessel but with the greater and universal demiurge that was anciently called Eros—the power springing in plants and hurling the planets, giving the "glistening great rhubarb leaves" their fierce identity, fecundating and stretching the lilies. The smear of yellow pollen on Mrs. Morel's face is a grossly humorous irony. This passage is a typifying instance of the spontaneous identification Lawrence constantly found between image and meaning, between real things and what they symbolize.

Our particular culture has evolved deep prohibitions against the expression, or even the subjective acknowledgment of the kind of phallic reality with which Lawrence was concerned— and with which ancient religions were also concerned. Certainly one factor in the uneasiness that Lawrence frequently causes us is the factor of those cultural prohibitions. But these prohibitions themselves Lawrence saw as disease symptoms, though the disease was far more extensive and radical than a taboo on the phallus. It was a spiritual disease that broke down the sense of identity, of "separate selfhood," while at the same time it broke down the sense of rhythm with universal nature. Paul Morel, working his fairly unconscious, adolescent, sexual way toward Miriam, finds that rhythm and that selfhood in the spatial proportions of a wren's nest in a hedge:

> He crouched down and carefully put his finger through the thorns into the round door of the nest.
> "It's almost as if you were feeling inside the live body of the bird," he said, "it's so warm. They say a bird makes its nest round like a cup with pressing its breast on it. Then how did it make the ceiling round, I wonder?"

When Paul takes his first country walk with Clara and Miriam, the appearance of a red stallion in the woods vividly realizes in unforced symbolic dimension the power which will drive Paul from Miriam to Clara, while the image also realizes the great horse itself in its unique and mysterious identity:

> As they were going beside the brook, on the Willey Water side, looking through the brake at the edge of the wood, where pink campions glowed under a few sunbeams, they saw, beyond the tree-trunks and the thin hazel bushes, a man leading a great bay horse through the gullies. The big red beast seemed to dance romantically through that dimness of green hazel drift, away there where the air was shadowy, as if it were in the past, among the fading bluebells that might have bloomed for Deirdre. . . .
> The great horse breathed heavily, shifting round its red flanks, and looking suspiciously with its wonderful big eyes upwards from under its lowered head and falling mane. . . .

A simple descriptive passage like the following, showing a hen pecking at a girl's hand, conveys the animal dynamics that is the urgent phase of the phallic power working in the boy and the girl, but its spontaneous symbolism of a larger reality is due to its faithfulness to the way a hen does peck and the feeling of the pecking—due, that is, to the actuality or "identity" of the small, homely circumstance itself:

> As he went round the back, he saw Miriam kneeling in front of the hencoop, some maize in her hand, biting her lip, and crouching in an intense attitude. The hen was eying her wickedly. Very gingerly she put forward her hand. The hen bobbed for her. She drew back quickly with a cry, half of fear, half of chagrin.
>
> "It won't hurt you," said Paul.
>
> She flushed crimson and started up.
>
> "I only wanted to try," she said in a low voice.
>
> "See, it doesn't hurt," he said, and, putting only two corns in his palm, he let the hen peck, peck, peck at his bare hand. "It only makes you laugh," he said.
>
> She put her hand forward, and dragged it away, tried again, and started back with a cry. He frowned.
>
> "Why, I'd let her take corn from my face," said Paul, "only she bumps a bit. She's ever so neat. If she wasn't, look how much ground she'd peck up every day."
>
> He waited grimly, and watched. At last Miriam let the bird peck from her hand. She gave a little cry—fear, and pain because of fear—rather pathetic. But she had done it, and she did it again.
>
> "There, you see," said the boy. "It doesn't hurt, does it?"

There is more terse and obvious symbolism, of the kind typical in Lawrence, in that sequence where Clara's red carnations splatter their petals over her clothes and on the ground where she and Paul first make love, but we acquire the best and the controlling sense of Lawrence's gift for the image, as dramatic and thematic expression, in those passages where his urgency is to see *things* and to see them clearly and completely in their most individualizing traits, for the character of his vision is such that, in truly seeing them as they are, he sees through them to what they mean.

We frequently notice the differentiating significance of a writer's treatment of nature—that is, of that part of "nature" which is constituted by earth and air and water and the non-human creatures; and we find that attitudes toward nature are deeply associated with attitudes toward human "good," human destiny, human happiness, human salvation, the characteristic problems of being human. One might cite, for instance, in *Tom Jones*, Fielding's highly stylized treatment of outdoor nature (as in the passage in which Tom dreams of Sophia beside the brook, and Mollie Seagrim approaches): here nature has only generalized attributes for whose description and understanding certain epithets in common educated currency are completely adequate—brooks murmur, breezes whisper, birds trill; nature is really a linguistic construction, and this rationalization of nature is appropriate in Fielding's universe since everything there exists ideally as an object of *ratio*, of reasoning intelligence. We notice in Jane Austen's *Pride and Prejudice* (in the description of Darcy's estate, for example) that outdoor nature again has importance only as it serves to express rational and social character —wherefore again the generalized epithet that represents nature as either the servant of intelligence or the space where intelligence operates. In George Eliot's *Adam Bede*, where there is relatively a great deal of "outdoors," nature is man's plowfield, the acre in which he finds social and ethical expression through work; this is only a different variety of the conception of nature as significant by virtue of what man's intelligential and social character makes of it for his ends.

With Emily Brontë, we come nearer to Lawrence, though not very near. In *Wuthering Heights*, nature's importance is due not to its yielding itself up to domestication in man's reason, or offering itself as an instrument by which he expresses his conscience before God or society, but to its fiercely unregenerate difference from all that civilized man is—a difference that it constantly forces on perception by animal-like attacks on and disruptions of human order. In Hardy, nature is also a daemonic entity in its own right, and not only unrationalizable but specifically hostile to the human reason. It is worth noting that, among all English novelists, Hardy and Lawrence have the most faithful touch for the things of nature and the greatest evocative genius in bringing them before the imagination. But there are certain definitive differences of attitude. Both Emily Brontë's and Hardy's worlds are dual, and there is no way of bringing the oppositions of the dualism together: on the one side of the cleavage are those attributes of man that we call "human," his reason, his ethical sensibility; and on the other side is "nature" —the elements and the creatures and man's own instinctive life that he shares with the nonhuman creatures. The opposition is resolved only by destruction of the "human": a destruction that is in Emily Brontë profoundly attractive, in Hardy tragic. But Lawrence's world is multiple rather than dual. Everything in it is a separate and individual "other," every person, every creature, every object (like the madonna lilies, the rhubarb plants, the wren's nest, the stallion); and there is a creative relationship between people and between people and things so long as this "otherness" is acknowledged. When it is denied—and it is denied when man tries to rationalize nature and society, or when he presumptuously assumes the things of nature to be merely instruments for the expression of himself, or when he attempts to exercise personal possessorship over people—then he destroys his own selfhood and exerts a destructive influence all about him.

In *Sons and Lovers*, only in Morel himself, brutalized and spiritually maimed as he is, does the germ of selfhood remain intact; and—this is the correlative proposition in Lawrence—in him only does the biological life force have simple, unequivocal assertion. Morel wants to live, by hook or crook, while his sons want to die. To live is to obey a rhythm involving more than conscious attitudes and involving more than human beings— involving all nature; a rhythm indifferent to the greediness of reason, indifferent to idiosyncrasies of culture and idealism. The image associated with Morel is that of the coalpits, where he descends daily and from which he ascends at night blackened and tired. It is a symbol of rhythmic descent and ascent, like a sexual rhythm, or like the rhythm of sleep and awaking or of death and life. True, the work in the coalpits reverses the natural use of the hours of light and dark and is an economic distortion of that rhythm in nature—and Morel and the other colliers bear the spiritual traumata of that distortion; for Lawrence is dealing with the real environment of modern men, in its complexity and injuriousness. Nevertheless, the work at the pits is still symbolic of the greater rhythm governing life and obedience to which is salvation. Throughout the book, the coalpits are always at the horizon:

> On the fallow land the young wheat shone silkily. Minton pit waved its plumes of white steam, coughed, and rattled hoarsely.
> "Now look at that!" said Mrs. Morel. Mother and son stood on the road to watch. Along the ridge of the great pit-hill crawled a little group in silhouette against the sky, a horse, a small truck, and a man. They climbed the incline against the heavens. At the end the man tipped the waggon. There was an undue rattle as the waste fell down the sheer slope of the enormous bank. . . .
> "Look how it heaps together," [Paul says of the pit] "like something alive almost—a big creature that you don't know. . . . And all the trucks standing waiting, like a string of beasts to be fed. . . . I like the feel of *men* on things, while they're alive. There's a feel of men about trucks, because they've been handled with men's hands, all of them."

Paul associates the pits not only with virility but with being alive. The trucks themselves become alive because they have been handled by men. The symbolism of the pits is identical with that of Morel, the father, the irrational life principle that is unequally embattled against the death principle in the mother, the rational and idealizing principle working rhythmlessly, greedily, presumptuously, and possessively.

The sons' attitude toward the father is ambivalent, weighted toward hate because the superior cultural equipment of the mother shows his crudeness in relief; but again and again bits of homely characterization of Morel show that the children —and even the mother herself—sense, however uncomfortably, the attractiveness of his simple masculine integrity. He has, un-injurable, what the mother's possessiveness has injured in the sons:

> "Shut that doo-er!" bawled Morel furiously.
> Annie banged it behind her, and was gone.
> "If tha oppens it again while I'm weshin' me, I'll ma'e thy jaw rattle," he threatened from the midst of his soapsuds. Paul and the mother frowned to hear him.
> Presently he came running out of the scullery, with the soapy water dripping from him, dithering with cold.
> "Oh, my sirs!" he said. "Wheer's my towel?"

It was hung on a chair to warm before the fire, otherwise he would have bullied and blustered. He squatted on his heels before the hot baking-fire to dry himself.

"F-ff-f!" he went, pretending to shudder with cold.

"Goodness, man, don't be such a kid!" said Mrs. Morel. "It's *not* cold."

"Thee strip thysen stark nak'd to wesh thy flesh i' that scullery," said the miner, as he rubbed his hair; "nowt b'r a ice-'ouse!"

"And I shouldn't make that fuss," replied his wife.

"No, tha'd drop down stiff, as dead as a door-knob, wi' thy nesh sides."

"Why is a door-knob deader than anything else?" asked Paul, curious.

"Eh, I dunno; that's what they say," replied his father. "But there's that much draught i' yon scullery, as it blows through your ribs like through a five-barred gate."

"It would have some difficulty in blowing through yours," said Mrs. Morel.

Morel looked down ruefully at his sides.

"Me!" he exclaimed. "I'm nowt b'r a skinned rabbit. My bones fair juts out on me."

"I should like to know where," retorted his wife.

"Iv-ry-wheer! I'm nobbut a sack o' faggots."

Mrs. Morel laughed. He had still a wonderfully young body, muscular, without any fat. His skin was smooth and clear. It might have been the body of a man of twenty-eight, except that there were, perhaps, too many blue scars, like tattoo-marks, where the coal-dust remained under the skin, and that his chest was too hairy. But he put his hands on his sides ruefully. It was his fixed belief that, because he did not get fat, he was as thin as a starved rat.

Paul looked at his father's thick, brownish hands all scarred, with broken nails, rubbing the fine smoothness of his sides, and the incongruity struck him. It seemed strange they were the same flesh.

Morel talks the dialect that is the speech of physical tenderness in Lawrence's books.[4] It is to the dialect of his father that Paul reverts when he is tussling with Beatrice in adolescent erotic play (letting the mother's bread burn, that he should have been watching), and that Arthur, the only one of the sons whom the mother has not corrupted, uses in his love-making, and that Paul uses

4 This observation is made by Diana Trilling in her Introduction to *The Portable D. H. Lawrence* (New York: The Viking Press, Inc., 1947).

again when he makes love to Clara, the uncomplex woman who is able for a while to give him his sexual manhood and his "separate selfhood." The sons never use the dialect with their mother, and Paul never uses it with Miriam. It is the speech used by Mellors in *Lady Chatterley's Lover*; and, significantly perhaps, Mellors' name is an anagram on the name Morel.

Some of the best moments in the children's life are associated with the father, when Morel has his "good" periods and enters again into the intimate activity of the family—and some of the best, most simply objective writing in the book communicates these moments, as for instance the passage in Chapter 4 where Morel is engaged in making fuses:

> . . . Morel fetched a sheaf of long sound wheat-straws from the attic. These he cleaned with his hand, till each one gleamed like a stalk of gold, after which he cut the straws into lengths of about six inches, leaving, if he could, a notch at the bottom of each piece. He always had a beautifully sharp knife that could cut a straw clean without hurting it. Then he set in the middle of the table a heap of gun-powder, a little pile of black grains upon the white-scrubbed board. He made and trimmed the straws while Paul and Annie filled and plugged them. Paul loved to see the black grains trickle down a crack in his palm into the mouth of the straw, peppering jollily downwards till the straw was full. Then he bunged up the mouth with a bit of soap—which he got on his thumb-nail from a pat in a saucer —and the straw was finished.

There is a purity of realization in this very simple kind of exposition that, on the face of it, resists associating itself with any *symbolic* function—if we tend to think of a "symbol" as splitting itself apart into a thing and a meaning, with a mental arrow connecting the two. The best in Lawrence carries the authenticity of a faithfully observed, concrete actuality that refuses to be so split; its symbolism is a radiation that leaves it intact in itself. So, in the passage above, the scene is intact as homely realism, but it radiates Lawrence's controlling sense of the characterful integrity of objects—the clean wheat straws, the whitely scrubbed table, the black grains peppering down a crack in the child's palm, the bung of soap on a thumbnail—and that integrity is here associated with the man Morel and his own integrity of warm and absolute maleness. Thus it is another representation of the creative life force witnessed in the independent objectivity of things that are wholly concrete and wholly themselves.

The human attempt to distort and corrupt that selfhood is reflected in Miriam's attitude toward flowers:

> Round the wild, tussocky lawn at the back of the house was a thorn hedge, under which daffodils were craning forward from among their sheaves of grey-green blades. The cheeks of the flowers were greenish with cold. But still some had burst, and their gold ruffled and glowed. Miriam went on her knees before one cluster, took a wild-looking daffodil between her hands, turned up its face of gold to her, and bowed down, caressing it with her mouth and cheeks and brow. He stood aside, with his hands in his pockets, watching her. One after another she turned up to him the faces of the yellow, bursten flowers appealingly, fondling them lavishly all the while. . . .
> "Why must you always be fondling things!" he said irritably. . . . "Can you never like things without clutching them as if you wanted to pull the heart out of them? . . . You're always begging things to love you. . . . Even the flowers, you have to fawn on them—"
> Rhythmically, Miriam was swaying and stroking the flower with her mouth. . . .
> "You don't want to love—your eternal and abnormal craving is to be loved. You aren't positive, you're negative. You absorb, absorb, as if you must fill yourself up with love, because you've got a shortage somewhere."

The relationship of the girl to the flowers is that of a blasphemous possessorship which denies the separateness of living entities—the craving to break down boundaries between thing and thing, that is seen also in Miriam's relationship with Paul, whom she cannot love without trying to absorb him. In contrast, there is the flower imagery in Chapter 11, where Paul goes out into the night and the garden in a moment of emotional struggle:

> It grew late. Through the open door, stealthily, came the scent of madonna lilies, almost as if it were prowling abroad. Suddenly he got up and went out of doors.
> The beauty of the night made him want to shout. A half-moon, dusky gold, was sinking behind the black sycamore at the end of the garden, making the sky dull purple with its glow. Nearer, a dim white fence of lilies went across the garden, and the air all round seemed to stir with scent, as if it were

alive. He went across the bed of pinks, whose keen perfume came sharply across the rocking, heavy scent of the lilies, and stood alongside the white barrier of flowers. They flagged all loose, as if they were panting. The scent made him drunk. He went down to the field to watch the moon sink under.

A corncrake in the hay-close called insistently. The moon slid quite quickly downwards, growing more flushed. Behind him the great flowers leaned as if they were calling. And then, like a shock, he caught another perfume, something raw and coarse. Hunting round, he found the purple iris, touched their fleshy throats and their dark, grasping hands. At any rate, he had found something. They stood stiff in the darkness. Their scent was brutal. The moon was melting down upon the crest of the hill. It was gone; all was dark. The corncrake called still.

The flowers here have a fierce "thereness" or "otherness" establishing them as existences in their own right—as separate, strange selves—and the demiurgic Eros is rudely insistent in their scent. Paul's perception of that independent life puts him into relation with himself, and the moment of catalytic action is marked by the brief sentence: "At any rate, he had found something." The "something" that he finds is simply the iris, dark, fleshy, mysterious, alien. He goes back into the house and tells his mother that he has decided to break off with Miriam.

Darkness—as the darkness of this night in the garden—has in Lawrence a special symbolic potency. It is a natural and universal symbol, but it offers itself with special richness to Lawrence because of the character of his governing vision. Darkness is half of the rhythm of the day, the darkness of unconsciousness is half of the rhythm of the mind, and the darkness of death is half of the rhythm of life. Denial of this phase of the universal tide is the great sin, the sin committed by modern economy and modern rationalism. In acceptance of the dark, man is renewed to himself—and to light, to consciousness, to reason, to brotherhood. But by refusal to accept that half of the rhythm, he becomes impotent, his reason becomes destructive, and he loses the sense of the independence of others which is essential to brotherhood. In Chapter 13 of *Sons and Lovers* there is a passage that realizes something of what we have been saying. It occurs just after Paul has made love to Clara in a field:

All the while the peewits were screaming in the field. When he came to, he wondered what was near his eyes, curving and strong with life in the dark, and what voice it was speaking. Then he realized it was the grass, and the peewit was calling. The warmth was Clara's breathing heaving. He lifted his head, and looked into her eyes. They were dark and shining and strange, life wild at the source staring into his life, stranger to him, yet meeting him; and he put his face down on her throat, afraid. What was she? A strong, strange, wild life, that breathed with his in the darkness through this hour. It was all so much bigger than themselves that he was hushed. They had met, and included in their meeting the thrust of the manifold grass-stems, the cry of the peewit, the wheel of the stars. . . .

. . . after such an evening they both were very still. . . . They felt small, half afraid, childish, and wondering, like Adam and Eve when they lost their innocence and realized the magnificence of the power which drove them out of Paradise and across the great night and the great day of humanity. It was for each of them an initiation. . . . To know their own nothingness, to know the tremendous living flood which carried them always, gave them rest within themselves. If so great a magnificent power could overwhelm them, identify them altogether with itself, so that they knew they were only grains in the tremendous heave that lifted every grass-blade its little height, and every tree, and living thing, then why fret about themselves? They could let themselves be carried by life, and they felt a sort of peace each in the other. There was a verification which they had had together. Nothing could nullify it, nothing could take it away; it was almost their belief in life.

But then we are told that "Clara was not satisfied. . . . She thought it was he whom she wanted. . . . She had not got him; she was not satisfied." This is the impulse toward personal possessorship that constantly confuses and distorts human relationships in Lawrence's books; it is a denial of the otherness of people, and a denial, really, of the great inhuman life force, the primal "otherness" through which people have their independent definition as well as their creative community. Paul had felt that "his experience had been impersonal, and not Clara"; and he had wanted the same impersonality in Clara, an impersonality consonant with that of the manifold grass stems and the peewits' calling the wheel of the stars. André Malraux, in his preface to the French translation of *Lady Chatterley's Lover*, says that this "couple-advocate," Lawrence, is concerned not with his own individuality or that of his mate, but with "being": "Lawrence has no wish to be either happy or great,"

Malraux says; "he is only concerned with being." [5] The concern
with being, with simple being-a-self (as distinguished from imposing the ego or abdicating selfhood in the mass), can be
understood only in the context of twentieth century man's
resignation to herd ideologies, herd recreations, herd rationalizations. Lawrence's missionary and prophetic impulse, like
Dostoevsky's, was to combat the excesses of rationalism and individualism, excesses that have led—paradoxically enough—to
the release of monstrously destructive irrationals and to the
impotence of the individual. He wanted to bring man's self-
definition and creativity back into existence through recognition
of and vital relationship with the rhythms that men share with
the nonhuman world; for he thought that thus men could find
not only the selves that they had denied, but also the brotherhood they had lost.

The darkness of the phallic consciousness is the correlative
of a passionate life assertion, strong as the thrust of the grass
stems in the field where Paul and Clara make love, and as the
dynamics of the wheeling stars. "In the lowest trough of the
night" there is always "a flare of the pit." A pillar of cloud by
day, the pit is a pillar of fire by night: and the Lord is at the
pit top. As a descent of darkness and an ascent of flame is associated with the secret, essential, scatheless maleness of the
father, so also the passionate self-forgetful play of the children
is associated with a fiery light in the night—an isolated lamp-
post, a blood-red moon, and behind, "the great scoop of darkness, as if all the night were there." It is this understanding of
the symbolism of darkness in Lawrence that gives tragic dignity
to such a scene as that of the bringing home of William's coffin
through the darkness of the night:

> Morel and Paul went, with a candle, into the parlour.
> There was no gas there. The father unscrewed the top of the
> big mahogany oval table, and cleared the middle of the room;
> then he arranged six chairs opposite each other, so that the
> coffin could stand on their beds.
> "You niver seed such a length as he is!" said the miner,
> and watching anxiously as he worked.
> Paul went to the bay window and looked out. The ash-

5 In *Criterion*, XII:xlvii (1932–33), 217.

tree stood monstrous and black in front of the wide darkness. It was a faintly luminous night. Paul went back to his mother.

At ten o'clock Morel called:

"He's here!"

Everyone started. There was a noise of unbarring and unlocking the front door, which opened straight from the night into the room.

"Bring another candle," called Morel. . . .

There was the noise of wheels. Outside in the darkness of the street below Paul could see horses and a black vehicle, one lamp, and a few pale faces; then some men, miners, all in their shirt-sleeves, seemed to struggle in the obscurity. Presently two men appeared, bowed beneath a great weight. It was Morel and his neighbour.

"Steady!" called Morel, out of breath.

He and his fellow mounted the steep garden step, heaved into the candlelight with their gleaming coffin-end. Limbs of other men were seen struggling behind. Morel and Burns, in front, staggered; the great dark weight swayed.

"Steady, steady!" cried Morel, as if in pain. . . .

The coffin swayed, the men began to mount the three steps with their load. Annie's candle flickered, and she whimpered as the first men appeared, and the limbs and bowed heads of six men struggled to climb into the room, bearing the coffin that rode like sorrow on their living flesh.

Here the darkness appears in another indivisible aspect of its mystery—as the darkness of death. Perhaps no other modern writer besides Rilke and Mann has tried so sincerely to bring death into relationship with life as Lawrence did, and each under the assumption that life, to know itself creatively, must know its relationship with death; a relationship which the ethos of some hundred and fifty years of rationalism and industrialism and "progress" have striven to exorcise, and by that perversion brought men to an abject worship of death and to holocausts such as that of Hiroshima. *Sons and Lovers* ends with Paul a derelict in the "drift toward death," which Lawrence thought of as the disease syndrome of his time and of Europe. But the death drift, the death worship, is for Lawrence a hideous distortion of the relationship of death to life. In the scene in which William's coffin is brought home, the front door "opened straight from the night into the room." So, in their rhythmic proportions, life and death open straight into each other, as do the light of consciousness and the darkness of the unconscious, and the usurpation of either one is a perversion of the other. Stephen Spender calls Lawrence "the most hopeful modern writer." His "dark gods," Spender says,

> . . . are symbols of an inescapable mystery: the point of comprehension where the senses are aware of an otherness in objects which extends beyond the senses, and the possibility of a relationship between the human individual and the forces outside himself, which is capable of creating in him a new state of mind. Lawrence is the most hopeful modern writer, because he looks beyond the human to the nonhuman, which can be discovered within the human.[6]

6 "The Life of Literature," *op. cit.*

15·How to Pick Flowers

by Mark Spilka

Father Tiverton has observed, quite shrewdly, that Lawrence had to die as a son before he could become a great artist. That death is chronicled, he thinks, at the end of *Sons and Lovers*, as Paul Morel refuses to follow his mother towards the grave:

> But no, he would not give in. Turning sharply, he walked towards the city's gold phosphorescence. His fists were shut, his mouth set fast. He would not take that direction, to the darkness, to follow her. He walked towards the faintly humming, glowing town, quickly. [Modern Library, p. 491]

Paul's death as a son implies his birth here as a man, and the potential birth of Lawrence himself as man and artist. It is a tenable theory, and from a biographical point of view, an important one.[1]

But there are a number of other ways, equally important, in which *Sons and Lovers* serves as the matrix for all of Lawrence's future work. The structural rhythms of the book are based, for example, upon poetic rather than narrative logic: the language backs and fills with the struggle between Walter and Gertrude Morel; in the scenes between Paul and Miriam Leivers, the tempo is labored and strained; then it quickens

Reprinted from The Love Ethic of D. H. Lawrence, 1955, *by Mark Spilka, by permission of the author and Indiana University Press.*

1 Father William Tiverton (Martin Jarrett-Kerr), *D. H. Lawrence and Human Existence* (New York: Philosophical Library, 1951), pp. 23–25, 35, 37.

perceptibly when Paul is with Clara Dawes. In each case, the emotional predicament determines the pace of the language, so that the novel surges along, always in key with the inward tensions of the protagonists: and this will prove the general rule in future novels.

But Lawrence makes a more crucial connection in this book between language and emotion: for the symbolic scenes are extremely literal, and the symbols seem to function as integral strands in the web of emotional tensions. They are seldom used in the Elizabethan sense, as mere omens of supernatural pleasure or displeasure; instead they seem to express some close relationship between man and nature. Thus Mrs. Morel holds her unwanted baby, Paul, up to the sun, the literal source of life, in a gesture of renunciation; and Morel himself stands fascinated, after a violent quarrel with his wife, as the drops of her blood soak into their baby's scalp—and this literal sealing of the blood-tie breaks his manhood; later on, the young lad Paul stares fixedly at the blood-red moon, which has roused in him his first violent sexual passion—and roused it as a force, not as a symbol. In each case, the relation between man and nature is direct and vital, and sun, blood, and moon are more "integral" than symbolic. This too will prove the general rule in future novels, though almost no one seems to have recognized this rather overwhelming truth about Lawrence's use of symbols.[2]

In *The Later D. H. Lawrence*, for example, Professor William Tindall treats Lawrence as a symbolist, and he tries to align him with the *correspondence* tradition established by Baudelaire. But the French symbolists were searching for the spiritual infinite, and Lawrence was not: his symbols operate at a different level of language than theirs, and for different ends; they are not suggestive evocations of timeless spiritual reality, but material and focal expressions of those vague but

2 The outstanding exception here is Dorothy Van Ghent, who speaks of the concrete reality of Lawrence's symbols. [See her essay "On Sons and Lovers," earlier in this volume.] See also Frederick Hoffman's view that Lawrence's symbols merely keep affective states alive, *Freudianism and the Literary Mind* (Baton Rouge: Louisiana State University Press, 1945), pp. 178–79.

powerful forces of nature which occur, quite patently, in time.[3] In the short story "Sun," for example, a woman moves from the sterile touch of her husband to life-giving contact with the sun.

> It was not just taking sun-baths. It was much more than that. Something deep inside her unfolded and relaxed, and she was given. By some mysterious power inside her, deeper than her known consciousness and will, she was put into connection with the sun, and the stream flowed of itself, from her womb. She herself, her conscious self, was secondary, a secondary person, almost an onlooker. The true Juliet was this dark flow from her deep body to the sun. [*The Later D. H. Lawrence*, Knopf, p. 348]

A symbolical flow? No, not even a face-saving *correspondance*. Lawrence means what he says here, though embarrassed critics like Tindall will always blithely cancel out his meaning: "the heroine in *Sun*," he writes, "responds with her little blazing consciousness to the 'great blazing consciousness' of heaven. There she lies naked, laughing to herself, with a flower in her navel. Her behavior may seem odd—but only when the symbolic receives a literal interpretation" (p. xv). But there is no other interpretation. The story stands or falls on the woman's living contact with the sun. The connection is organic and dramatic, and what Tindall really finds odd here is the thought that man can live in anything but an alien universe.

Most modern readers will side with Tindall in this respect, but Lawrence felt otherwise, and the only point I want to make is this: that he always wrote otherwise—as if the sun were not merely a gas ball but a source of life, and the moon not merely a satellite but a living force.

II

Strangely enough, he first began to write this way in *Sons and Lovers*, his third and supposedly his most conventional novel. It seems ironic, then, that Mark Schorer should criticise him for failing to use "technique as discovery" in this book— especially when he actually employs here his most characteristic techniques to discover things which Mr. Schorer overlooks, or

3 For a full account of the differences between Lawrence and the symbolists, see Spilka's article, "Was D. H. Lawrence a Symbolist?" *Accent*, XV (Winter, 1955), 49–60.

perhaps ignores, in his justly famous essay.[4] For Lawrence makes his first ambitious attempt, in *Sons and Lovers*, to place his major characters in active relation with a live and responsive universe: and this helps to account, I think, for the strange subjective power of the novel.

We get only a slight hint of this arrangement in the case of Walter Morel. As the book develops, he gradually breaks his own manhood; but this breakdown coincides with an actual shrinkage in physique, and this shrinkage seems to come from the direct contact between Morel and the forces of nature. Thus, instead of facing his problems at home, Morel loves to slip off with his friends for good times; on one of these drunken sprees he falls asleep in an open field, and then wakens, an hour later, feeling queer—and the physical breakdown begins here, with Morel in the act of denying his own manhood. During the bout of illness which follows, his wife begins to cast him off, and she turns to the children, for the first time, "for love and life." Admittedly, the incident is more illusive than real, but the natural contact is there, and it becomes more clearly evident at other points in the novel, when the forces of nature emerge as actual "presences." Before Paul's birth, for example, the drunken Morel shuts his wife out into the garden, and she feels these presences under the "blinding" August moon:

> She became aware of something about her. With an effort she roused herself to see what it was that penetrated her consciousness. The tall white lilies were reeling in the moonlight, and the air was charged with their perfume, as with a presence. Mrs. Morel gasped slightly in fear. She touched the big, pallid flowers on their petals, then shivered. They seemed to be stretching in the moonlight. She put her hand into one white bin: the gold scarcely showed on her fingers by moonlight. She bent down to look at the binful of yellow pollen; but it only appeared dusky. Then she drank a deep draught of the scent. It almost made her dizzy. [pp. 30–31]

Conscious only of the child within her, Mrs. Morel feels herself melting away: "After a time the child, too, melted with her in the mixing-pot of moonlight, and she rested with the

---

4 "Technique as Discovery," *Hudson Review*, I (1948), 68–87. [See also excerpts from this essay, earlier in this volume.]

hills and lilies and houses, all swum together in a kind of swoon." Later, when Morel lets her back into the house, she smiles faintly upon seeing her face in the bedroom mirror, "all smeared with the yellow dust of lilies." Both mother and unborn child have been enveloped by the powerful dark forces of life (they have not merged with the "infinite"), and the dust becomes a kiss of benediction for them both, the confirmation of their vitality. Later on, in *Aaron's Rod*, Lawrence would see the same flower, the lily, as a symbol of vital individuality— "Flowers with good roots in the mud and muck . . . fearless blossoms in air" (Seltzer, p. 273)—and Lilly, the Lawrence-figure in the book, would personify this vitality and aloofness in name and deed.

As these thoughts indicate, flowers are the most important of the "vital forces" in *Sons and Lovers*. The novel is saturated with their presence, and Paul and his three sweethearts are judged, again and again, by their attitude toward them, or more accurately, by their *relations* with them. The "lad-and-girl" affair between Paul and Miriam, for example, is a virtual communion between the two lovers and the flowers they both admire. And this communion begins with Paul's first words to the shy, romantic girl, on their meeting at Willey Farm:

> He was in the garden smelling the gillivers and looking at the plants, when the girl came out quickly to the heap of coal which stood by the fence.
> "I suppose these are cabbage-roses?" he said to her, pointing to the bushes along the fence. . . .
> "I don't know," she faltered. "They're white with pink middles."
> "Then they're maiden-blush."
> Miriam flushed. . . . [pp. 149–50]

As the book moves on, the identification of Miriam with maiden-blush is broadened to imply an unhealthy spirituality. Paul grows to hate her worshipful, fawning attitude toward life, an attitude which is consistently revealed by her "relations" with flowers: "When she bent and breathed a flower, it was as if she and the flower were loving each other. Paul hated her for it. There seemed a sort of exposure about the action, something too intimate" (p. 205). This hatred bursts into open re-

sentment as their affair draws toward an end. One day Paul
lashes out at the girl, at Willey Farm, for caressing daffodils:

> Can you never like things without clutching them as if
> you wanted to pull the heart out of them? . . .
> You wheedle the soul out of things. . . . I would never
> wheedle—at any rate, I'd go straight. . . .
> You're always begging things to love you . . . as if you
> were a beggar for love. Even the flowers, you have to fawn on
> them . . . [p. 257]

In another context, Lawrence attacks Wordsworth himself
for a similar offense—for attempting to melt down a poor
primrose "into a Williamish oneness":

> He didn't leave it with a soul of its own. It had to have his
> soul. And nature had to be sweet and pure, Williamish. Sweet-
> Williamish at that! Anthropomorphized! Anthropomorphism,
> that allows nothing to call its soul its own, save anthropos.
> . . . [*The Later D. H. Lawrence*, p. 209]

But the primrose was alive in its own right, for Lawrence;
it had "its own peculiar primrosy identity . . . its own individuality." And once again his approach to nature is primitive and direct, an affirmation of the "religious dignity" of life
"in its humblest and in its highest forms." For if men, animals
and plants are all on the same level, at the primitive stage,
then none of them can readily usurp the others' souls.

We can safely say, then, that Miriam is Wordsworth, at
least in her attitude toward nature, or toward flowers. She is
finally damned by Paul as a nun, and certainly this recalls those
famous lines by Wordsworth: "It is a beauteous evening, calm
and free;/The holy time is quiet as a nun/Breathless with adoration. . . ." Of course, the metaphor is appropriate within context, but Lawrence would never reduce nature to the bloodless
spirituality of a nun, with no vitality of its own.

Yet in the early stages of *Sons and Lovers*, Paul Morel, the
Lawrence-figure, has actually joined with Miriam in such bloodless communions over flowers. He has even taken pride in bringing them to life in the girl's imagination, and their love has its
beginning "in this atmosphere of subtle intimacy, this meeting
in their common feeling for something in nature. . . ." But as
we know, Miriam's approach to nature is ultimately deadly, and

this is the key to the dissembling of their love: she loves Paul as she loves flowers, she worships him as she worships them, and Paul feels suffocated by such adoration. This feeling is heavily underscored, for example, in the early "lad-and-girl" courtship scenes: one evening, as the two of them walk through the woods, Miriam leads Paul on, eagerly, to a wild-rose bush she has previously discovered.

> They were going to have a communion together—something that thrilled her, something holy. He was walking beside her in silence. They were very near to each other. She trembled, and he listened, vaguely anxious. . . . Then she saw her bush.
> "Ah!" she cried, hastening forward.
> It was very still. The tree was tall and straggling. It had thrown its briers over a hawthorn-bush, and its long streamers trailed thick, right down to the grass, splashing the darkness everywhere with great split stars, pure white. In bosses of ivory and in large splashed stars the roses gleamed on the darkness of foliage and stems and grass. Paul and Miriam stood close together, silent, and watched. Point after point the steady roses shone out to them, seeming to kindle something in their souls. The dusk came like smoke around, and still did not put out the roses.
> Paul looked into Miriam's eyes. She was pale and expectant with wonder, her lips were parted, and her dark eyes lay open to him. His look seemed to travel down into her. Her soul quivered. It was the communion she wanted. . . . [pp. 189–90]

But once the communion "takes," once Paul has brought the roses into her soul (for their anthropomorphic slaughter), he turns aside, feeling pained, anxious, and imprisoned. They part quickly, and he stumbles away toward home—"as soon as he was out of the wood, in the free open meadow, where he could breathe, he started to run as fast as he could. It was like a delicious delirium in his veins."

A few pages later, Lawrence describes a similar scene between Paul and his mother, and the contrast is brilliantly revealing. Mrs. Morel has just discovered three deep blue scyllas under a bush in the garden. She calls Paul to her side excitedly:

> "Now just see those! . . . I was looking at the currant-bushes, when, thinks I to myself, 'There's something very blue; is it a bit of sugar-bag?' and there, behold you! Sugar-

bag! Three glories of the snow, and such beauties! But where
on earth did they come from?"

"I don't know. . . ."

"Well, that's a marvel, now! I *thought* I knew every weed
and blade in this garden. But *haven't* they done well? You see,
that gooseberry-bush just shelters them. Not nipped, not
touched! . . ."

"They're a glorious color! . . ."

"Aren't they! . . . I guess they come from Switzerland,
where they say they have such lovely things. Fancy them
against the snow! . . ."

She was full of excitement and elation. The garden was
an endless joy to her. . . . Every morning after breakfast
she went out and was happy pottering about in it. And it was
true, she knew every weed and blade. [pp. 194–95]

The vitality, the animation, the healthy glow of the life-
flame, is typical of Mrs. Morel. Always, when Paul brings her
flowers, the scene is gay, lively, warm, or poignant. If the cold
family parlor "kills every bit of a plant you put in [it]," outside,
in the garden or in the open fields, mother and son are always
in bright and vital contact with the nodding heads of sur-
rounding flowers. Indeed, even near death this paradoxically
destructive woman fosters sunflowers in her garden (p. 443).

But the most powerful of the floral scenes takes place between Paul and his rival sweethearts, Miriam Leivers and Clara
Dawes. And here Richard Aldington makes a terrible (and
perhaps typical) blunder, in his *Portrait of a Genius But* . . . :
he attempts to show Lawrence's willfulness and inconsistency
(his *but-ness*) by referring to the way Paul and Miriam (i.e.,
Lawrence and Jessie Chambers) touch flowers: "what was
wrong for her was right for him if he happened to want to do
it." [5] But this is to miss the whole beauty of the most important
revelation scene in *Sons and Lovers*, the scene in which Paul,
Miriam, and Clara are together on Lawrence's favorite battle-
ground: an open field in the country. Paul and Clara have just
been formally introduced; he is passionately attracted to her, and
eventually he will become her lover. But Miriam is aware of this

5 D. H. Lawrence: Portrait of a Genius But . . . (New York: Duell,
Sloan & Pearce, 1950), pp. 47–48, 60. Dorothy Van Ghent also clarifies
some of the passages Aldington misreads in her comments on flower
imagery, *The English Novel*, pp. 256–57.

attraction, and she has actually arranged the whole meeting as a test; for she believes that her hold on Paul's "higher" nature, his soul, will prevail over his desires for "lower" things—Clara's body. And her belief seems to be borne out when the three of them come to an open field, with its many "clusters of strong flowers." Ah! cries Miriam, and her eyes meet Paul's. They commune. Clara sulks. Then Paul and Miriam begin to pick flowers:

> He kneeled on one knee, quickly gathering the best blossoms, moving from tuft to tuft restlessly, talking softly all the time. Miriam plucked the flowers lovingly, lingering over them. He always seemed to her too quick and almost scientific. Yet his bunches had a natural beauty more than hers. He loved them, but as if they were his and he had a right to them. She had more reverence for them: they held something she had not. [p. 279]

And there is the crux of the matter: the flowers hold life as Paul himself holds life: his contact with the "God-stuff" is spontaneous and direct—he is alive and organic, and the flowers are his to take. But negative, spiritual, sacrificial Miriam "wheedle[s] the soul out of things"; she kills life and has no right to it. What is wrong for her is actually right for him, since life kindles life and death kills it—which is the essence of Lawrencean communion.

But the revelation process now extends to Clara Dawes. She has already been sketched out as a disconsolate suffragette, and now she states, militantly, that flowers shouldn't be picked because it kills them. What she means, in effect, is that *she* doesn't want to be "picked" or taken by any man; she has separated from her husband, and for her the flowers become as proud and frigid, in their isolation, as she would like to be in hers. But since Paul believes that life belongs to the living, he begins to argue the point with her; then, as the scene unfolds, he shifts from rational argument to pagan flower dance:

> Clara's hat lay on the grass not far off. She was kneeling, bending forward still to smell the flowers. Her neck gave him a sharp pang, such a beautiful thing, yet not proud of itself just now. Her breasts swung slightly in her blouse. The arching curve of her back was beautiful and strong; she wore no stays. Suddenly, without knowing, he was scattering a handful of cowslips over her hair and neck, saying:

> "Ashes to ashes, and dust to dust,
> If the Lord won't have you the devil must."

The chill flowers fell on her neck. She looked up at him with almost pitiful, scared grey eyes, wondering what he was doing. Flowers fell on her face, and she shut her eyes.

Suddenly, standing there above her, he felt awkward.

"I thought you wanted a funeral," he said, ill at ease.

Clara laughed strangely, and rose, picking the cowslips from her hair. She took up her hat and pinned it on. One flower had remained tangled in her hair. He saw, but would not tell her. He gathered up the flowers he had sprinkled over her. [pp. 280–81]

Because of this pagan ritual, Paul and Clara now engage in their first warm, spirited conversation—about a patch of blue-bells poised in fear at the edge of the wood, like a man about to go outward into life, or like a woman about to enter the dark woods of love. Both images are clearly implied as the scene ends; both reveal character and situation, and on a deeper level, the poised flowers hint at one of Lawrence's favorite major themes—that Western man, living too much in the open spaces of the mind, must sooner or later confront the darker depths of emotion. And the key to all this revelation is how to pick flowers: Miriam, with false reverence; Paul with love, like a lover; and Clara not at all—but at least she respects the life in them, and later, when she is fully "awakened" by Paul, she will pick them, and the flowers, in their turn, will "defend" her—whereas Miriam's sheltered blooms will quickly die (pp. 380–81). All of which, if it proves nothing else, at least indicates that logic (in this case Mr. Aldington's logic) is not much of a match for the sure intuition of a creative artist.

III

But since flowers are the burden of this argument, the point must be pressed still further: the "picking scene" floods out to the rest of the book, that is, in either direction—backward, to the benedictive dust on Mrs. Morel's nose, or forward, to the first love scene between Paul and Clara, and to the final parting of Paul and Miriam in the closing paragraphs of the novel. For Paul, blessed by lily dust, must now claim the flower of life which caught in Clara's hair, and he must also place the flowers

of death in Miriam's arms. In the first case, the scarlet carnations which he buys for Clara became an active force when he
takes her on a trip to the countryside. Once there, the would-be
lovers find a secluded spot near the bank of the Trent river, and
for the first time they make love. The flowers give benediction
to their union:

> When she arose, he, looking on the ground all the time, saw
> suddenly sprinkled on the black, wet beech-roots many scarlet
> carnation petals, like splashed drops of blood; and red, small
> splashes fell from her bosom, streaming down her dress to her
> feet.
> "Your flowers are smashed," he said. [p. 365]

The smashing works both ways, however, for this is the
"baptism of fire in passion" which Paul has been seeking. Here
too is the first sign of the vision of love which Lawrence would
develop, in time, to full and confident expression as an ethic of
renewal. Paul and Clara, because of their affair, will now come
into their fullness as man and woman. And this is what Paul
seems to be driving at, later on, when he explains to Miriam
that Clara had been only half-alive with her husband, and that
she needed to be fully awakened:

> "That's what one *must have*, I think . . . the real, real flame
> of feeling through another person—once, only once, if it only
> lasts three months. See, my mother looks as if she'd *had* every-
> thing that was necessary for her living and developing. There's
> not a tiny bit of a feeling of sterility about her."
> "No," said Miriam.
> "And with my father, at first, I'm sure she had the real
> thing. She knows; she has been there. You can feel it about her,
> and about him, and about hundreds of people you meet every
> day; and, once it has happened to you, you can go on with
> anything and ripen."
> "What has happened, exactly?" asked Miriam.
> "It's so hard to say, but the something big and intense
> that changes you when you really come together with somebody
> else. It almost seems to fertilize your soul and make it that you
> can go on and mature."
> "And you think your mother had it with your father?"
> "Yes; and at bottom she feels grateful to him for giving
> it her, even now, though they are miles apart."
> "And you think Clara never had it?"
> "I'm sure." [pp. 372–73]

Paul's convictions are soon borne out: for once this "fertilization" process occurs, Clara is able to take back her husband, and Paul himself becomes man enough to resist the deathward pull from his mother's grave: "Together they had received the baptism of life; but now their missions were separate." The sign of this baptism, the active confirmation of it, was the scattering of red petals across their first bed—for the flowers *participated* in the mystery rite.

As the book ends, Paul makes his final break with Miriam, and even their last meeting, in his Nottingham rooms, is presided over by a bowl of freesias and scarlet anemones, "flaunting over the table." Because of the stifling nature of Miriam's love, Paul refuses to marry her. For her part, Miriam knows that "without him her life would trail on lifeless." But as they leave the rooms, Paul impulsively presents her with the flowers:

> "Have them!" he said; and he took them out of the jar, dripping as they were, and went quickly into the kitchen. She waited for him, took the flowers, and they went out together, he talking, she feeling dead. [p. 490]

This final contrast between the two is again determined by their active and direct relation to a natural force. For Paul, who is emotionally vital, these are the flowers of life; for Miriam, who feeds wholly on the spirit and on personal affinity, they are the rootless flowers of death. Some fifteen years later, Lawrence would expand upon the general significance of Miriam's failure, using the same powerful floral imagery from this final scene in *Sons and Lovers:*

> Oh, what a catastrophe, what a maiming of love when it was made a personal, merely personal feeling, taken away from the rising and the setting of the sun, and cut off from the magic connection of the solstice and the equinox! This is what is the matter with us. We are bleeding at the roots, because [like Miriam] we are cut off from the earth and sun and stars, and love is a grinning mockery, because, poor blossom, we plucked it from its stem on the tree of Life, and expected it to keep on blooming in our civilised vase on the table. ("A Propos of Lady Chatterley's Lover," *Sex, Literature and Censorship,* Twayne, p. 109)

16 · Counterfeit Loves

by Mark Spilka

Sons and Lovers is interpreted, much too often, in terms of the "split" theory which Lawrence once outlined in a letter to Edward Garnett.[1] According to that letter, William and Paul Morel are unable to love normally when they come to manhood, because their dominant mother holds them back, so that a split occurs between body and soul—their sweethearts getting the former; their mother, the latter; while the boys themselves are shattered, inwardly, in the course of the struggle.

Admittedly, this theory accounts for much of the surface tension of the novel; but as Mark Schorer has pointed out, it seems to conflict with a second and wholly different scheme of motivation. Unless I am badly mistaken, this second scheme is more important than the first. For there seem to be *two* psychologies at work in *Sons and Lovers*, one imposed upon the other, though without destroying its effectiveness. We know, for example, that Lawrence had heard about Freud before he wrote the final draft of the novel.[2] We also know that the Garnett letter refers to the final draft, and that previous versions of the book had followed somewhat different lines. So Lawrence may well have written the book, at first, in accord with his own developing psychology, and then rewritten it in

Reprinted from The Love Ethic of D. H. Lawrence, *1955, by Mark Spilka, by permission of the author and Indiana University Press.*

1 *The Letters of D. H. Lawrence,* ed. Aldous Huxley (New York: Viking, 1932), pp. 78–79.
2 See Frederick Hoffman, *Freudianism and the Literary Mind,* p. 153.

garbled accord with Freud's: hence the confusion, and the effect of superimposition, which bothers Mr. Schorer and many other readers. But if this is so, then the novel takes its strength from Lawrence's psychology and its weakness (inadvertently) from Freud's. The "split" theory, for example, is more Freudian than Lawrencean; it involves a kind of Freudian triangle—mother-son-sweetheart—while the conflict in all future novels centers upon a single man and woman, a specific couple, whose relationship is judged or resolved in terms of its own vitality. We have already seen such conflicts, incidentally, in the floral scenes in *Sons and Lovers*, where vitality, or the full glow of the life-flame, is the chief criterion in Paul's specific relations with his mother, and with Miriam and Clara—where each affair is judged, in other words, in terms of its effect upon the life-flow, or the "livingness," of the man and woman involved. And as a matter of fact, each of Paul's three loves is actually significant in itself, since each contributes something vital to his development, yet finally proves destructive and inadequate. So all three loves—spiritual, oedipal, and possessive—resemble the counterfeit loves of later stories, and this in spite of the obvious Freudian twist which Lawrence seems to give them in his final draft.

Romantic Miriam Leivers, for example, with her love of intellect, her heavy dumb will, and her attempt to abstract the soul right out of Paul's body, has something in common with Hermione Roddice, that harsh creature of will and intellect in *Women in Love*. There is common ground, too, between what Clara Dawes wants out of Paul—possession, imprisoning personal love—and the princess-slave relationship in later stories like "The Captain's Doll." In the same vein, Mrs. Morel resembles the later and less appealing mothers in Lawrence's short stories (say, Pauline Attenborough in "The Lovely Lady," or Rachel Bodoin in "Mother and Daughter") who sap the life from their children, regardless of outside competition, because oedipal love is sterile in itself. The truth is, then, that *Sons and Lovers* is mainly an exploration of destructive or counterfeit loves—with a garbled Freudian "split" imposed upon it. At least this helps to explain the unique emotional tenor of the book: for in spite of all confusion there is a strange new reading experience here, a unique event in the realm of fiction, and in the realm of morality as well. Indeed, if *Sons and Lovers* is (as Harry Moore tells us) "the last novel of the nineteenth century," it is also one of the first novels of the twentieth. The book is only outwardly conventional; it draws its greatest strength from Lawrence's radical new insight, moral as well as psychological, into the complex nature of emotional conflict.

II

Jessie Chambers cites a number of significant lines which appeared in the first draft of *Sons and Lovers*, but which were eliminated in the final version:

> "What was it he (Paul Morel) wanted of her (Miriam)? Did he want her to break his mother down in him? Was that what he wanted?"
> And again: "Mrs. Morel saw that if Miriam could only win her son's sex sympathy there would be nothing left for her." (*D. H. Lawrence: A Personal Record*, Cape, p. 191)

In the final draft of the book, and in Lawrence's letter to Garnett, this conflict is *stated* somewhat differently: if Miriam should win Paul's *soul*, then there would be nothing left for Mrs. Morel; as for his sex sympathy, the mother wants her to win that, if she will only leave his soul in her possession. Yet Lawrence makes it perfectly clear, through dramatic portions of the book, that Miriam's failure to attract Paul, physically, has led to her defeat in the spiritual conflict, and we see at once that the excised lines hold true to the actual situation. The girl's sexual failure is deeply rooted, for example, in her own emotional make-up. As Lawrence amply demonstrates, she is unable to lose herself in any simple pleasurable occasion, her body is tense and lifeless, her abnormal spiritual intensity is coupled with a genuine fear of things physical:

> She walked with a swing, rather heavily, her head bowed forward, pondering. She was not clumsy, and yet none of her movements seemed quite *the* movement. Often, when wiping the dishes, she would stand in bewilderment and chagrin because she had pulled in two halves a cup or a tumbler. It was as if, in her fear and self-mistrust, she put too much strength into the effort. There was no looseness or abandon about her. Every-

thing was gripped stiff with intensity, and her effort, overcharged, closed in on itself.

She rarely varied from her swinging, forward, intense walk.
Occasionally she ran with Paul down the fields. Then her eyes
blazed naked in a kind of ecstasy that frightened him. But she
was physically afraid. If she were getting over a stile, she gripped
his hands in a little hard anguish, and began to lose her presence of mind. And she could not persuade her to jump from
even a small height. [pp. 182–83]

Lawrence even suggests the future sexual problem, in an
early scene, when Miriam shows Paul the swing in her father's
barn. Characteristically, she sacrifices the first turn to him, and
he flies through the air, "every bit of him swinging, like a bird
that swoops for joy of movement." Then he turns the swing
over to the reluctant girl, and begins to set her in motion.

She felt the accuracy with which he caught her, exactly
at the right moment, and the exactly proportionate strength of
his thrust, and she was afraid. Down to her bowels went the
hot wave of fear. She was in his hands. Again, firm and inevitable came the thrust at the right moment. She gripped the
rope, almost swooning.

"Ha!" she laughed in fear. "No higher!"

"But you're not a *bit* high," he remonstrated.

"But no higher."

He heard the fear in her voice, and desisted. Her heart
melted in hot pain when the moment came for him to thrust
her forward again. But he left her alone. She began to breathe.
[pp. 179–80]

Yet both Paul and Miriam are prudes in their early courtship. She recoils from "the continual business of birth and begetting" on the farm, and he takes his cue from her. Their own
friendship is always pitched, moreover, at an intensely spiritual
and intellectual level, so that even the simplest contact seems
repellent: "His consciousness seemed to split. The place where
she was touching him ran hot with friction. He was one in-
ternecine battle, and he became cruel to her because of it."
Again, when the two chaste lovers are out for a walk one night,
Paul suddenly stands transfixed at the sight of an enormous
orange moon; his blood concentrates "like a flame in his chest,"
but this time Miriam shrinks away from actual contact: "it was
as if she could scarcely stand the shock of physical love, even a

passionate kiss, and then he was too shrinking and sensitive to give it."

Thus the chief "split" between Paul and Miriam comes from the abstract nature of their love, and not from the mother's hold upon the young man's soul. And the final responsibility for this split belongs with Miriam. When the friendship between the young couple wanes, for example, Paul resigns himself to the old love for his mother. But in the spring of his twenty-third year, he returns to the girl for another try at sensual love. This time, he seeks "the great hunger and impersonality of passion" with her, and though she agrees to this, she decides to submit herself religiously, as if to a sacrifice. Even as their love-making becomes more frequent, she continues to clench herself for the "sacrifice," as she had clenched herself on the swing in earlier days. So the lovers part once more, with this final confirmation that Miriam's frigidity is rooted in her own nature, and not in mere ignorance of sex. Her purity is nullity rather than innocence; she lacks real warmth, and Paul, in his youthful inexperience, is unable to rouse it in her. Although they meet again, after his mother's death, they are still divided by her incompleteness. Paul is shattered and adrift toward death himself; he wants her to respond to him out of warmth, out of womanly instinct. But she merely offers the old familiar sacrifice, and Paul rejects it: "he did not hope to give life to her by denying his own."

Yet if Miriam lacks warmth, she has strength of will to spare. She endures Paul's insults, his cruel probings, his wrong-headed arguments; she lets him go, time and again, out of the conviction that she holds the ultimate key to his soul. And she does have the ability to stimulate him in his work, to arouse his own spiritual nature to fever pitch, and to serve as the necessary "threshing floor" for his ideas. Because of this ability, she believes "he cannot do without her"; but her belief results in a significant lapse—a kind of self-betrayal—when Paul decides to break away: "Always—it has always been so," she cries out. "It has been one long battle between us—you fighting away from me." The statement shocks Paul profoundly; he reasons that if she had known this all along, and had said nothing, then their love "had been monstrous."

He was full of a feeling that she had deceived him. She had despised him when he thought she worshipped him. She had let him say wrong things, and had not contradicted him. She had let him fight alone. . . . All these years she had treated him as if he were a hero, and thought of him secretly as an infant, a foolish child. Then why had she left the foolish child to his folly? His heart was hard against her. [p. 350]

The exposure of this duplicity (contempt disguised by reverence) shows Miriam in her truest colors. Quite plainly she resembles the willful Hermione Roddice of *Women in Love*, though she is never so poised, skillful, and predatory as Hermione. But the heavy dumb will is undeniably there, and this, coupled with her fierce desire to be a man, to succeed through intellectual knowledge, makes her a decided forerunner of those feminine creatures of intellect and will whom Lawrence would later deplore as spiritual vampires. Thus Miriam is a nun, in Paul's eyes, who would reduce the world to a nunnery garden: on the one hand, her excessive spirituality smothers his spirit; on the other, it destroys her own capacity to respond, sympathetically, to his newly-awakened need for sensual love. And so she defeats herself in the struggle for Paul's heart, by thwarting his deep male instinct to be loved, impersonally, as a man, rather than as a mind or soul or personality. And she loses to Paul's mother by default, but she is not really defeated, at the deepest level of the conflict, by Mrs. Morel.[3]

III

Nor is Clara Dawes defeated by Paul's mother, though she fits in better with the older woman's plans: she takes care of Paul's sexual needs, that is, and leaves plenty of him over for Mrs. Morel. So the mother is "not hostile to the idea of Clara"; in fact, she finds the relationship rather wholesome, after the soul-sucking affair with Miriam. She even likes Clara, but judges her as somehow not large enough to hold her son. Paul reaches a similiar verdict about his mistress, independently, when he gives her back to her husband. But since Clara brings

3 Lawrence's chapter titles are instructive here. In "The Defeat of Miriam" Mrs. Morel defeats Miriam. But in "The Test on Miriam," a later chapter, Miriam herself fails the "test."

him a potentially fuller love than either Miriam or his mother, we must examine her role in the book with special care. She is, after all, the first imperfect version of the Lawrencean woman, the "lost girl" in search of true womanhood.

Paul is 23 when he meets Clara, and she is about 30. He responds at once to her slumbering warmth, and senses that her aloofness is just a defensive pose. For her part, Clara admires his animal quickness: he brings her the promise of renewed vitality, and they draw close together and make love, once Paul has broken away from Miriam. Thus Paul receives the impersonal love he needs, "the real, real flame of feeling through another person," and Clara comes to full awakening as a woman. We can almost feel this transformation, for example, in a scene which follows their initial consummation in Clifton Grove. Now the lovers enter Clifton village, take tea at the house of an old lady, and rouse her to gaiety through their special warmth. As they are about to leave, the woman comes forward timidly "with three tiny dahlias in full blow, neat as bees, and speckled scarlet and white."

> She stood before Clara, pleased with herself, saying:
> "I don't know whether—" and holding the flowers forward in her old hand.
> "Oh, how pretty!" cried Clara, accepting the flowers.
> "Shall she have them all?" asked Paul reproachfully of the old woman.
> "Yes, she shall have them all," she replied, beaming with joy. "You have got enough for your share."
> "Ah, but I shall ask her to give me one!" he teased.
> "Then she does as she pleases," said the old lady, smiling.
> And she bobbed a little curtsey of delight. [p. 367]

As her delight would seem to indicate, this is a communion scene, and one which neatly affirms the inward change in both of the lovers. The reward of flowers, the life-symbol, to Clara is signficant enough; but it is the "true and vivid relationship" with the old woman—her bright response to the lovers' mutual warmth—which gives us an immediate sense of inward change. "By life," writes Lawrence, "we mean something that gleams, that has the fourth-dimensional quality" (*Phoenix*, Viking, p. 529).

In the months that follow, this "gleam" or fourth-dimensional quality informs the relations between Paul and Clara. When he pins berries on her coat, she watches his quick hands, "and it seemed to her she had never *seen* anything before. Till now, everything had been indistinct." When he embraces her, she feels glad, erect, and proud again: "It was her restoration and her recognition." She falls passionately in love with him, and he with her ("as far as passion went"), till their love becomes an actual immersion in the "fourth dimension." One night, for instance, they take each other in an open field:

> It was all so much bigger than themselves that he was hushed. They had met, and included in their meeting the thrust of the manifold grass-stems, the cry of the peewit, the wheel of the stars. . . .
>
> And after such an evening, they were both very still, having known the immensity of passion. . . . To know their own nothingness, to know the tremendous living flood which carried them always, gave them rest within themselves. If so great a magnificent power could overwhelm them, identify them altogether with itself, so that they knew they were only grains in the tremendous heave that lifted every grass-blade its little height, and every tree, and every living thing, then why fret about themselves? They could let themselves be carried by life, and they felt a sort of peace each in the other. There was a verification which they had had together. Nothing could nullify it, nothing could take it away; it was almost their belief in life. [pp. 414–15]

Later on, Lawrence drops the "almost" out of that final phrase, and develops his belief in life from sexual love, or from the connection with the life-force which sexual love implies. But in *Sons and Lovers*, his belief has barely taken shape, and the conflict between Paul and Clara is never well-defined. Nevertheless, the lines of definition are there, and Lawrence makes good use of them. Thus Clara is soon dissatisfied with impersonal love; like Miriam, she wants to grasp hold of Paul and to possess him personally. So she begins to crowd her love into the daytime hours at Jordan's factory. She presses Paul for little personal intimacies, but he shrinks away from this: "The night is free to you," he says. "In the daytime I want to be by myself. . . . Love-making stifles me in the daytime." But Paul is even more disturbed about another failing: he believes that Clara is unable to "keep his soul steady," that he is simply beyond her, in his

creative and intellectual self, and in the breadth and depth of
his emotional entanglement—which anticipates a later belief:
that men and women must be in balance with each other, as
individuals with distinct "life-flows" of their own, before genuine
love can flourish. In *Sons and Lovers*, Clara falls short on this
count: her "balance" with Paul is scarcely stable, and the growing uneasiness in their affair can be traced, for the most part, to
her own inadequacy as an independent being. But even their
common bond in passion begins to weaken, under this double
burden of "imbalance" and possessive love:

> They did not often reach again the height of that once when
> the peewits called. Gradually, some mechanical effort spoilt
> their loving, or, when they had splendid moments, they had
> them separately, and not so satisfactorily. . . . Gradually
> they began to introduce novelties, to get back some of the
> feeling of satisfaction. They would be very near, almost dan-
> gerously near to the river, so that the black water ran not far
> from his face, and it gave a little thrill; or they loved sometimes
> in a little hollow below the fence of the path where people
> were passing occasionally, on the edge of the town, and they
> heard footsteps coming, almost felt the vibration of the tread,
> and they heard what the passers-by said—strange little things
> that were never intended to be heard. And afterwards each of
> them was rather ashamed, and these things caused a distance
> between the two of them. [p. 427]

This disintegration in love is soon followed by an unexpected but climactic incident. Paul meets Clara's husband one
night in a lonely field; Dawes has been waiting for him there
and a wild battle follows, in which both opponents are badly
damaged. Afterwards, the affair with Clara continues, but only
on a mechanical plane: for Dawes has fought with the desperate
strength of a man who wants his woman back, and Paul, for
all his blind resistance, does not want the woman badly. And so
he sheds his dying love in the battle, and a bit later on, he
makes his restitution: he finds Dawes in the hospital at Shef-
field, befriends him, and gradually brings husband and wife
together again. Since Clara really needs her stable, personal,
daytime lover, she agrees to the reunion. However that may be,
she fails with Paul because of her own shortcomings, for (along
with her possessiveness) she lacks the capacity, the breadth of
being, to take on the full burden of his troubled soul.

IV

But if both Miriam and Clara defeat themselves, this tells us something important about Mrs. Morel: it is not her interference which destroys her sons, but the strength and peculiar nature of her love. If we switch for a moment to electrical terms, her sons are drawn to her, away from the weaker poles of attraction, because she is the strongest force in the field—and easily the most vital woman in the novel.[4] She is warm and lively, for example, with those she loves, for the early months with her husband were months of passionate fulfillment. Though intellectual herself, she was first attracted to Morel by "the dusky, golden softness of his sensuous flame of life"—and this passion for manly, sensual men continues throughout the book. She approves, for example, of "the feel of *men* on things," and she takes immediately to the good-looking Mr. Leivers. After her first visit to his farm, she reveals a latent wish to the young lad Paul: "Now *wouldn't* I help that man! . . . *Wouldn't* I see to the fowls and the young stock. And *I'd* learn to milk, and *I'd* talk with him, and *I'd* plan with him. My word, if I were his wife, the farm would be run, I know!"

She also likes the quiet, compact miner, Mr. Barker, who takes good care of his pregnant wife, buys the week's groceries and meats on Friday nights, and keeps a level head. "Barker's little," she tells her husband, "but he's ten times the man you are." And the remark, however vindictive, holds true, for Morel has lost his manhood, and Lawrence gives us ample evidence of this throughout the novel. Unable to live up to his wife's high ideals, afraid of her mind, her will, and above all, her status as "that thing of mystery and fascination, a lady," Morel quarrels with her about money, he takes to drink, begins to mistreat her, and eventually, rather than face the problem in his own home, he retreats from the battle and breaks his own manhood. To be sure, there is a dual responsibility here, since Mrs. Morel has

4 Seymour Betsky reaches a similar conclusion in his contribution to *The Achievement of D. H. Lawrence*, ed. Harry T. Moore and Frederick Hoffman (Norman: University of Oklahoma Press, 1953), p. 138: "The Morel sons realize that their own mother is a considerably more remarkable woman than any they meet outside the home."

actually driven him to destroy himself. But the fact remains that Lawrence holds his men accountable, in the end, for their own integrity of being, and this will prove an important theme in future novels. The chief irony in *St. Mawr*, for example, is the lack of manhood in the modern world, which drives the heroine to preserve her horse, St. Mawr, as "the last male thing in the universe."

At this point in *Sons and Lovers*, Mrs. Morel turns to her children for fulfillment. And here we run into one of the curious strengths of the book, for the companionship between mother and sons is described, at first, in completely wholesome terms. The destructive potential is there, of course, and Lawrence marks it out as he goes along; but on the whole this is a healthy relationship, and it remains so until the boys come of age. Thus William and Paul are actually kindled to life by their mother's affection; along with the other children, they love to gather about her to discuss the day's events; or they gather berries for Mrs. Morel; they bake bread, blanch walnuts, fetch the father's pay, and exult with her over bargains bought at the marketplace. Indeed, even when Paul falls sick and sleeps with his mother, Lawrence treats the occasion in terms of innocence and health:

> Paul loved to sleep with his mother. Sleep is still most perfect, in spite of hygienists, when it is shared with a beloved. The warmth, the security and peace of soul, the utter comfort from the touch of the other, knits the sleep, so that it takes the body and soul completely in its healing. Paul lay against her and slept, and got better; whilst she, always a bad sleeper, fell later on into a profound sleep that seemed to give her faith. [p. 82]

Thus, in spite of the general discord in the home, there is also a healthy side to the children's lives, and this helps to account, I think, for the delightful quality of the early scenes between Paul and his mother. On their trip to Nottingham, for instance, Mrs. Morel seems "gay, like a sweetheart," and the two of them feel "the excitement of lovers having an adventure together." But instead of two lovers, we see nothing more at Jordan's factory than an anxious mother and a shy, fumbling boy, who botches a "trial" translation for his potential employer. Paul finally gets the job, but there are still more embarrassing moments ahead: a long wait for a currant tart brings anguish to the pair; or their zest at a flower shop attracts the stares of its employees. But incidents like these are scarcely oedipal. There is the same sheer immersion in simple pleasures, for example, when Paul and his mother visit the Leivers' farm: on their way across the fields, they stop to admire a horse, a small truck, and a man silhouetted against the sky; Paul calls her attention to a heron floating above them; he jests at her clumsy manner of mounting stiles; and later, on the way home, their hearts ache with happiness. The early scenes between Paul and his mother are almost always like this—innocent, gay, full of warmth, and marked by lively talk.

But the tenor begins to change once William, the eldest son, dies in London of pneumonia and erysipelas. The death comes as a terrible blow to Mrs. Morel, who loved him passionately, and thought of him almost as "her knight who wore *her* favour in the battle." Now she loses all interest in life, and remains shut off from the family. But a few months later, Paul comes down with pneumonia too. "I should have watched the living, not the dead," she tells herself, and rouses her strength to save him:

> Paul was very ill. His mother lay in bed at nights with him; they could not afford a nurse. He grew worse, and the crisis approached. One night he tossed into consciousness in the ghastly, sickly feeling of dissolution, when all the cells in the body seem in intense irritability to be breaking down, and consciousness makes a last flare of struggle, like madness.
> "I s'll die, mother!" he cried, heaving for breath on the pillow.
> She lifted him up, crying in a small voice:
> "Oh, my son—my son!"
> That brought him to. He realized her. His whole will rose up and arrested him. He put his head on her breast, and took ease of her love.
> "For some things," said his aunt, "it was a good thing Paul was ill that Christmas. I believe it saved his mother."
> [pp. 167–68]

This scene is an important one, but it is not as oedipal as it seems. What Lawrence describes here is a legitimate communion, in his eyes. We have already seen the deeply positive stress which he places upon sleep with the beloved, and upon the healing qualities of loving touch. We have also seen the basic health of the mother-son relationship. Now that health is verified, for when Lawrence writes that Paul "realized" his mother, he means that Paul has finally reached her, objectively, in valid, wholesome love. Paul is saved—saved, paradoxically, to be almost destroyed by the oedipal love which follows this event. For the beauty and richness of the scene is this: Lawrence has marshalled all the forces of destruction at precisely the same point at which he has just affirmed, dramatically, all that previous liveliness and love between Paul and his mother: William, the first son-lover, has been destroyed; now Paul will take his place in his mother's heart; he will *become* her second lover, he will in turn be sapped of his vitality, but at the moment he has just become her most beloved son.

In the years that follow, the relations between Paul and his mother are sometimes rich in satisfaction. He wins prizes for her with his artwork, and she looks upon them as part of her fulfillment. Paul sees it this way too: "All his work was hers." But there are quarrels over his love affairs, and Paul becomes increasingly unhappy. Then, late in the book, he finds "the quick of his trouble": he has loved both Miriam and Clara, but he can belong to neither of them while his mother lives; so long as she holds him, he can never "really love another woman." Thus Lawrence invokes the "split" theory, the pull between mother and sweethearts, to explain his hero's debilitation. But as we have already seen, this theory fails to account for the actual nature of Paul's affairs. We must look elsewhere, then, for the "quick" of his troubles; more specifically, we must look ahead to *Psychoanalysis and the Unconscious* (Seltzer, 1921), where Lawrence was finally able to straighten out his views on oedipal love.

In this frontal attack on Freudian psychology, Lawrence decided that the incest-craving is never the normal outcome of the parent-child relationship, but always the result of impressions planted in the child's unconscious mind by an unsatisfied parent. But therefore oedipal love is mechanistic, and if mechanistic, then destructive and abnormal in itself. In one of the late stories, for example, an avaricious mother sends an unspoken whisper through her household—*There must be more money!*—and her young boy destroys himself in his attempts to get it. Now significantly enough, this pattern is already at work in *Sons and Lovers*, though here the whisper runs—*There must be fulfillment!*—as when Paul lies on the sofa, recovering from an early bout with bronchitis:

> He, in his semi-conscious sleep, was vaguely aware of the clatter of the iron on the iron-stand, of the faint thud, thud on the ironing-board. Once roused, he opened his eyes to see his mother standing on the hearthrug with the hot iron near her cheek, listening, as it were, to the heat. Her still face, with the mouth closed tight from suffering and disillusion and self-denial, and her nose the smallest bit on one side, and her blue eyes so young, quick, and warm, made his heart contract with love. When she was quiet, so, she looked brave and rich with life, but as if she had been done out of her rights. It hurt the boy keenly, this feeling about her that she had never had her life's fulfilment: and his own incapability to make [it?] up to her hurt him with a sense of impotence, yet made him patiently dogged inside. It was his childish aim. [p. 80]

Here, then, is the planting of the incest germ, the unwitting imposition of the idea of fulfillment in the young boy's mind. Later on, when Paul becomes the actual agent of his mother's fulfillment, this idea leads inevitably to the incest-craving (through what Lawrence calls "a logical extension of the existent idea of sex and love," *Psychoanalysis*, p. 24), and from thence to the disintegration of his essential being. For the proof of this theory, take the constant wrangling with his mother; his fury at her old age; the almost violent quarrel with his father; his own mad restlessness; his obvious "will to die"; and, after the fight with Dawes, the complete blankness of his life. He is closer to his mother now than at any stage in the book, and the only thing which saves him from destruction is her own impending death. For Mrs. Morel falls ill with cancer now, and Paul cares for her, handling all the details with the doctors, as if he were the father. He is dazed and isolated from those around him; his grief stays with him like a mechanical thing which can't be shut off; he wants his mother to die, but she holds on to life, as always, with her powerful will; finally, he gives her an overdose of morphia, and this kills her. He has openly played the lover in these last days, and his mother, though reduced to a strange, shrivelled-up little girl, is almost the young wife. But the very desperation of the situation gives it dignity: this is their special, private, intimate grief over an impossible dream, and the magnificence of the woman, and the devotional quality of Paul's love, render the deathbed scenes poignant and innocent.

Paul gives Clara back to her husband after this; he rejects Miriam, and is himself on the deathward drift, following his mother's spirit. And it is here, in the final pages, that his debilitation is most clearly the result, not of any split between mother and sweethearts, but of his powerful, sterile, obsessive and mechanistic love for his mother.

v

Thus, it is not the "split" theory which gives *Sons and Lovers* its marvelous power, but the successful dramatization of three destructive forms of love—oedipal, spiritual, and "unbalanced-possessive." It seems almost as if Paul were caught, at various times, within the swirling waters of three terrible whirlpools, each of which drags him down toward a form of death-in-life; and it is not so much the violent shifts from one pool to the next which harm him, but the damage he sustains within each separate pool: and the most deathward swirl of them all is with his mother.

These three disintegrative loves, when viewed separately, help to account for the emotional depth of the book. But there is still Paul's "death" as a son to account for, and his subsequent rebirth as a man, which Lawrence dimly hints at in the final lines. Paul is alone at night in the fields outside Nottingham, and wants only to follow his mother toward the grave—

> But no, he would not give in. Turning sharply, he walked towards the city's gold phosphorescence. His fists were shut, his mouth set fast. He would not take that direction, to the darkness, to follow her. He walked towards the faintly humming, glowing town, quickly.

As Harry Moore points out, Paul's return to life hinges upon the final word, "quickly," which means *livingly* rather than *rapidly*: "The last word in *Sons and Lovers* is an adverb attesting not only to the hero's desire to live but also to his deep ability to do so." [5] And it is this quickness, this vitality, which has enabled Paul to turn away, first from Miriam, then Clara, and now, finally, from his mother. For if Paul has failed in his three loves, he has also drawn from them the necessary strength to live. We know, for example, that Paul is a promising young artist, and Lawrence also tells us something significant about his art: "From his mother he drew the life-warmth, the strength to produce; Miriam urged this warmth into intensity like a white light." Now Clara must be considered, for she adds to this life-warmth and creative vision the gift of manhood, the "baptism of fire in passion" which will enable Paul "to go on and mature." Indeed, *nothing* can nullify this verification which he and Clara have had together—"it was almost their belief in life":

> As a rule, when he started love-making, the emotion was strong enough to carry with it everything—reason, soul, blood—in a great sweep, like the Trent carries bodily its back-swirls and intertwinings, noiselessly. Gradually, the little criticisms, the little sensations, were lost, thought also went, everything borne along in one flood. He became, not a man with a mind, but a great instinct. His hands were like creatures, living; his limbs, his body, were all life and consciousness, subject to no will of his, but living in themselves. Just as he was, so it seemed the vigorous, wintry stars were strong also with life. He and they struck with the same pulse of fire, and the same joy of strength which held the bracken-frond stiff near his eyes held his own body firm. It was as if he, and the stars, and the dark herbage, and Clara were licked up in an immense tongue of flame, which tore onwards and upwards. Everything rushed along in living beside him; everything was still, perfect in itself, along with him. This wonderful stillness in each thing in itself, while it was being borne along in a very ecstasy of living, seemed the highest point of bliss. [pp. 426–27]

This combination of hurling along in the sea of life, yet remaining still and perfect in oneself, is the nucleus of Lawrencean belief, though we see here only a first rough version of

5 *The Life and Works of D. H. Lawrence* (New York: Twayne, 1951), p. 105. Compare Mark Schorer's contention, in "Technique as Discovery," that Paul returns to life "as nothing in his previous history persuades us that he could unfalteringly do." Yet there is nothing "unfaltering" about Paul's choice, and there is *much* in his previous life which enables him to make it.

things to come. Nevertheless, at the end of *Sons and Lovers*, we know, we have experienced the fact that Paul Morel has achieved a kind of half-realized, or jigsaw success, consisting of mixed elements of life-warmth, creative vision, incipient manhood, and most important of all, a belief (almost) in life itself: and this is the nutritive force which enables him, at the end, to become a man, and to turn quickly toward the glowing city, away from his mother.

17 · The Unattainable Self

by Louis Fraiberg

I

Sons and Lovers achieves a large measure of success as a novel despite the fact that the author's vision exceeds his means. In this early book, written during a period of self-discovery, Lawrence was seeing himself and the world afresh and beginning to feel his powers as a literary artist. He discarded two earlier starts which he had made on the book and began it again in the light of newly developing insights. To an impressive degree it demonstrates the capacity to move its readers through an externalization of the author's experience embodied in an appropriate form which, though it is far from technically perfect, is nevertheless very effective.

It is a tragedy of fate, the agent of destiny being the character of the protagonist. Because of the rigid patterns of emotional life imposed upon him during childhood, Paul Morel is never able thereafter to break away from the consequences of a misidentification of two polar opposites, and this determines the future direction of his life. Although he attempts through love and through work to find the meaning of human existence and to place himself in a creative relationship to it, he fails. He manages to experience passion but only fleetingly, and he does not reap the fruits of it, the sense of self, which Lawrence be-

Reprinted from Twelve Original Essays on Great English Novels, *edited by Charles Shapiro, by permission of the author and Wayne State University Press.*

lieves to be the reward of submission to and identification with the great life force.

This notion that the psychic imprints of childhood can never be revised—apparently an oversimplification of the Freudian ideas to which Lawrence was introduced during the writing of the book—becomes the key to one level of the action. On another level Lawrence's mystique of sexual experience, for which Paul is the spokesman, serves this purpose, but as a theory it is open to question on some of its own terms, as we shall see. These two frames of reference for behavior, although applied simultaneously to Paul, are not harmoniously interwoven, and their interaction therefore contributes less than it might to the power of the book.

Among the elements that do bind it together structurally, and so enhance its impact upon the reader, are the flower symbolism [1] and the Oedipal relationships.[2] In a letter written shortly after the book's completion, Lawrence himself emphasized the split between physical and spiritual love that brings about Paul's downfall; this conflict provides unity on a third level.[3] All these—and perhaps some others in addition—contribute to such success as the novel achieves.

Each of the interpretations is valid within its own limitations. The purpose of this study is to examine the vicissitudes of the hero's career without specific commitment to any of these views and to demonstrate that what happens to Paul Morel is not quite what Lawrence says is happening. It is going too far to say, as some do, that Lawrence is too close to this book, that he is using the writing of it as a form of psychotherapy, or at least as emotional catharsis. There is some truth in this view, as has been shown by Harry T. Moore [4] and Mark Schorer,[5] but

1 Mark Spilka, *The Love Ethic of D. H. Lawrence* (Bloomington, Indiana, 1955), pp. 37–89. [See excerpts in this volume.]

2 Daniel Weiss, "Oedipus in Nottinghamshire," *Literature and Psychology*, VII (August, 1957), 33–42. [See excerpt from subsequent book in this volume.]

3 Aldous Huxley, ed., *The Letters of D. H. Lawrence* (New York, 1932), pp. 78–79.

4 *The Life and Works of D. H. Lawrence* (New York, 1951).

5 "Technique as Discovery," in John W. Aldridge, ed., *Critiques and Essays in Modern Fiction* (New York, 1952). [See also portions of the essay in this volume.]

it needs to be further defined and documented before we can accurately assess its value.

It seems safe to say, however, that in the portrayal of Paul Morel, Lawrence has not sustained to the point of artistic perfection the keeping of the optimum aesthetic distance from his fictional counterpart and that, consequently, some of Paul's experiences are not wholly integrated into the multi-layered structure to which I have alluded.

Paul is a consistent character—whether his life does or does not approximate Lawrence's own—and his fate is both dramatically believable and emotionally valid. When he fails, by the touchstone of Lawrence's passion-maturity theory, this is also believable and valid. But character and ideology do not always work together in this book. This detracts somewhat from its effect, but to identify their chief discrepancies, as will be done here, is not to imply any derogation of its merits. It is rather to suggest that during its composition Lawrence was still perfecting his vision of the world and learning his craft.

II

The self is the product of inborn tendencies, assimilated parental influences and the discoveries made about both the outer and inner worlds in one's progress toward adulthood. In *Sons and Lovers*, Paul's heredity is only of slight consequence, the power of his mother over him is decisive, and most of his essays in search of an identity are either ineffectual or so threatening to the emotional status quo that the maternal influence crushes them. This state of affairs is the outcome of the "irreversible" emotional events of his childhood.

Paul's character is shaped by forces to which he merely responds; he is not the master of his own destiny but a victim of circumstance. The battle between his mother and father sets up in him a complementary attraction and repulsion. He is overwhelmed with love by his mother, a love which he reciprocates to the point where she "absorbs" him; and he is terrorized by his father's violence toward her, which causes him to reject the elder Morel both as a father and as a model of masculinity. If there is originally any possibility of Paul's self-discovery as a boy and self-determination as a man, it is lost in the interplay of the powerful primitive forces before which the quiet, rather passive child is helpless.

When Mrs. Morel is pregnant with Paul she too experiences something of this, which serves as a foreshadowing of her son's fate. "What have I to do with it?" she asks, and Lawrence adds, "Sometimes life takes hold of one, carries the body along, accomplishes one's history, and yet is not real, but leaves oneself as it were slurred over." This poses a problem for the reader. On the one hand, "sometimes" the self is not involved in its destiny, but on the other, it is necessary for life to "take hold of one," perhaps for one to submit to life, in order to realize selfhood. It is a paradox which is not resolved in the book. Both processes take place, but the latter is out of tune with what happens to Paul and the former with Lawrence's thesis.

Mrs. Morel, the dominant person in Paul's life, was a woman with a strong masculine component in her makeup. Influenced by her father who "was to her the type of all men . . . puritan, high-minded, and really stern," she valued intelligence and suffered her first alienation from her husband when she realized that he was unable to participate in the discussions of religion, philosophy and politics that she enjoyed. "The pity was, she was too much his opposite." In the face of this, the passion which bound the marriage together in its early days proved to be not enough. Gertrude Morel was determined to attain an identity of her own, and she partially succeeded, though at a terrible price.

> She could not be content with the little he might be; she would have him the much that he ought to be. So, in seeking to make him nobler than he could be, she destroyed him. She injured and hurt and scarred herself, but she lost none of her worth. She also had the children.

Thereupon, her motherliness took the distorted form of hatred of her husband and absorption of her sons, first William, then Paul. It was as though the passion which she could no longer feel for Morel was split into two streams. One, transformed into contempt, hostility and loathing, remained in a perverse way the only bond between them. The other, the residue of her love for him, engulfed the sons.

The bitter and explosive family atmosphere, the degradation of the father ("his manhood broke"), the establishment of the mother as the nucleus around whom the children clustered, all these were accomplished facts while Paul was still a small boy. Confronted with this imbalance, he responded in the only way he could—by becoming thoroughly bewildered about his own role. Instead of a father on whom he might model himself there was only a hated, rejected and despised figure who was not altogether a man, whose contribution to the emotional education of his children was chiefly the power to feel only anger and despair intensely. Whatever other feelings he inspired in them from the broken fragments of his manhood were far overshadowed by the strength of this negation. William and Paul, receiving mainly these from him, were thus denied the opportunity to develop a normal aggressiveness which could be utilized and controlled to build a competent and creative character, to find a satisfying self. Instead of a mother whose love could be renounced temporarily in order later to reaffirm it from the base of a growing masculine personality there was only the all-consuming woman whose possession of their souls transformed her sons into her would-be but impotent lovers. Paul's love for his mother, magnified out of all proportion by her demands, and her assumption of the leading role in the family swept him into an identification made up of incompatible masculine and feminine elements. Both it and his hostility against his father were excessive, other emotional avenues were blocked, and Paul was irrevocably deprived of any chance to reach normal maturity.

To be sure, there had been some predisposition for this. "Paul, always rather delicate and quiet . . . trotted after his mother like her shadow. He was usually active and interested but sometimes he would have fits of depression." This was during the period of her preference for William, but even then the the fits "caused a shadow in Mrs. Morel's heart, and her treatment of Paul was different from that of the other children." Her special feeling for him brought an eager and effective response. "When she fretted he understood, and could have no peace. His soul seemed always attentive to her." Paul's innate tendencies were thus reinforced and exploited by his mother and his feet placed early on the path he was thereafter to follow.

The first half of the novel is concerned largely with this one-sided picture of Paul's stunted self, though it becomes more complex as the inner conflicts begin to manifest themselves in behavior. In his groping for individuality in the manner of a child, we see some of the difficulties which Lawrence has in being unable to reconcile his emerging artistic vision of the significance of human experience with his artistic compulsion to report that experience naturalistically. As the book goes on, Paul is tormented by a series of ambivalences which he flounderingly tries to resolve. At times he thinks he has done so, but he never really can, and each time he is compelled to admit defeat without knowing what has beaten him and to go his tortured way from one unhappy relationship to another. This failure of his efforts, though necessary to Lawrence's plan, is so rationalized that it mirrors one of the failures of the novel.

It has been said that this book does not have a conventional structure, and this is true on one level. It is built on a number of instances of intensely realized experience each having a thematic significance. But psychologically the series is not a sequence, even though it appears on the surface to be one. The chronological plan of the novel—the essential part of which is Paul's life between childhood and the end of adolescence—does not work because the events do not bring associated changes in character. Paul's responses are fixed. He cannot develop; he can only repeat his suffering. Each attempt to find himself through a relationship with a woman is part of a series which is potentially meaningful (Mother: Miriam: Clara: Mother) but which actually fails. The book is structurally flawed because the failure is always for the same reason and the action is therefore too repetitive for any forward movement to take place. At the end of each episode Paul is back where he started; the situation is different but he is not. His experiences are thus deprived of the meaning they might have had as related parts of a dramatic succession, and while the reader is carried forward on one level, he is held back on the other that ought to accompany it.

The reason for this seems to me to be that Lawrence is still short of the full artistic control of his vision which later—in *Lady Chatterley's Lover*, for example—makes possible the marriage of form and idea and the production of an articulated aesthetic whole. This is entirely outside the question whether one agrees or disagrees with his thesis; it seems to be related to the fact that he has not yet himself fully assimilated it. There is consequently a partial gap between his accurate naturalistic reporting (or invention) of his characters' behavior and its artistic significance. The latter he indicates with more success by the flower symbolism and by other means, which he uses with great skill individually; but the relationships even between them are imperfect. There are thus a number of separate parts of the book which are not pulling together, either for Paul or for the reader.

Once Paul's childhood is past, therefore, the order in which the love incidents occur is not important. His character is set, and he is doomed to repeat himself compulsively, endlessly and tragically. *Sons and Lovers* thus has the outer shape of a picaresque novel, the adventurous travels of the unformed soul among women. Its inner shape is that of the mirror image of a saint's life: it is the equivalent of a search for grace which can never be attained, though at times glimpsed and even touched. In Lawrence's mystique, faith is more efficacious than works, but mystical immersion is better than either.

Paul's childhood, then, produced a boy who was ill-equipped to become a man, either psychologically or in terms of Lawrence's cosmos, although the latter supposedly has no relationship to the former. The experiencing of a moment of spiritual communion either occurs or it does not occur; there is no halfway. On the other hand, once attained, it is never lost. "That is what one *must have*, I think . . . the real, real flame of feeling through another person—once, only once, if it only lasts three months. . . . and once it has happened to you, you can go on with anything and ripen," says Paul to Miriam. But no such ripening takes place in his mother, who has presumably experienced this feeling, and it certainly does not in his father, her partner. In Paul the confusion between his masculine and feminine identifications also makes this impossible.

As a boy he had been withdrawn in significant ways. He retreated into the coziness of the relationship with his mother and suffered greatly when he was forced to emerge from its protection even temporarily, as when he went each Friday to bring home his father's pay. It was much more to his liking that "Friday was the baking night and market night. It was the rule that Paul should stay home and bake" while he awaited his mother's return from the market. On these occasions there was the acting-out of a partial reversal of roles, as though he were the housewife waiting for her husband. But more important than the act itself was the feeling which accompanied it: "He loved her homecoming." This served further to confirm him in his misidentification.

The end of his childhood was signalized by his successful search for a job—under his mother's guidance, as might be expected. But the necessity of staying away from home during working hours proved even more painful than his trips to the pay office at the mine had been. "Now that he felt he had to go out into life, he went through agonies of shrinking self-consciousness." But he managed to find a tolerable substitute for the lost home atmosphere among the sewing girls in whose department he spent as much time as his duties would allow. "Paul liked the girls best. The men seemed common and rather dull. He liked them all, but they were uninteresting." It was not long before he was established in the factory and getting along quite well. But the reason was not, as would be hoped, that he was beginning to find himself in the responsibilities of growing independence and manhood—quite the contrary. "The factory had a homely feel." There was no growth, no substantive change, only a reaching back for what he had left behind.

At this point in the book there is a glimpse of the role of work in the development of masculine character, but it is only a passing mention, and Lawrence proceeds thereafter to minimize it as a possibly significant part of Paul's experience.

> Paul always enjoyed it when . . . all the men united in labor. He liked to watch his fellow clerks at work. The man was the work and the work was the man, one thing, for the time being. It was different with the girls. The real woman never seemed to be there at the task, but as if left out, waiting.

Although there are later a few hints that Paul's interest in work might contribute positively to his sense of self, Lawrence does not follow them up. Paul is depicted mainly as an observer and commentator rather than as a participant; often, as in this pas-

sage, the text abruptly switches to another subject. Here it is
the separateness of woman from anything not useful biologically
and its obverse, a favorite idea of Lawrence's, the stultifying
effect of modern life on normal development. He goes almost so
far as to deny any creative possibilities for the individual in society.

This is not altogether explicit in *Sons and Lovers.* Paul rejects the chance of achieving at least a small measure of fulfillment even from his routinized work. He stands aside and
adopts an almost feminine passivity. He brings his wages home
to his mother, superficially a man's role, but the resemblance
ends there, for he uses this merely to add a new link to the un-
breakable relationship. "Then he told her the budget of the day.
His life-story like an Arabian Nights, was told night after night
to his mother. It was almost as if it were her own life." Or as if
he had never left home. This excessive sharing—a two-way process—is emphasized again and again. Paul and his mother are
one, the corollary to which is that Paul will never be himself.

> His ambition, as far as this world's gear went, was quietly to
> earn his thirty or thirty-five shillings a week somewhere near
> his home, and then, when his father died, have a cottage with
> his mother, paint and go out as he liked, and live happy ever
> after. . . . He thought that *perhaps* he might also make a
> painter, the real thing. But that he left alone.

In this fantasy he achieves the classical Oedipal goal of death
of the father and possession of the mother, but with a difference.
The father is to die somehow, conveniently, not through the
son's agency, and the mother is to be possessed not as a lover
but as a female companion. One element of reality intrudes itself:
painting, which might *perhaps* lead to an independent achievement and thereby contribute to a true masculine self-realization, is rejected and precisely for this reason.

So Paul reaches the end of childhood with all the major
battles except one already lost. His natural passivity has been
accentuated and exploited by his mother for her own ends; he
has been alienated from his father; the creative development of
his masculinity through work has not begun and will not take
place in the remainder of the book. This contribution to growth
appears to be of little interest to Lawrence, who cares only for

Paul's struggle to disentangle himself from his mother and sees that only in cosmic-biological terms, as though no others were possible. What matters to him is the relation of man to the natural forces that brought him into being.

Accordingly, in the attempts of Paul to love Miriam and Clara there is a reading of love as a sinking—not a rising—into oneness with nature. But though at moments Paul attains this apparent spiritual success, it leads him not to peace but to frustration, and ultimately he is forced to recognize its equation with death, thus defeating Lawrence's attempt to establish passion as the road to selfhood. The search for life and its meaning perversely becomes for Paul the inadvertent but welcome union with death, the obliteration of self. This is both a logical and fictional contradiction, and it prevents the book from achieving full aesthetic integration. Its power to move the reader, then, depends in part on the fact that the issue is settled (but not closed) in the first half. The second half derives its dramatic value from Paul's inner conflict, from the intensity with which significant moments of experience are depicted, and from the fidelity of many incidents to life.

III

The concluding half of the book describes the failure of Paul's search for a viable self, a failure which stems as much from his over-attachment to his mother as from the inconsistency in Lawrence's theory. If full communion through relationship with another person is the precondition for mature selfhood, then by definition it is irrelevant whether there is a prior attachment to one's mother. But Lawrence has made this attachment crucial for Paul. The psychological, the immediately human, side of the story interferes with the attainment of the mystically human goal that the theory is concerned with. Whether considered novelistically or naturalistically, then, Paul is in an impossible position: he is forever prevented from achieving a satisfactory masculine identification. The problem in *Sons and Lovers*, however, is not identification but identity.

We have already seen that Paul failed to establish the childhood conditions for a healthy development toward an adult selfhood on Freud's terms; his attempts to reach it on Lawrence's terms will also fail. The reason for this is not that there is any weakness in Lawrence's ability to render human nature but that he has not woven the representational into a harmonious pattern with the theoretical.

Miriam is too unfleshly a being to afford Paul the experience of mutual discovery which a first love can bring. She is virginal almost in a saint-like way: although her emotional life is rich, it is split off from sexuality. Paul cannot cope with her since for him strong emotion and physical love ought theoretically to accompany each other. In the early part of their relationship, as his awareness of his need for physical love grows, he suppresses it "into a shame." For her part, she wants only spiritual communion with him, which he rejects because that is all she offers. The paradoxical result of this frustration is to send him in a direction in which salvation might, in part, be attainable. Since their love cannot yet culminate in physical passion, he takes pride in his art and shows her some of his designs. "There was for him the most intense pleasure in talking about his work with Miriam. All his passion, all his wild blood, went into this intercourse with her, when he talked and conceived his work." The sexual imagery in this passage indicates his perversion of work from its normal function to that of a substitute. Sexually thwarted by Miriam, he tries to invest his art with the emotion properly belonging to a physical relationship with her, but this proves futile. Satisfied in neither direction, he is easily drawn back into his mother's orbit by an open act of seduction:

> "And I've never—you know, Paul—I've never had a husband—not really—"
> He stroked his mother's hair, and his mouth was on her throat.

In this newly restored situation, where the love of mother and son can be expressed more overtly than before, Paul is left with only one truly masculine means of expression. But this is in distorted form: he can oppose and hate his father. The elder Morel comes into the room just following the climax of this scene, while Paul and his mother are still embracing each other. " 'At your mischief again?' he said venomously." This is almost an outright recognition of sexual rivalry, and a quarrel follows.

Morel is about to strike his wife and Paul is about to defend her by attacking him when she providentially faints. It is the only way the fight could have been prevented. Since Paul's feelings are not discharged in action, no reconciliation takes place, and his relationship with his father remains based on hatred and nourished by it so that it grows more intense than ever. The psychic power in Paul that might have helped to bring him into harmony with himself is once again directed toward destruction, and his unresolvable confusion remains.

Inevitably he breaks with Miriam—although he later returns to her for a short time—since he will not submit himself wholly to her, knowing that passion on such terms cannot benefit him. But he also recognizes that his mother insists on the same bargain, and so he tries once more to find a love which will accept him without absorbing him, which will enable him to achieve passion and so free him. He turns to Clara who seems to promise better things. In some ways she is the very opposite of Miriam. She is worldly, independent, intelligent, socially and politically alive; she does not suffer from Miriam's inhibiting spirituality. Most especially, she is a married woman who is separated from her husband and so an accessible sexual object. If Paul is at last to experience passion, she is an eminently suitable partner.

But first she sends him back to Miriam. His acquiescence in this is a crucial event because now for the first time two conflicting tendencies in Paul are confronted with one another, and the results are important both for his fate and for Lawrence's theory. Paul had entered a period of despondency the serious nature of which his mother recognized. She remonstrated with him, she struggled with him, "she seemed to fight for his very life against his own will to die." To such a pass had his search for the fullness of life brought him. But her efforts were useless. The parting from Miriam, necessary though it had been, had deprived him of vital spirit. "He had that poignant carelessness about himself, his own suffering, his own life, which is a form of slow suicide." But there was still a sufficient remnant of vitality left to make another effort. The trouble now was that Paul would never again be able to press toward life without being haunted by death; never again would he be able to free himself from the confusion between them in his mind.

Heroically overcoming her repugnance and doubt, Miriam finally yielded to him. It was a union of desperate urgency for him and of tragic renunciation for her. She was fully aware that he would not find what he was seeking and so would leave her once more, this time for good. "She relinquished herself to him, but it was a sacrifice in which she felt something of horror. This thick-voiced, oblivious man was a stranger to her." Thus, instead of being united to her in their first act of love, he was parted from her, and har own sense of separateness confirmed the fact that she had lost him. Her feeling of horror was the recognition of his little death, a sample of his dedication, in the very act of love, to ultimate death.

As she had foreseen, there was no satisfaction for him. "He was physically at rest, but no more." What she did not know was the cause of the failure, his association of love with death and the beginning of a positive pleasure in the equation.

> He did not mind if the raindrops came on him; he would have lain and got wet through: he felt as if nothing mattered, as if his living were smeared away into the beyond, near and quite lovable. This strange, gentle reaching-out to death was new to him. . . . To him now, life seemed a shadow, day a white shadow; night, and death, and stillness, and inaction, this seemed like *being*. To be alive, to be urgent and insistent —that was *not-to-be*. The highest of all was to melt out into the darkness and sway there, identified with the great Being.

He had argued with her that "possession was a great moment in life" because of the concentration of strong emotions there, convinced that somehow in the experiencing of these emotions he would become free to discover and ripen his real self. To this she had demurred; her realization was accomplished in different ways. She did not easily accept defeat, however, and had fought to rescue him from the mindlessness of his passion to awareness of her that would make humanity and love possible. In their love-making she had been vigilant never to permit him

> any relaxing, never any leaving himself to the great hunger and impersonality of passion; he must be brought back to a deliber-

ate, reflective creature. As if from a swoon of passion she called him back to the littleness, the personal relationship. . . . His eyes, full of the dark, impersonal fire of desire, did not belong to her.

And after their virginal carnality, in which was forged the terrible bond that kept them superficially linked while inwardly each rejected the other, Paul gave voice to its meaning for him.

> "To be rid of our individuality, which is our will, which is our effort—to live effortless, a kind of conscious sleep—that is very beautiful, I think; that is our after-life—our immortality."

In his very first experience of passion, therefore, he was on the road to losing, not finding, himself, and he had begun to ascribe to not-being, to death, the value properly belonging to life. Imagining that he was on the threshold of obtaining his desire, he arranged a course of sterile lovemaking with Miriam to which she was able to lend only her body. Again and again during their week together he returned hoping to experience the depth of feeling whose meaning he had so misinterpreted, but each repetition of the act only diminished the intensity felt during the climax and forced on him an awareness of its true quality. The futility of his attempt became more and more obvious, although he did not give up easily. "For a second he wished he were sexless or dead. Then he shut his eyes again to her, and his blood beat back again." He exhausted himself to no purpose.

Full love was not possible for him; "there remained afterwards always the sense of failure and of death. If he were really with her, he had to put aside himself and his desire. If he would have her, he had to put her aside." The test on Miriam had failed. Paul's quest for life and the meaning of self had taken the downward path toward death and the obliteration of self. But it was a long and tortuous path. He was left tantalizingly unfulfilled, each time with a tiny taste of what fulfillment could mean. Unfortunately for him, the obstacle to complete fulfillment was at the same time the agent of destruction, and so each new attempt only confirmed his failure. He had taken what seemed like a decisive step, but it had not brought the results he had hoped for.

As he rode home [from his week with Miriam] he felt that he
was finally initiated. He was a youth no longer. But why had
he the dull pain in his soul? Why did the thought of death,
the after life, seem so sweet and consoling?

The solution would be attempted again, this time with Clara,
and again it would fail.

IV

It began auspiciously enough. Their first lovemaking was
easy and natural, like a true marriage—and yet he was not
wholly free from concern. " 'Not sinners, are we?' he said, with
an uneasy little frown." Clara's reassurance sent him home
temporarily appeased, but he was still groping for an understanding of the prize which now seemed to be within his grasp.

He had reason to feel unsure of it; the same canker that
had corroded his relationship with Miriam affected the apparent
success with Clara, and he was at last compelled to acknowledge
it.

"You know, mother, I think there must be something the
matter with me, that I *can't* love. When she's there, as a rule,
I *do* love her. Sometimes, when I see her just as *the woman*,
I love her, mother; but then, when she talks and criticizes, I
often don't listen to her.

Just as before, he could not accept Clara as a person with her
own valuable qualities—valuable to him as well—but only as
a convenient vehicle for his spurious passion. And he could
not love her because passion was not enough. It did not provide a union with her; she remained only a catalyst for his self-
destruction. Even worse than this, by committing himself to
the search for realization solely through this impersonal means,
he had cut himself off from other ways that promised better
chances of success. In communion with the vital center of life,
which should have brought clarity of purpose, he found paradox
and confusion. No, this was not the road to the self.

Part of the difficulty lay in Lawrence's view of the communion to be obtained through passionate sexuality. As described in *Sons and Lovers* it consists of a surrender to the
experience, the "little death" of sexual intercourse, which then
leads to a kind of nirvana.

> As a rule, when he started lovemaking, the emotion was strong enough to carry with it everything—reason, soul, blood—in a great sweep. . . . Gradually the little criticisms, the little sensations, were lost, thought also went, everything borne along in one flood. He became, not a man with a mind, but a great instinct. . . . everything was still, perfect. . . . This wonderful stillness in each thing in itself, while it was being borne along in a very ecstasy of living, seemed the highest point of bliss.

This describes the physical experience and its aftermath, but it attempts to give it significance on too primitive a level. Paul reaches "the highest point of bliss" through two negations of what is necessary for the achieving of true self-realization. First, mind is swallowed up by instinct; the human is thus degraded into the merely biological, which Lawrence then tries to give a value of the highest rank. Man's powers of mind become "the little criticisms," and they are simply lost in the torrent of all-devouring instinct, which is here equated with the greatest good. Second, at the peak of the experience, what gives the ecstasy its meaning, according to Lawrence, is not the surge of life but its opposite, stasis, which can only be interpreted as the immediate apprehension of death. These are not presented as balanced forces complementing each other; the sub-human triumphs.

In Paul, too, negation has long been dominant, and it has taken the form of the very preference for instinctual experience that Lawrence here regards as success in life. He never resolves this contradiction in *Sons and Lovers*.

Paul's position is now impossible, as is demonstrated once more, this time in his fight with Dawes, Clara's estranged husband. In this struggle Paul is pure "instinct without reason or feeling." He is on the point of choking Dawes to death when he stops himself and limply allows his antagonist to kick him into unconsciousness. Having failed in the search for himself through love and through passion, Paul is left with the ability to express himself only through hostile, aggressive, destructive acts. In the fight with Dawes he halts at the brink of murder and turns his desire to kill against himself by the expedient of submitting to the other's attack. The Oedipal pattern is, of course, obvious here, but it is not our present concern, which is the warping of Paul's personality. He now enters a period of estrangement from his mother, and the deterioration of his relations with Clara proceeds unchecked. In the sullen grip of destructive passion, he nevertheless tries again to find the joy he had momentarily felt in sexual union, but his sporadic couplings with Clara only succeed in driving them farther apart.

> . . . she grew to dread him. He was so quiet, yet so strange.
> . . . She began to have a kind of horror of him. . . . He
> wanted her—he had her—and it made her feel as if death
> itself had her in its grip. She lay in horror. . . .

Clara, like Miriam before her, sensed the perversion of his values and recoiled from his commitment to death, feeling the same loathing as her predecessor. It was hopeless, and he finally cut his ties with Clara altogether, going so far as to give her back to Dawes, his conqueror. Then, in a perverse way, the hostility he had felt for his sexual partner was transferred to his mother, who was now dying of cancer. Its clash with his excessive love for her gave rise to an irrepressible and insoluble final conflict.

The act which sealed his fate, however, and made it forever impossible to break his childhood bonds was the mercy-killing of his mother. It was the final tragedy, worked out with the inevitability of fate, which gave death the victory over love and completed the destruction of Paul's character. Mrs. Morel was growing steadily worse. Her pain was so great that her children could not bear to watch.

> "She'll live over Christmas," said Annie. They were both
> full of horror.
> "She won't," he replied grimly. "I s'll give her morphia."
> . . ."
> That evening he got all the morphia pills there were, and
> took them downstairs. Carefully he crushed them to powder.
> "What are you doing?" said Annie.
> "I s'll put them in her night milk."
> Then they both laughed together like two conspiring children. On top of all their horror flickered this little sanity.

Miriam and Clara had felt horror at the chill of his embraces. Now he himself was feeling it in an act of love and murder. Perhaps its merciful aspect woke him for a moment to its impact.

He had been most tender, even erotic, with his mother in her illness; when she died he embraced and kissed her like a lover, but he was revolted by the coldness of her mouth. "He bit his lip with horror. Looking at her, he felt he could never, never let her go." Nevertheless, a moment later he turned away and matter-of-factly began making the necessary arrangements.

Unable to mourn normally and freely to express a healing grief, he was prevented by his knowledge that in killing her he had killed something of himself. To his guilt was added a feeling of self-loss. The deed had sprung not simply from the wish to spare her further pain but likewise from his all-but-conscious recognition that he was governed forever by the impulse to deny the rights of others in him, to sever the connections which might bind him and them to life, and to seek instead a false union in the greater-than-human universality which he felt fleetingly in moments of surrender to strong emotion. Even this, as we have seen, could be attained only at the cost of isolating himself from his partner and thus separating rather than uniting, denying rather than fulfilling. Both Miriam and Clara had seen what he was not fully able to see, that his apparent grasping of life was actually its rejection.

Committed to the cult of transcendent experience, Paul was condemned to the Faustian penalty, the loss of his soul. He was caught in the fatal contradictions of Lawrence's theory as well as those of his own personality. The highest experience had turned out to be the negation of experience, and an inner war was launched in which polar opposites were equated without their contradictions being reconciled. The possibility that Paul might attain recognition of a viable self and develop it in a creative masculine direction succumbed to the converging assaults of the contending forces. All that was left for him was the decline into death.

The tone of the final passage of the book is somber, as befits a tragedy. Paul's struggle has come to nothing. He is apathetic, and he recognizes the meaning of his despondency. "What am I doing? . . . Destroying myself." But though the battle is lost, the defeated side is not wholly exterminated. Something indefinable in him, "a stroke of hot stubbornness inside his chest resisted his own annihilation." A few remaining flickers signal his automatic but hopeless resistance, never strong enough to overcome the long-prepared defeat. And so the book ends with Paul refusing to surrender but overwhelmed because the means of victory have been denied him from the beginning.

He looks up at the night sky and sees his own minuteness and insignificance. Life itself has no permanent place here.

> Everywhere the vastness and terror of the immense night which is roused and stirred for a brief while by the day, but which returns, and will remain at last eternal, holding everything in its silence and its living gloom. . . . On every side the immense dark silence seemed pressing him, so tiny a spark into extinction. . . .

His desire to live is now no more than a feeble, reflexive gesture against fate. For a moment the memory of his mother returns to him, and he briefly thinks of saving himself through identification with her. But this would mean a self-annihilating identification with death. He is thwarted everywhere. No other choice is left.

The last paragraph of the book, which has seemed to some an affirmation of victory for life and for Paul, can yield this meaning only if the plain tendency of all that has gone before is ignored or if the book is regarded as leading to a sequel in which all will be reversed. It reads, in part:

> But no, he would not give in. Turning sharply, he walked towards the city's gold phosphorescence. His fists were shut, his mouth set fast. He would not take that direction, to the darkness. . . . He walked towards the faintly humming, glowing town, quickly.

This certainly reads like an affirmation, but it contradicts everything that has happened to Paul up to now. It is probable that it reflects what has happened to Lawrence himself, his attainment of a satisfying sexual relationship and the finding of his artistic powers, which however, lapse here long enough to let him write an incongruous conclusion to Paul's story. As Mark Schorer says in "Technique as Discovery," Paul here does what "nothing in his previous history persuades us that he could unfalteringly do."

What appears to have taken place is a split between Lawrence the man and Lawrence the writer. As has often been suggested, he could not always sufficiently separate himself from his material. Paradoxically, one of his strengths as a writer is this very capacity to derive artistic truth from a fictionalization of the events of his own life. Fictional success depends on the achieving of a proper distance from the personal emotion so that the work may acquire a certain autonomy, an artistic harmony and wholeness largely independent of its author. Put another way, it depends on a fusion of the experiences depicted in the book with the author's novelistic intentions so that theme, symbols, characters and action become parts of an integrated whole.

In *Sons and Lovers* Lawrence has not been altogether successful in this. True, the theme provides one kind of unity; the symbolism of nature underlying and accompanying the action helps fix it into one kind of novelistic pattern; the Oedipal conflicts help bring the book into correspondence with one kind of observed experience. But in this book—only his third—the theme is imperfectly worked out. Lawrence's vision of a larger significance for man's existence is not yet fully formed, and it contains inner contradictions.

As a character in a novel Paul is somewhat lacking in interest. His childhood mis-identification has caused him to acquire too simple a perception of himself: instead of a balance of love and hate he suffers an imperfect fusion of them which can be overtly expressed only intermittently as one momentarily displaces the other. His is the ambivalence of dissociation, not of integration or of the kind of internal conflict which holds the reader by the resolution of tensions. The psychological truth about Paul has not been transmuted into adequate fictional terms. The book is not even a study of disintegration, for Paul's character was not a properly functioning one to begin with. The trouble is that the characterization is too flat and that the contest is over too soon. As a consequence, no changes—either developmental or disintegrative—can take place. The entire second half of the book is devoted to the reiteration of this fact by showing the compulsive, repetitive nature of Paul's relationship with three different women none of whom succeeds in altering the sameness of his response to love.

If salvation, in Lawrence's view, comes from the attainment of a separate, mature self through shared passion, then it is made impossible for Paul because of his almost Pavlovian conditioning. If the experience of passion is supposed to lead to the greatest good, then the book confuses the issue by equating the outcome of passion with death. If the dramatic impact of a novel depends on the significant choices made by the characters, then this is weakened here since Paul's psychological fate is imposed upon him from without and he is rendered incapable of choosing. If a tragedy ought to rise progressively from climax to climax until the final resolution is reached, then in *Sons and Lovers* there is a flattening-out of this effect because the issue is settled before we are halfway through, and the remainder is merely a confirmation, thrice repeated, of what we already know. Lawrence has provided the inevitability, but he has failed to provide the equally necessary surprise.

This is not a finished book. Paul's oscillation between life and death is not permitted to stop, as we have seen, even at the very end. This can make sense only if the book is regarded as a kind of prologue to the rest of the Lawrence canon, a position which is difficult to defend. The key to its understanding seems rather to lie in the changes for the better which took place in Lawrence's own life during its composition. Genius though we may call him, during this time he was not yet a finished—or mature—artist. His achievement in *Sons and Lovers* is a partial triumph of his own passion and developing skill over the intransigence of his materials.

18 · Sons, Lovers and Mothers

by Alfred Kazin

Sons and Lovers was published fifty years ago. In these fifty years how many autobiographical novels have been written by young men about the mothers they loved too well, about their difficulties in "adjusting" to other women, and about themselves as the sensitive writers-to-be who liberated themselves just in time in order to write their first novel? Such autobiographical novels—psychological devices they usually are, written in order to demonstrate freedom from the all-too-beloved mother—are one of the great symbols of our time. They are rooted in the modern emancipation of women. Lawrence himself, after a return visit in the 1920's to his native Nottinghamshire, lamented that the "wildness" of his father's generation was gone, that the dutiful sons in his own generation now made "good" husbands. Even working-class mothers in England, in the last of the Victorian age, had aimed at a "higher" standard of culture, and despising their husbands and concentrating on their sons, they had made these sons images of themselves. These mothers had sought a new dignity and even a potential freedom for themselves as women, but holding their sons too close, they robbed them of their necessary "wildness" and masculine force. So the sons grew up in bondage to their mothers, and the more ambitious culturally these sons were—Frank O'Connor says that

Introduction to the Modern Library edition of Sons and Lovers, by D. H. Lawrence. © Copyright 1962 by Random House, Inc. Reprinted by permission. The essay first appeared in Partisan Review, Summer, 1962.

Sons and Lovers is the work of "one of the New Men who are
largely a creation of the Education Act of 1870"—the more likely
they were to try for their emancipation by writing a novel. The
cultural aspiration that explains their plight was expected to
turn them into novelists.

Sons and Lovers (which is not a first novel) seems easy to
imitate. One reason, apart from the relationships involved, is the
very directness and surface conventionality of its technique.
James Joyce's *A Portrait of the Artist As a Young Man*, published only three years after *Sons and Lovers*, takes us immediately into the "new" novel of the twentieth century. It
opens on a bewildering series of images faithful to the unconsciousness of childhood. Proust, who brought out the first volume
of his great novel, *A la recherche du temps perdu*, in the same
year that Lawrence published *Sons and Lovers*, imposed so
highly stylized a unity of mood on the "Ouverture" to *Du côté
de chez Swann*, that these impressions of childhod read as if
they had been reconstructed to make a dream. But *Sons and
Lovers* opens as a nineteenth-century novel with a matter-of-fact
description of the setting—the mine, the landscape of "Bestwood," the neighboring streets and houses. This opening could
have been written by Arnold Bennett, or any other of the ex-
cellent "realists" of the period whose work does not summon
up, fifty years later, the ecstasy of imagination that Lawrence's
work, along with that of Joyce and Proust, does provide to us.
Lawrence is writing close to the actual facts. In his old-fashioned
way he is even writing *about* the actual facts. No wonder that a
young novelist with nothing but *his* own experiences to start
him off may feel that Lawrence's example represents the
triumph of experience. Literature has no rites in *Sons and
Lovers*; everything follows as if from memory alone. When the
struggle begins that makes the novel—the universal modern story
of a "refined" and discontented woman who pours out on her
sons the love she refuses the husband too "common" for her—
the equally universal young novelist to whom all this has happened, the novelist who in our times is likely to have been all
too mothered and fatherless, cannot help saying to himself—
"Why can't I write this good a novel out of myself? Haven't I

suffered as much as D. H. Lawrence and am I not just as sensitive? And isn't this a highly selective age in which 'sensitive' writers count?"

But the most striking thing about Lawrence—as it is about Paul Morel in *Sons and Lovers*—is his sense of his own authority. Though he was certainly not saved from atrocious suffering in relation to his mother, Lawrence's "sensitivity" was in the main concerned with reaching the highest and widest possible consciousness of everything—"nature," family, society, books—that came within his experience as a human being. His sense of his own powers, of himself as a "medium" through which the real life in things could be discovered for other people, was so strong that his personal vividness stayed with his earliest friends as a reminder of the best hopes of their youth; it was instantly recognized by literary people in London when they read his work. You can easily dislike Lawrence for this air of authority, just as many people dislike him for the influence that he exerted during his lifetime and that has grown steadily since his death in 1930. There is already an unmistakeable priggish conceit about Paul Morel in this novel. Here is a miner's son who is asked by his mother if his is a "divine discontent" and replies in this style: "Yes, I don't care about its divinity. But damn your happiness! So long as life's full, it doesn't matter whether it's happy or not. I'm afraid your happiness would bore me." But even this contains Lawrence's sense of his own authority. He saw his talent as a sacred possesion—he was almost too proud to think of his career as a *literary* one. This sense of having a power that makes for righteousness—this was so strong in Lawrence, and so intimately associated with his mother's influence, that the struggle he describes in *Sons and Lovers*, the struggle to love another woman as he had loved his mother, must be seen as the connection he made between his magic "demon," his gift, and his relationship to his mother.

Freud once wrote that he who is a favorite of the mother becomes a "conqueror." This was certainly Freud's own feeling about himself. The discoverer of the Oedipus complex never doubted that the attachment which, abnormally protracted, makes a son feel that loving any woman but his mother is a "desecration," nevertheless, in its early prime features, gives a particular kind of strength to the son. It is a spiritual strength, not the masculine "wildness" that Lawrence was to miss in contemporary life. Lawrence's own feeling that he was certainly somebody, the pride that was to sustain him despite horribly damaged lungs through so many years of tuberculosis until his death at forty-five; the pride that carried him so far from a miner's cottage; the pride that enabled him, a penniless schoolteacher, to run off with a German baroness married to his old teacher and to make her give up her three children; the pride that thirty years after his death still makes him so vivid to us as we read—this pride had not its origin but its *setting*, in the fierce love of Mrs. Arthur Lawrence for "Bert," of Mrs. Morel for her Paul.

Lawrence, who was so full of his own gift, so fully engaged in working it out that he would not acknowledge his gifted contemporaries, certainly did feel that the "essential soul" of him as he would have said, his special demon, his particular gift of vision, his particular claim on immortality, was bound up with his mother. Not "love" in the psychological sense of conscious consideration, but love in the mythological sense of a sacred connection, was what Lawrence associated with his mother and Paul with Mrs. Morel. Lawrence's power over others is directly traceable to his own sense of the sacredness still possible to life, arising from the powers hidden in ordinary human relationships. The influence he had—if only temporarily—even on a rationalist like Bertrand Russell reminds one of the hold he kept on socialist working-class people he had grown up with and who certainly did not share Lawrence's exalted individualism. Lawrence's "authority," which made him seem unbearably full of himself to those who disliked him, was certainly of a very singular kind. He had an implicit confidence in his views on many questions—on politics as on sex and love; he was able to pontificate in later life about the Etruscans, of whom he knew nothing, as well as to talk dangerous nonsense about "knowing through the blood" and the leader principle. Yet it is Lawrence's struggle to retain all the moral authority that he identified with his mother's love that explains the intensity of *Sons and Lovers*, as it does the particular intensity of Lawrence's style in this book, which he later criticized as too violent. Yet behind this style lies Lawrence's lifelong belief in what he called "quickness," his need to see the "shimmer," the life force in everything, as opposed to the "dead crust" of its external form. Destiny for Lawrence meant his privileged and constant sense of the holiness implicit in this recognition of the life force. Destiny also meant his recognition, as a delicate boy who had already seen his older brother Ernest (the "William" of *Sons and Lovers*) sicken and die of the struggle to attach himself to another woman, that his survival was somehow bound up with fidelity to his mother. Lawrence had absolute faith in his gift, but it was bound up with his physical existence, which was always on trial. He felt that it was in his mother's hands. The gift of life, so particularly precious to him after his near-fatal pneumonia at seventeen (when his brother died), could be easily lost.

With so much at stake, Lawrence put into ultimate terms, life or death, the struggle between Paul Morel's need to hold onto his mother and his desire to love Miriam Leivers as well. The struggle in *Sons and Lovers* is not between love of the mother and love of a young woman; it is the hero's struggle to *keep* the mother as his special strength, never to lose her, not to offend or even to vex her by showing too much partiality to other women. This is why the original of "Miriam Leivers," Jessie Chambers, says in her touching memoir (*D. H. Lawrence: A Personal Record*, by "E.T.") that she had to break with Lawrence after she had seen the final draft of the book, that "the shock of *Sons and Lovers* gave the death-blow to our friendship," for in that book "Lawrence handed his mother the laurels of victory."

That is indeed what Lawrence did; it would not have occurred to him to do anything else. And Jessie Chambers also honestly felt that she minded this for Lawrence's sake, not her own, since by this time there was no longer any question of marriage between them. Jessie, who certainly loved Lawrence for his genius even after she had relinquished all personal claim on him, had launched Lawrence's career by sending out his poems. When Lawrence, after his mother's death, wrote a first draft of *Sons and Lovers*, he was still unable to work out his situation in a novel. Jessie encouraged him to drop this unsatisfactory version of the later novel and to portray the emotional struggle directly. At his request, she even wrote out narrative sections which Lawrence revised and incorporated into his novel. (Lawrence often had women write out passages for his novels when he wanted to know how a woman would react to a particular situation; Frieda Lawrence was to contribute to his characterization of Mrs. Morel.) Lawrence sent Jessie parts of the manuscript for her comments and further notes. After so much help and even collaboration, Jessie felt betrayed by the book. Lawrence had failed to show, she said, how important a role the girl had played in the development of the young man as an artist. "It was his old inability to face his problem squarely. His mother had to be supreme, and for the sake of that supremacy every disloyalty was permissible."

Lawrence is quoted in Harry T. Moore's biography, *The Intelligent Heart,* as saying of Miriam-Jessie, she "encouraged my demon. But alas, it was me, not he, whom she loved. So for her too it was a catastrophe. My demon is not easily loved: whereas the ordinary me is. So poor Miriam was let down." Lawrence's tone is exalted, but he certainly justified himself in *Sons and Lovers* as a novelist, not as a "son." That is the only consideration now. Jessie Chambers herself became an embittered woman. She tried to find her salvation in politics, where the fierce hopes of her generation before 1914 for a new England were certainly not fulfilled. But Lawrence, taking the new draft of *Sons and Lovers* with him to finish in Germany after he had run off with Frieda, was able, if not to "liberate" himself from his mother in his novel, to write a great novel out of his earliest life and struggles.

That is the triumph Jessie Chambers would not acknowledge in *Sons and Lovers,* this she could not see—the Lawrence "unable to face his problem squarely" made a great novel out of the "problem," out of his mother, father, brother, the miners, the village, the youthful sweetheart. Whatever Jessie may have thought from being too close to Lawrence himself, whatever Lawrence may have said about his personal struggles during the six-week frenzy in which he launched the new draft, Lawrence felt his "problem" not as something to be solved, but as a subject to be represented. All these early experiences weighed on him with a pressure that he was able to communicate—later he called it "that hard violent style full of sensation and presentation." Jessie Chambers herself described Lawrence's accomplishment when she said, speaking of the new draft of *Sons and Lovers* that she drove Lawrence to write, "It was his power to transmute the common experiences into significance that I always felt to be Lawrence's greatest gift. He did not distinguish between small and great happenings. The common round was full of mystery, awaiting interpretation. Born and bred of working people, he had the rare gift of seeing them from within, and revealing them on their own plane."

Lawrence's particular gift was this ability to represent as valuable anything that came his way. He had the essential religious attribute of *valuing* life, of seeing the most trivial things as a kind of consecration. In part, at least, one can trace this to the poverty, austerity and simplicity of his upbringing. Jessie Chambers once watched Lawrence and his father gathering watercress for tea. "Words cannot convey Lawrence's brimming delight in all these simple things." Delight in simple things is one of the recurring features of the working-class existence described in *Sons and Lovers*. We can understand better the special value that Lawrence identified with his mother's laboriousness and self-denial in the scene where Mrs. Morel, wickedly extravagant, comes home clutching the pot that cost her fivepence and the bunch of pansies and daisies that cost her fourpence. The rapture of the commonest enjoyments and simplest possessions is represented in the mother and father as well as in the young artist Paul, the future D. H. Lawrence. This autobiographical novel rooted in the writer's early struggles is charged with feeling for his class, his region, his people. Lawrence was not a workingman himself, despite the brief experience in the surgical appliances factory that in the novel becomes Paul Morel's continued job. Chekhov said that the working-class writer purchases with his youth that which a more genteel writer is born with. But Lawrence gained everything, as a writer, from being brought up in the working class, and lost nothing by it. In *Sons and Lovers* he portrays the miners without idealizing them, as a socialist would; he relishes their human qualities (perhaps even a little jealously) and works them up as a subject for his art. He does not identify himself with them; his mother, too, we can be sure from the portrait of Mrs. Morel, tended to be somewhat aloof among the miners' wives. But Lawrence knows *as a writer* that he is related to working people, that he is bound up with them in the same order of physical and intimate existence, that it is workers' lives he has always looked on. Some of the most affecting passages in this novel are based on the force and directness of working-class speech. " 'E's niver gone, child?" Morel says to his son when William dies. Paul answers in "educated" and even prissy English, but the voice of the mines, the fields and the kitchens is rendered straight and unashamed. Lawrence, who knew how much he had lost as a man by siding with his mother in the conflict, describes the miner Morel getting his own breakfast, sitting "down to an hour of joy," with an irresistible appreciation of the physical and human picture involved: "He toasted his bacon on a fork and caught the drops of fat on his bread; then he put the rasher on his thick slice of bread, and cut off chunks with a clasp-knife, poured his tea into his saucer, and was happy."

The writer alone in Lawrence redeemed the weaknesses of being too much his mother's son. We see the common round of life among the miners' families very much as the young Lawrence must have seen it, with the same peculiar directness. His mental world was startlingly without superfluities and wasted motions. What he wrote, he wrote. The striking sense of authority, of inner conviction, that he associated with his mother's love gave him a cutting briskness with things he disapproved. But this same immediacy of response, when it touched what he loved, could reach the greatest emotional depths. The description of William Morel's coffin being carried into the house is a particular example of this. "The coffin swayed, the men began to mount the three steps with their load. Annie's candle flickered, and she whimpered as the first men appeared, and the limbs and bowed heads of six men struggled to climb into the room, bearing the coffin that rode like sorrow on their living flesh." Lawrence's power to move the reader lies in this ability to summon up all the physical attributes associated with an object; he puts you into direct contact with all its properties *as* an object. Rarely has the realistic novelist's need to *present*, to present vividly, continually, and at the highest pitch of pictorial concentration—the gift which has made the novel the supreme literary form of modern times—rarely has this reached such intense clarity of representation as it does in *Sons and Lovers.* There are passages, as in Tolstoy, that make you realize what a loss to directness of vision our increasing self-consciousness in literature represents. Lawrence is still face to face with life, and he can describe the smallest things with the most attentive love and respect.

Lawrence does not describe, he would not attempt to describe, the object as in *itself* it really is. The effect of his prose is always to heighten our consciousness of something, to relate it to ourselves. He is a romantic—and in this book is concerned with the most romantic possible subject for a novelist, the growth of the writer's own consciousness. Yet he succeeded as a novelist, he succeeded brilliantly, because he was convinced that the novel is the great literary form, for no other could reproduce so much of the actual motion or "shimmer" of life, especially as expressed in the relationships between people. Since for Lawrence the great subject of literature was not the writer's own consciousness but consciousness between people, the living felt relationship between them, it was his very concern to represent the "shimmer" of life, the "wholeness"—these could have been mere romantic slogans—that made possible his brilliance as a novelist. He was to say, in a remarkable essay called "Why The Novel Matters," that "Only in the novel are *all* things given full play, or at least, they may be given full play, when we realize that life itself, and not inert safety, is the reason for living. For out of the full play of all things emerges the only thing that is anything, the wholeness of a man, the wholeness of a woman, man alive, and live woman." It was *relationship* that was sacred to him, as it was the relationships *with* his mother, her continuing presence in his mind and life, that gave him the sense of authority on which all his power rested. And as a novelist in *Sons and Lovers* he was able to rise above every conventional pitfall in an autobiographical novel by centering his whole vision on character as the focus of a relationship, not as an absolute.

After *Sons and Lovers,* which was his attempt to close up

the past, Lawrence was to move on to novels like *The Rainbow*
(1915) and *Women In Love* (1920), where the "non-human
in humanity" was to be more important to him than "the old-
fashioned human element." The First World War was to make
impossible for Lawrence his belief in the old "stable ego" of
character. Relationships, as the continuing interest of life, became in these more "problematical," less "conventional" novels,
a version of man's general relationship, as an unknown in himself, to his unexplained universe. But the emphasis on growth
and change in *Sons and Lovers*, the great book that closes Lawrence's first period, is from the known to the unknown; as Frank
O'Connor has said, the book begins as a nineteenth century
novel and turns into a twentieth century one. Where autobiographical novels with a "sensitive" artist or novelist as hero
tend to emphasize the hero's growth to self-knowledge, the history of his "development," the striking thing about *Sons and
Lovers*, and an instance of the creative mind behind it, is that
it does not hand the "laurels of victory" to the hero. It does not
allow him any self-sufficient victory over his circumstances. With
the greatest possible vividness it shows Paul Morel engulfed in
relationships—with the mother he loves all too sufficiently, with
the "spiritual" Miriam and Clara, neither of whom he can love
whole-heartedly—relationships that are difficult and painful,
and that Lawrence leaves arrested in their pain and conflict.
When Jessie Chambers said of the first draft of *Sons and Lovers*
that "Lawrence had carried the situation to the point of dead-
lock and had stopped there," she may have been right enough
about it as an aborted novel. But Lawrence's primary interest
and concern as a novelist, his sense of the continuing *flow* of
relationship between people, no matter how unclear and painful,
no matter how far away it was from the "solution" that the
people themselves may have longed for, is what makes this
whole last section of the novel so telling.

But of course it is the opening half of *Sons and Lovers* that
makes the book great. The struggle between husband and wife
is described with a direct, unflinching power. Lawrence does not
try to bring anything to a psychological conclusion. The marriage is a struggle, a continuing friction, a relationship where
the wife's old desire for her husband can still flash up through

her resentment of his "lowness." That is why everything in the "common round" can be described with such tenderness, for the relationship of husband and wife sweeps into its unconscious passion everything that the young Lawrence loved, and was attached to. Living in a mining village on the edge of old Sherwood Forest, always close to the country, Lawrence was as intimate with nature as any country poet could have been, but he was lucky to see rural England and the industrial Midlands in relation to each other; the country soothed his senses, but a job all day long in a Nottingham factory making out orders for surgical appliances did not encourage nature worship. "On the fallow land the young wheat shone silkily. Minton pit waved its plumes of white steam, coughed, and rattled hoarsely." Lawrence is a great novelist of landscape, for he is concerned with the relationships of people living on farms, or walking out into the country after the week's work in the city. He does not romanticize nature, he describes it in its minute vibrations. In *Sons and Lovers* the emotional effect of the "lyrical" passages depends on Lawrence's extraordinary ability to convey movement and meaning even in non-human things. But in this book nature never provides evasion of human conflict and is not even a projection of human feelings; it is the physical world that Lawrence grew up in, and includes the pit down which a miner must go every day. Paul in convalescence, sitting up in bed, would "see the fluffy horses feeding at the troughs in the field, scattering their hay on the trodden yellow snow; watch the miners troop home—small, black figures trailing slowly in gangs across the white field."

This miniature, exquisite as a Japanese watercolor, is typical of *Sons and Lovers*—the country lives and seethes, but it has no mystical value. It is the landscape of Nottinghamshire and Derbyshire, and in the book it is still what it was to Lawrence growing up in it, an oasis of refreshment in an industrial world. The countryside arouses young lovers to their buried feelings and it supplies images for the "quickness," the vital current of relationship, that Lawrence valued most in life. It is never sacred in itself. When you consider that this novel came out in 1913, at the height of the "Georgian" period, when so many young poets of Lawrence's generation were mooning over nature, it is striking that *his* chief interest is always the irreducible ambiguity of human relationships. Lawrence's language, in certain key scenes, certainly recalls the emotional inflation of fiction in the "romantic" heyday preceding the First World War. But the style is actually exalted rather than literary. There is an unmistakably scriptural quality to Lawrence's communication of extreme human feeling. Mr. Morel secretly cut young William's hair, and Mrs. Morel feels that "this act of masculine clumsiness was the spear through the side of her love." The Lawrences were Congregationalist, like American Puritans. They were close to the Lord. The strong sense of himself that Lawrence was always to have, the conviction that what he felt was always terribly important just in the way he felt it, is imparted to Mrs. Morel herself in the great scene in which the insulted husband, dizzy with drink, locks her out of the house. The description of Mrs. Morel's feelings is charged with a kind of frenzy of concern for her; the language sweeps from pole to pole of feeling. Mrs. Morel is pregnant, and her sense of her moral aloneness at this moment is overwhelming. "Mrs. Morel, seared with passion, shivered to find herself out there in a great white light, that fell cold on her, and gave a shock to her inflamed soul." Later we read that "After a time the child, too, melted with her in the mixing-pot of moonlight, and she rested with the hills and lilies and houses, all swum together in a kind of swoon."

In this key scene of the mother's "trouble" (which must have been based on things that Lawrence later heard from his mother), the sense we get of Mrs. Morel, humiliated and enraged but in her innermost being haughtily inviolate, gives us a sense of all the power that Lawrence connected with his mother and of the power in the relationship that flowed between them. In *Sons and Lovers* he was able to re-create, for all time, the moment when the sympathetic bond between them reached its greatest intensity—and the moment when her death broke it. Ever after, Lawrence was to try to re-create this living bond, this magic sympathy, between himself and life. He often succeeded in creating an exciting and fruitful version of it—in relationship to his extraordinary wife Frieda; to a host of friends, disciples, admirers and readers throughout the world; even to his own novels and stories, essays and articles and poems and letters. Unlike Henry James, James Joyce, Marcel Proust, T. S. Eliot, Lawrence always makes you feel that not art but the quality of the lived experience is his greatest concern. That is why it is impossible to pick up anything by him without feeling revivified. Never were a writer's works more truly an allegory of his life, and no other writer of his imaginative standing has in our time written books that are so open to life. Yet one always feels in Lawrence his own vexation and disappointment at not being able to reproduce, in the full consciousness of his genius, the mutual sympathy he had experienced with his mother. One even feels about Lawrence's increasing vexation and disappointment that it tore him apart physically, exhausted and shattered him. Wandering feverishly from continent to continent, increasingly irritable and vulnerable to every human defect and cultural complacency, he seems finally to have died for lack of another place to aim at; for lack, even, of another great fight to wage. His work itself was curiously never enough for him, for he could write so quickly, sitting anywhere under a tree, that the book seemed to fly out of his hand as soon as he had made it; and he was so much the only poet in his imaginative universe that he could not take other writers seriously enough to rejoice in his own greatness. He was searching, one feels, for something infinitely more intangible than fame, or a single person, or a "God"—he was searching for the remembered ecstasy of experience, the quality of feeling, that is even more evanescent than the people we connect with it. Lawrence kept looking for this even after he had reproduced it in *Sons and Lovers*, whose triumph as art was to give him so little lasting satisfaction. Art could not fulfill Lawrence's search, and only death could end it. But the ecstasy of a single human relationship that he tried to reproduce never congealed into a single image or idol or belief. Imaginatively, Lawrence was free; which is why his work could literally rise like a phoenix out of the man who consumed himself in his conflict with himself.